RESEARCHING SEXUAL VIOLENCE AGAINST WOMEN

BOOKS UNDER THE GENERAL EDITORSHIP OF JON R. CONTE, PH.D.

Hate Crimes: Confronting Violence Against Lesbians and Gay Men
edited by Gregory M. Herek and Kevin T. Berrill

Legal Responses to Wife Assault: Current Trends and Evaluation
edited by N. Zoe Hilton

The Male Survivor: The Impact of Sexual Abuse
by Matthew Parynik Mendel

The Child Sexual Abuse Custody Dispute: Annotated Bibliography
by Wendy Deaton, Suzanne Long, Holly A. Magaña, and Julie Robbins

The Survivor's Guide
by Sharice A. Lee

Sexual Abuse in Nine North American Cultures: Treatment and Prevention
edited by Lisa Aronson Fontes

The Impact of Mandated Reporting on the Therapeutic Process: Picking Up the Pieces
by Murray Levine, Howard J. Doueck, and Associates

Intimate Betrayal: Understanding and Responding to the Trauma of Acquaintance Rape
by Vernon R. Wiehe and Ann L. Richards

Preventing Child Maltreatment Through Social Support: A Critical Analysis
by Ross A. Thompson

Researching Sexual Violence Against Women: Methodological and Personal Perspectives
edited by Martin D. Schwartz

Sibling Abuse: Hidden Physical, Emotional, and Sexual Trauma
by Vernon R. Wiehe

Children Acting Sexually Aggressively: Coming to Understand Them
by Sharon K. Araji

RESEARCHING SEXUAL VIOLENCE AGAINST WOMEN

Methodological and Personal Perspectives

Martin D. Schwartz
editor

SAGE Publications
International Educational and Professional Publisher
Thousand Oaks London New Delhi

For information address:

SAGE Publications, Inc.
2455 Teller Road
Thousand Oaks, California 91320
E-mail: order@sagepub.com

SAGE Publications Ltd.
6 Bonhill Street
London EC2A 4PU
United Kingdom

SAGE Publications India Pvt. Ltd.
M-32 Market
Greater Kailash I
New Delhi 110 048 India

Printed in the United States of America

Library of Congress Cataloging-in-Publication Data

Main entry under title:

Researching sexual violence against women: methodological and personal perspectives / editor, Martin D. Schwartz.
p. cm.
Includes bibliographical references (p.) and index.
ISBN 0-8039-7369-1 (cloth: acid-free paper). — ISBN 0-8039-7370-5 (pbk.: acid-free paper)
1. Rape—Research. 2. Rape—Research—Psychological aspects. 3. Dating violence—Research. 4. Sexual harassment of women—Research. 5. Women—Crimes against—Research. I. Schwartz, Martin D.
HV6558.R47 1997
362.883—dc21

97 98 99 00 01 02 03 10 9 8 7 6 5 4 3 2 1

Acquiring Editor: C. Terry Hendrix
Editorial Assistant: Dale Grenfell
Production Assistant: Karen Wiley
Typesetter/Designer: Christina Hill
Cover Designer: Candice Harman
Indexer: Molly Leggett
Print Buyer: Anna Chin

Contents

Preface

We have witnessed in the 1990s two countervailing trends in research on rape, sexual harassment, and other violence against women. First, there has been an enormous backlash movement throughout North America, with many men and a few women arguing that feminists have greatly exaggerated the problem. Much of the attack has obscured the major issues in favor of hard-to-follow petty complaints about the nature of scholarly research design. At the same time, however, more and more scholars and students have turned their attention to this problem. The amount of research and data available to us has been increasing dramatically.

These, then, are the two major reasons that this book of original essays has been written. The authors here unanimously reject the backlash movement and in general stand strongly behind the work that has been attacked. They believe that large numbers of women suffer from a variety of forms of sexual coercion. In fact, as we shall see below, one of the important things this book provides (in Part I) is an important resource for the reader who wishes to find out about the various studies that have been done on sexual assault on North American campuses.

In Part II of this book, we look at the sociology of emotion, and particularly at the problem that researchers face in dealing with the emotions they experience while producing the research we applaud in Part I. Certainly everyone knows that academics can become rather passionate about frog warts, the techniques of Mayan architecture, or whether Bacon actually wrote some of Shakespeare's sonnets. Yet the potential for emotional upheaval and personal attack is much greater in the field of violence against women. Researchers must learn how to control or channel their own emotions. Particularly if they are women, they are sure to be challenged, attacked, ridiculed, sexualized, or accused of being lesbians (as if this is relevant) at the same time that they are literally mad with frustration at the events they are studying.

How does one learn to deal with these problems? Why is a book like this necessary? A relative lack of mentors is one of the difficulties of conducting research in a new field, such as campus sexual assault. Most academic research programs can provide advice on when logistic regression is a better tool than discriminant function analysis, but few have mentors who can talk about how to handle your uncontrollable tears late at night after a day of conducting interviews with victimized women. Few think to prepare researchers on what to do with their emotions or how to handle sexual harassment in the field.

Thus, the second part of this book consists of chapters by three experienced researchers who talk as much about their own emotions and their emotion work as their research. They discuss how they manage to continue as researchers and offer advice for people starting out in this very emotion-laden field.

The third and final goal of this book is to help fill the gap in the methodological literature of studying sexual assault and sexual harassment of women. Although more and more studies are appearing, there still are few materials available to scholars entering this field to help them over hurdles of research design or even to just steel their nerve. Part III of this book introduces the reader to a variety of experienced researchers who explain how they resolved some important feminist research problems or discuss how their inability to resolve them left them wiser and willing to share this wisdom.

In the material below, I will discuss each of these three points in more detail, along with the materials in this book.

The Backlash Against Sexual Assault Research

Interestingly, the 1980s were fairly good times for feminist researchers into sexual assault. Led by Mary Koss, researchers discovered that there are numerous "hidden" victims who do not report their victimization either to the police or to health officials, making them invisible in official statistics. The findings of these researchers were new, different, to some minds a bit "racy," and against the conventional wisdom. All in all, this is exactly what much of the news media looks for in a story. Some of this research got extensive media play.

Unfortunately, many people do not want to believe that there are large numbers of women who have been victimized by men. Neil Gilbert (1991), for example, strongly attacked Koss, insisting that any discovery of hidden victims was a "phantom epidemic." However, Gilbert's ability to make such claims suffered from two difficulties: He himself never studied or conducted any research on rape, and virtually all of the existing data *did* show that such victimization exists. This does not mean that there is no room here for dispute. There are disputes in every field. Thinking of any scientific advance that did not involve disputes between qualified scientists on each side contesting the "truth" is difficult. The difference here is that only one side has data. Those people who represent the backlash—who argue that there are not large numbers of victimized women—are for the most part people without data, without experience in survey research, and generally without any background whatsoever in the field. What they do have are a media system and a public ready and willing to believe anyone who argues that men are not victimizing women in large numbers (see, e.g., Podhoretz, 1991).

What is most interesting about this is that all of North America is currently in the throes of a major political move that demands the harshest possible penalties against all types of offenders (Clear, 1994). Most Americans support executions, and even modern politicians argue that U.S. prison sentences—the longest in the world—are just a slap on offenders' wrists. Meanwhile, perhaps the most sacred political symbol of the mid-1990s is the crime victim, with much of this antioffender rhetoric being invoked on the victim's behalf. In the United States, most states and the federal government have passed "victim rights" legislation, generally with the image of white women attacked by strangers as the movement's most potent image (Weed, 1995). Yet for some reason, many of these same politicians and their supporters are convinced that feminists are exaggerating when they insist that women are victimized by people they know.

The key issue for Koss and others is that much rape is hidden, sometimes even from the victims themselves. Susan Estrich (1987) explains how this can happen. Few North Americans deny that there is such a thing as rape or that it should be punished. The problem is that many people feel there is, on the one hand, "real rape," which is commonly portrayed as some greasy guy jumping out from behind a bush; then, there are other rapes that are not so "real." Thus, unless the woman was of blameless character and attacked by a stranger, many people will simply deny that a rape has taken place. Women, who have grown up in the same society and heard the same messages as men all of their lives, may also doubt that an event can be termed *rape* if the woman invited the man to her apartment or voluntarily entered the dormitory room where the rape took place (Sanday, 1996).

One of the issues that most annoyed critics such as Gilbert is that so many of Koss's respondents said that, although they were in a situation that met the legal definition of forcible rape, they did not say that the word *rape* applied to what happened. This shows, the argument goes, that feminists are trying to expand the definition of rape as part of their campaign to change the rules regarding how men and women relate to each other. Gilbert's specific attack, which brought him some small amount of fame and success, was to argue as truth the untested theoretical supposition that some people might have misunderstood one or two of Koss's questions.

Still, no matter how much Gilbert, Podhoretz, and other men have tried, there is only a limited media market for a man who attacks women on this issue. Therefore, Katie Roiphe became the darling of the *New York Times* and much of the Eastern press for her extraordinary book, *The Morning After* (1993). The arguments in her book were based completely on Gilbert's, but they were put into a wrapping of a feminist attacking feminists. What was most interesting was not that this book was published at all but that Roiphe was featured everywhere, from the cover of the *New York Times Sunday Magazine* to many of the top conservative television talk shows. After all, this particular expert was a young graduate student in literature who had never held a job, had never done research, and had made no claim to have interviewed any women except her own personal friends at Harvard and Princeton. The book itself is based on misrepresentations, mistakes, and misunderstandings (Muehlenhard, Sympson, Phelps, & Highby, 1994). Why did America's media reach out to embrace someone who obviously knew little about the subject and ignore those who had long labored in the field? The "feminists against feminists" theme was again picked up by the media when Christine Hoff-Sommers (1994) continued the attack.

In some ways, the same thing happened in Canada. Walter DeKeseredy describes his own work, in which he asked a national sample of college and university men and women about their experiences. This expensive research, partially designed to see if Koss's findings applied also in Canada, was at first covered heavily by the media because DeKeseredy and Kelly found widespread victimization of women on college campuses. Soon, however, some of Canada's top media figures began to argue that DeKeseredy's figures had to be wrong, evidently because they were too high. The researchers began to receive hate mail and threats.

Research on Sexual Assault on College Campuses

Why do we keep finding large numbers of victimized women, even in the face of a national media blitz arguing that these women could not possibly exist? In Chapter 1, Koss and Hobart Cleveland, both at the University of Arizona, explain that date rape exists mainly because society does not censure it and may in fact encourage it. They provide one of the better summaries of the most current data. Koss's original research is not discussed in great detail in this volume, but the chapter by Jacquelyn White and John Humphrey, of the University of North Carolina at Greensboro, discusses in detail one way to both replicate and improve on it. Virtually all studies of sexual violence have been based on cross-sectional research—usually by the use of anonymous questionnaires. Here, these two authors describe their rationale for and use of longitudinal research. Although they present quite a number of excellent rationales for this decision, perhaps the best is that by using multiple measures over a long period of time, such surveys tend to blunt any criticisms that the respondents may have been confused enough by any one single question to change the direction of the general findings. This, of course, is one of the key attacks on Koss made by Gilbert and Roiphe.

In Chapter 3, DeKeseredy, of Carleton University in Ottawa, not only describes the Canadian national survey discussed above but also attempts to help researchers entering this field by discussing the ways in which he improved upon the original work.

Perhaps the attack on Koss's findings that most hurt survivors and front-line advocates for victims was the claim by critics that most women were not even victimized or harmed by what Koss was measuring—that Koss was labeling as rape what the women themselves were calling a bad date. Patricia Frazier and Lisa Seales, of the University of Minnesota, address these attacks by Gilbert and Roiphe by reporting that in two different studies, women who were raped suffered from a great deal of distress whether or not they personally applied the word *rape* to their experiences. Denying the status of *rape victim* to women whose experiences do not fit the researcher's definition of "real rape," as Gilbert and Roiphe would do, does not relieve these women of any distress and denies them the opportunity for help and support.

Along the same lines, Victoria Pitts (Brandeis University) and Martin Schwartz argue that the most important factor in whether women report their experiences as rape might be the actions and support of their friends and relatives. In a study of what the "most helpful person" told women who had experiences that fit Ohio's definition of sexual assault, Pitts and Schwartz found that although all of these women were given love and support, the ones who were specifically told it was not their fault were the ones who reported their experiences as rape. Like Frazier and Seales, Pitts and Schwartz argue that blaming the victim, even in a loving way, denies these women the knowledge of how to direct their anger and keeps them from seeking help.

Emotion and Rearching Violence Against Women

To anyone attending teaching workshops and discussions, it is apparent that many people think that proper training means that one can and should dispense with one's own feelings when working in a professional context. Even though most sociologists today take as a matter of faith that there is very little value-free research and teaching, they still generally hold that this does not mean that one can weep with one's students. Betsy Stanko, of Brunel University in England, another of the authors who has been studying rape since the 1970s, uses her chapter to move beyond the abstract description of her earlier work to discuss her own emotions—anger, pain, fear, sadness, and frustration. She suggests capturing one's emotions as data and talks about how to foster personal support.

Susan Hippensteele is in a fairly unique position. A well-trained research psychologist who is a leader in the study of ethnoviolence, she is also a frontline activist who holds the title of victim advocate at the University of Hawaii. She analyzes the problem of simultaneously being both a committed activist and a careful research scientist. She shows us how difficult it is to isolate racism from sexism and homophobia and gives us some advice on how to follow in her footsteps.

Christine Mattley, of Ohio University, argues that part of the continuum of violence against women in North America is the pornography industry, which includes what might be called "telephone fantasy workers." In a unique field study, she managed to get employed by a telephone sex service and took almost 2,000 calls from clients. Here, she focuses on the emotions of the researcher: How do you deal with the (dis)courtesy stigma given to you by your employers and fellow employees back at the university? How does it feel to be sexualized, made the butt of jokes, and trivialized as a researcher because you have chosen to work with a deviant or stigmatized (albeit legal) group?

Jennifer Huff's chapter complements Mattley's in many ways, although Mattley discusses her treatment in the academy whereas Huff discusses her treatment in the field. Specifically, Huff found that being sexually harassed by her research subjects made it difficult for her to gather data. Those who are experienced in the study of sexual harassment will recognize in her work some classic signs of self-blame, worry, and uncertainty about whether it might be easier to drop the project than to continue. She does not have a magic formula for ending sexual harassment, but she does feel that training in dealing with it should be a part of the standard training of field researchers.

Doing Research on Violence Against Women

One of the most inappropriately used words in feminist research methods is *participatory research.* Many researchers, particularly in professional schools, have found it "catchy" to refer to research subjects as "coresearchers," for example, when they are nothing of the sort. However, Claire Renzetti, editor of the top journal in this field, *Violence Against Women,* has accomplished perhaps the best-known feminist participatory research in the United States with her study of lesbian battering. Here she discusses in detail the advantages of her research method over standard positivist research for studying violence against women.

Jody Miller, of the University of Missouri, St. Louis, takes many of these same questions and relates them to the issues discussed in the emotions research section. Miller has published research from her studies of violence against prostitutes in some of the field's top journals, and this piece is only superficially about prostitutes. She addresses a number of essential questions about feminist research, including her own reaction to stories of rape, the problem of middle-class women studying a deviant group, and the difficulty of following the advice of many feminist researchers.

As a man who does research on campus sexual assaults, I have a particular interest in the chapter by Dawn Currie and Brian MacLean. Having heard for almost 20 years the received wisdom that this research is best done by women because female victims will not volunteer information to men, it has always interested me that this presumption has never been tested. Here, Currie and MacLean, two of Canada's best-known and most respected criminological researchers, address this presumption empirically and conclude that training is more important than the sex of the researcher. Yet they move far beyond this finding to show how, in our constant concern with a researcher's sex, we forget that research is gendered in many more complex ways.

Kimberly Huisman, of the University of Southern California, takes on an important subject for field researchers. There is no question that the literature on violence against minority women is significantly weaker than the literature on violence against white women. Yet most researchers with an interest in this area are white. Can a white woman gain entry into a minority community? Should she? Will the data be of any value? Huisman draws on her experience in studying violence against Asian women to deal with these questions.

Acknowledgments

As with all works, thanks are due to a number of people for getting this project off the ground and together. Terry Hendrix of Sage watched it go through some interesting incarnations and drag on longer than anyone could possibly have imagined. Molly Leggett was an invaluable assistant not only because of her talent and intelligence but also because she always found the time to pitch in and help just when both she and I were at our busiest. Carol Blum, whom I got to know when she was planning the 1979 Take Back the Night March in Cincinnati, had nothing to do with this book, but everything to do with me. A number of people were kind enough to serve as blind referees for articles in this book, but I especially wish to thank Amanda Konradi, Kimberly Cook, Christine Mattley, Walter DeKeseredy, Molly Leggett, Lisa Clayton-Stockdale, and Jody Miller for their efforts. Finally, as usually happens when you get the very best people to write for you, many of the authors here really were too busy to write these chapters, and their willingness to stay with it and to produce such high-quality work shows their commitment to the idea behind the book, which itself *is* the idea behind the book!

PART

I

Introduction: Research on Sexual Assault on College Campuses

MARTIN D. SCHWARTZ

Much of the focus of this book will be on the person who wishes to do research on sexual assault or to understand the literature on it. In this part, we will not only discover what is the current state of knowledge in this field but also go in depth to experience with the authors two large-scale and three smaller scale research projects designed to further our understanding of rape.

This is one of those fields in which one person's research dominates all discussion. Virtually every study in this field since the mid-1980s builds on a foundation built by Mary Koss and her associates. Even the backlash authors who trivialize survivors' experiences seem to forget how many researchers are active; they key their attacks as if Koss were the only person working in this field. Thus, it is fitting that she takes the lead in this book by providing, with Hobart Cleveland, a review of the nature of the literature in this area. Essentially, they have written one of the most concise and clear "primers" in this field—to paraphrase an old commercial, the one article to read if you are reading only one.

Koss and Cleveland argue that college campuses are rape-supportive environments that give already sexually aggressive men the elbowroom they need to act on their impulses or desires. Furthermore, exactly the same environments make it difficult for women victimized by these men to report their experiences to college personnel, to law enforcement, and often even to friends and family. The fact that most men on campus believe that sexual aggression is normal makes it easier for a smaller number of aggressive men to see their assaults as "normal."

Furthermore, Koss and Cleveland explain to us something of the complex relationship of alcohol, rape, and male peer support groups, such as fraternities. They take on some thorny questions: Why are some women who have obviously been raped unwilling to apply that label to themselves? Why don't victimized women report their experiences to the police?

The next chapter in this part gives us some examples of how to put together a massive, macrolevel study of campus sexual assault. In Chapter 2, Jacquelyn White and John Humphrey address the problem that many questions are difficult or impossible to answer with questionnaires given one time, in one place, to one group of people. The latter are excellent for documenting how often sexual assault occurs and how widespread it is, but they tell us little about where and how such behavior develops and spreads. For example, are typical perpetrators one-time assaulters, who just "misunderstood" the victim's "communications," as is commonly claimed? Or do these men habitually "misunderstand" woman after woman?

In Chapter 3, Walter DeKeseredy takes on much the same task as Koss, but he uses a representative sample of 3,142 Canadian students. His study included both French- and English-speaking students from coast to coast, attending institutions ranging from community colleges to large urban research universities. Here he outlines his findings and shows how they are generally consistent with U.S. surveys. Although it is commonly assumed that Canadian society is safer than U.S. society, evidently this does not apply to the sexual assault of women on campus.

The final two chapters in this part have a narrower scope. In both cases, they attempt to speak directly to the attacks on Koss that were outlined in the preface to this book. Patricia Frazier and Lisa Seales (Chapter 4) are particularly interested in accusations that what researchers call rape is really seduction. The reason (the argument goes) why women don't report their victimization to the police is that they realize that they were not victimized. In two separate studies, Frazier and Seales found that women who were victimized by acquaintances were not different from women victimized by strangers, at least in terms of their psychological reactions. Although there are some differences, generally both sets of women are equally distressed.

In Chapter 5, Victoria Pitts and Martin Schwartz also report a local campus victimization study. Their concern was with why some students reported themselves to be rape victims whereas others did not. Although this certainly would not apply in all cases, it is certain from their findings that many women internalize what they are told by others. Those women told that they were to blame for what happened (in a context in which they felt they were being *helped*) said they *were not* victims. Those who were assured that they were not at fault said that they *were* victims.

CHAPTER

1

Stepping on Toes

Social Roots of Date Rape Lead to Intractability and Politicization

MARY P. KOSS
HOBART H. CLEVELAND

The early 1990s found rape research, especially as it was depicted in the public media, embroiled in an intensely politicized debate over the nature of date rape. This politicization can be contrasted to the environment of the early 1980s, before the last decade's wave of rape research changed the way we think of sexual violence. Then, rapes were seen as products of a psychopathic fringe of men. Some 15 years later, researchers faced a drastically different understanding of rape and sexual aggression, one that we ourselves helped bring about. Through surveys of college men and women, community surveys, and a growing body of qualitative data, scholars have documented that rape and other forms of sexual coercion are not limited to a disturbed minority but are found among all social strata. The levels of sexual coercion recorded by researchers would seem unlikely to endure in the face of unambivalent societal censure. Yet recent surveys point to similar or even higher levels of aggression than recorded almost 15 years earlier (i.e., contrast Abbey, Ross, McDuffie, & McAuslan, 1996, with Koss & Oros, 1982). Two general arguments could account for the endurance of date rape—either the research is seriously flawed or society does not censure it. Because the former argument has been addressed elsewhere (Gilbert, 1993; Koss, 1993; Koss & Cook, 1993), this chapter focuses on the latter assertion.

Using both qualitative and quantitative findings, we argue that abundant rape-supportive environments encourage sexually aggressive men to act on their impulses and discourage women from reporting experiences in which they feel they were victimized. To support this perspective, we first examine the ease with which coercive beliefs and aggressive behaviors fit within our cultural understanding of sexuality. Second, we discuss the social context in which the potentially sexually aggressive man lives, considering the mediating role played by peer-group support. Third, we consider the effects on women of being nested within these contexts, paying special attention to scripted notions of women's sexual roles and stereotypes of "deserving victims." After discussing the influences on, and behaviors of, both sexes, we conclude with a discussion of the dyadic aspects of sexual coercion, examining the role that each sex plays in determining the immediate environment of the other. We argue that it is this behavioral interdependence that leads to the intractability of date rape. In the course of making these arguments, we attempt to demonstrate both the reasons why this area of research has become politicized and the meaning that can be drawn from this politicization.

Prevalence and Normalcy of Date Rape

ABERRANT OR COMMON?

The findings of Koss and her colleagues and of other investigators (e.g., Koss, Gidycz, & Wisniewski, 1987; for a review, see Koss, 1993) have demonstrated that sexual aggression is far more prevalent than many have thought or have been willing to accept (Gilbert, 1993). According to data from a nationally representative sample of college men and women, a total of 53% of college women have experienced some degree of sexual coercion, with 12% of them reporting attempted rape and 15% reporting completed rape. These findings have been repeated many times both in the United States (e.g., Abbey et al., 1996) and in other countries (e.g., DeKeseredy & Kelly, 1993a; Gavey, 1991). For example, Abbey and colleagues examined a sample of 1,160 women from a large Midwestern university and found that 59% of respondents reported some form of adolescent or adult sexual assault experience, with 23% disclosing completed rape (Abbey et al., 1996). Perhaps more challenging to traditional beliefs than the overall frequency of sexual aggression is its source. Koss and colleagues (Koss, Dinero, Seibel, & Cox, 1988; Koss et al., 1987) reported that 8 of 10 rape victims knew their perpetrator and that 57% of rapes were committed on dates. Similarly, in Abbey's recent survey, 95% of sexual assaults were committed by someone the women knew (Abbey et al., 1996). Yet college women continue to be ill-served by their widespread belief that the greatest risk of sexual violence is posed by strangers (Norris, Nurius, & Dimeff, 1996).

THE NATURALISTIC FALLACY THAT FREQUENCY EQUALS NORMALCY

Although sexually aggressive men may not be the majority, we argue that their behavior is reasonable given the social context in which they operate. We do not suggest that sexual aggression is an average practice or is experienced by nearly everyone in the usual course of development, although this statement may be true of the lowest degrees of victimization, such as having one's sexual intentions misunderstood by the opposite sex. Even widespread prevalence, however, would not support acceptability or justifiability. Such reasoning represents participation in the "naturalistic fallacy," which is the erroneous conclusion that anything natural is the way it *should* be, that "is" equals "ought." Lack of testimony regarding the harmful effects of date rape feeds illusions that it is harmless. Researchers have repeatedly observed that rape victims, more so than victims of other crimes of comparable severity, keep their victimization hidden (Koss, 1988; Koss, Woodruff, & Koss, 1991; Williams, 1984). Moreover, the better acquainted a woman is with her perpetrator, the less likely she is to discuss her experience with anyone (Koss et al., 1988). Furthermore, the psychological distress experienced by women, such as symptoms of depression, anxiety, lowered quality of relationships with men, and sexual satisfaction, are equivalent across groups of rape victims regardless of whether the rapist was a stranger, casual friend, or acquaintance. The equivalence of harm across degrees of perpetrator relationship is inconsistent with our traditional ideas of what makes rapes traumatic; nor can these findings be reconciled with societal ambivalence toward date rape.

Most societies have methods that "legitimate, obfuscate, deny, and thereby perpetuate violence" (Heise, Pitanguy, & Germain, 1994, p. 1). Rape is socioculturally supported when there is no punishment of the man or when the rape is condoned as a punishment for the woman (Rozee, 1993). Although date rape is perpetrated and experienced by a minority of men and women, it is considered justifiable by substantial portions of both. For example, young adults and adolescents have reported that forced sex is acceptable if the victim and aggressor had been dating a long time (59%), if they had prior intimacy (61%), or if she had previously had sex with other men (31%; Kikuchi, 1988). One study of young adults and adolescents found that over 50% of the respondents agreed that "a women who goes to the home of a male is implying she is willing to have sex" (Hans & Vidmar, 1986, p. 204). An amendment to student conduct codes in which rape was defined as sexual intercourse that proceeded after one of the participants expressed objections was rejected by 39% of students surveyed (Turk & Muehlenhard, 1991). This finding is surprising because the definition is a conservative one that does not require explicit consent (saying yes) to sexual advances. Instead, it is a passive definition that endorses the appropriateness of assuming "yes" unless "no" is stated.

For many college students, permissibility and acceptability appear not to be constrained by the abstract concept of consent. Accordingly, the views of sexually aggressive men, who consider their sexual aggression "normal," are not independent from societal beliefs in the normalcy of sexual aggression. These beliefs create a social context in which both men and women are nested. The following sections attempt to understand these contextual influences, beginning with features that encourage potential perpetrators, then moving to forces that render victims silent witnesses to their assault, and ending with the immediate context of acquaintance rape within dyadic relationships.

The Social Contexts and Behaviors of Sexually Aggressive Men

The typical rape of a college woman involves an 18- to 19-year-old victim and is committed by one assailant, who the victim knew or was dating.

Commonly, the participants shared some degree of previous consensual intimacy prior to what she perceived as unwanted, forced sexual intercourse, and he perceived as legitimate seduction. Although victims on average described their lack of consent as very clear, perpetrators saw it as hazy or ambiguous. The amount of force used was moderate from the victims' perspective and minimal from the perpetrators'. At the time of the incident, most of the perpetrators were drinking or under the influence of a drug (73%), as were many of the victims (55%; Koss, 1988). Dates in which the man chose the activity, drove, and paid the expenses were more likely to end in rape compared to dates in which the division of activities was more equal (Muehlenhard & Linton, 1987). There is a striking similarity between the "average rape" and the contexts discussed previously that students use to justify forced sex (Kikuchi, 1988).

The sources contributing to the expression of sexual aggression may be broken down to a minimum of two elements: a man attracted to sexual aggression and forces that overcome inhibitions toward expression of aggression, including social contexts. Both elements are seen in the data from the higher-education contexts sampled by Koss and colleagues (e.g., Koss & Dinero, 1988, 1989a; Malamuth, Sockloskie, Koss, & Tanaka, 1991). Here we focus on social contexts but comment on how individual characteristics may influence self-selection into rape-supportive environments. Permissive social ecologies that offer men the opportunity to aggress and force women to accept their aggression are abundantly available on campuses and in communities across North America. At the most general level of analysis, these contexts do not vary much from place to place, as evident by the rates of sexual aggression that were not significantly different despite the size of the city where an institution of higher education was located; the size of the institution; whether it was a technical school, college, or university; or whether it was public or private. There were small effects showing that sexual aggression varied by region (Koss, 1988; Koss et al., 1987). These findings demonstrate that support for or release of sexual aggression is available across otherwise dissimilar college environments. Fraternity membership and athletic participation were not assessed in these studies because many of the types of institutions included in the national sample lacked such campus organizations but evidenced date rape nevertheless. Where fraternities and athletics exist, they may contribute conducive environments and supportive peer groups for sexual aggression, but they are not necessary or sufficient in and of themselves for sexual aggression to occur. We have discussed their relationship to sexual aggression elsewhere (Koss & Cleveland, in press; Koss & Gaines, 1993).

RAPE-FACILITATING PERCEPTIONS

If date rape were clearly rejected by social custom, law, and practice or if it were unambiguously and consistently sanctioned, sexually aggressive men would be censured or ostracized for commission of this act. Instead of censuring date rapists, the social environment can be seen as supporting the reward of sexually aggressive behaviors (Pineau, 1989). On a direct reinforcement level, "predatory" men report greater numbers of sexual encounters than nonaggressive men (e.g., Koss & Dinero, 1989a; Malamuth et al., 1991). These men experience reinforcement of sexual aggression among their peers through their perceptions that their status has been enhanced by forcing sex on a deserving woman. For example, men reported that their status with peers not only would not suffer but indeed would be enhanced if they forced sex on a woman they drank with at a bar (Kanin, 1985).

Sexually aggressive men's attitudes also facilitate their behaviors by allowing them to rationalize that the woman deserves what they are doing to her. For example, they view certain types of women, such as "bar pick-ups" and "known teases," as "fair targets" for sexual aggression (Kanin, 1985). By classifying some women as justifiable recipients of unwanted sex, sexually aggressive men are given permission to view coercive actions against these women not as extreme or unacceptable but as part of and consistent with "normal" sexuality. With this permission, it is understandable that sexually aggressive men are more likely to be proud of their coercive behaviors than ashamed or guilty (Koss, 1988). Unsurprisingly, few men who have forced sex on someone view their behavior as anything like rape (12%), and many intend to behave similarly again (47%; Koss, 1988).

HIGH-RISK INDIVIDUAL CHARACTERISTICS

Sexual aggression has a developmental course, although there is a strong tendency for past behavior to predict the future (White & Humphrey, 1994). Men who committed sexual assault during adolescence are four times more likely to commit sexual assault in college than men who had not previously acted aggressively. The importance of formative influences relative to features of the current social context has been demonstrated in the data collected by Koss and Dinero (1988; 1989a) and by Malamuth (1986). Malamuth found that 86% of the variance in naturalistic sexual aggression could be accounted for by individual characteristics, including psychological traits and past experiences, such as dominance as a sexual motive, hostility toward women, acceptance of interpersonal violence and rape myths, sexual abuse, consensual sexual experience, and their interactions (also see Malamuth & Dean, 1991). These findings suggest that sexually aggressive men have personality traits that prime them to accept rape myths and encourage them to act on these beliefs. Consistent with this idea is the recent finding by Malamuth and Brown (1994) that aggressive characteristics in men were associated with discounting the content of female communications. Specifically, those men high in aggressive characteristics perceived less negativity and more seductiveness when faced with hostile rejections from women (Malamuth & Brown, 1994).

PEER SUPPORT

Sexually aggressive men may seek out environments supportive of their preexisting beliefs and past behavior with women. Proximate (or situational) correlates of sexual aggression, such as alcohol use or joining and participating in a rape-supportive peer group, can be conceptualized as strategies that men who are prone to sexual aggression use to accomplish their goals. One of the most salient influences on social support comes from the aggressor's peer group (DeKeseredy & Schwartz, 1993). A peer group can help define the structures, resources, and opportunities that influence the negotiation of consensual sex. For example, a fraternity may offer men an environment that is conducive to meeting women in a social setting. For a man interested in sexual encounters, joining a fraternity can be very strategic. This has been confirmed by a recent survey of sorority women, who revealed that during the month preceding the survey they attended an average of 11.5 fraternity-sorority events (Norris et al., 1996). Similarly, joining a fraternity presents certain advantages to a man interested in an environment conducive to sexual seduction. To begin with, many of these frequent social events are governed by an expectation of heavy alcohol consumption (Norris et al., 1996). Fraternities also provide peers who practice and support highly masculine, sexually coercive behaviors (Boeringer, Shehan, & Akers, 1991; Koss & Gaines, 1993; Martin & Hummer, 1989). These peers play an important role in keeping sexually aggressive beliefs accessible so the aggressor is cognitively and emotionally primed to aggress (Shotland, 1992). In addition, in many settings fraternities offer physical space that the potential perpetrator can arrange and control to facilitate sexual encounters.

We do not suggest that fraternities have a patent on providing the resources and structures for a rape-supportive environment, however (DeKeseredy & Schwartz, 1993). They merely provide a transparent example of how peer groups provide support for sexual aggression. Other peer-group structures exist that may be rape supportive, such as athletic teams, the military, or male-dominated workplaces. These settings are sought out for a variety of reasons that go beyond obtaining sexual access to women. However, the individuals most affected by these settings are those with preexisting tendencies to be sexually aggressive that are strengthened and released by the peer group. A man can select to accomplish nonconsensual sexual connection via threats of bodily harm, physical force, by acting together with other males to isolate and overcome a vulnerable woman, or by taking advantage of the incapacity that results from a woman's intoxication. Depending on group values and physical resources, a sexually aggressive man will be encouraged or supported to pursue different coercive strategies.

ALCOHOL AS A STRATEGIC TACTIC

Research has shown consistently that alcohol consumption by the victim, perpetrator, or both, increases the risk of sexual assault (Koss & Dinero, 1988, 1989a, 1989b; Muehlenhard & Linton, 1987; Norris et al., 1996). The role of alcohol in the genesis of aggression has been reviewed at length, and it is clear that the link is far more complicated than its direct pharmacological effects or the result of release of inhibitions (Abbey, Ross, & McDuffie, 1995; Leonard, 1993). A larger portion of the variance in the causation of sexual aggression is accounted for by the formative experiences of youth than that attributed to alcohol use (Koss & Dinero, 1988). Alcohol use may be viewed as strategic or, using the term of DeKeseredy and Schwartz (1993), "instrumental." Men already intend to participate in, or are open to, sexually aggressive behaviors prior to alcohol use.

Some findings support our assertion that alcohol is used by men in dating situations as a purposeful strategy to gain sexual access. In a sample of members of the Greek community, heavy drinking was positively correlated with the belief that alcohol makes it easier to act out sexually (Baer, Kivlahan, & Marlett, 1995). This belief seems to be well founded, as calculated mean blood alcohol levels in sorority women were positively associated with reported number of sex partners ($r = .31$, $p = .01$), reduction in the ability of these women to remove themselves from sexually aggressive situations ($r = .42$, $p = .001$), and negatively associated with use of physical resistance ($r = .35$, $p = .01$; Norris et al., 1996). Considering factors such as alcohol use as strategies, rather than ultimate causal mechanisms, removes their exculpating power. Consider what would happen if alcohol could be removed from a university campus. Would the two thirds of sexually aggressive men who reported purposefully getting a date drunk to have sexual intercourse stop their sexual aggression, or would they simply adopt another coercive strategy (Kanin, 1985)?

INTENTIONAL CREATION OF RAPE-FACILITATIVE ENVIRONMENTS

Not only do sexually aggressive men seek out peer groups that support sexual aggression, they also manage their interactions with women to decrease female resistance. For example, by selecting women who are "fair targets" by virtue of their style of dress or sexual lifestyle, isolating them from others, and using alcohol as a seduction tool, the sexually aggressive man can enmesh a prospective victim in behavior that implicates her as a "bad victim." This makes it more likely that she will be blamed for the rape by not only men but women (Norris et al., 1996). This manipulation of the proximate context of rape reduces her likelihood of receiving support, thereby reducing the chances that his aggression will be reported. Evidence supports the assertion that men think strategically about alcohol and "seduction." Although unstudied, it is likely that sexually aggressive men also think strategically about isolating women and picking on women whose behavior feeds stereotypes of deserving victims. Anecdotal reports exist of some men and some campus peer groups that have gone to elaborate lengths to create opportunities for individual rape, gang rape, and other forms of sexual abuse. In some cases, strategic planning went to the extent of creating specialized chambers for the sexual assaults to be carried out, sometimes while being observed or videotaped by other men in the group.

ABSENT FEEDBACK FROM PUNISHMENT

The outcomes of criminal justice processing of rape cases suggest that rapists are unlikely to be sanctioned. A reported rape has a lower chance of leading to a conviction than other reported violent crimes, and this finding is especially true of acquaintance rape (Holmstrom & Burgess, 1978; McCahill, Meyer, & Fischman, 1979). Moreover, dispositions differ between aggravated and simple rapes (those with minimal to moderate force that often involve parties who are acquainted), with reports of the former being twice or more as likely to lead to indictments (Weniger, 1978; Williams, 1978). Conviction rates are zero when juries find what they consider contributory negligence by the victim and no use of a weapon or physical roughness (McCahill et al., 1979). We note that these citations are not current, but we have been unable to locate more recent figures that break down conviction rates for rape. Legal scholars have concluded that there exists "a near-total nullification of the crime of rape in cases where the parties knew each other and no aggravating factor was present" (Bryden & Lengnick, 1996, pp. 55-56). Susan Estrich (1987) says the effect of these decisions is to preserve male sexual access to women, unencumbered by fear of being punished. Even on campuses, where relatively low tolerance for the victimization of women students might be expected, reported rapes and sexual assaults are unlikely to lead to severe punishment by campus authorities (McMillen, 1990).

The Social Contexts and Behaviors of Female Victims

WOMEN AS GATEKEEPERS

Traditional sexual scripts differ for men and women. They dictate that men should be the aggressors and women the gatekeepers and that women eschew sexual activity outside of a committed relationship, whereas men are not only allowed but encouraged to seek such activities (Pineau, 1989). Sadly, these gender-based sexual scripts have survived the "sexual revolution." In supposedly gaining the freedom to say "yes," women have lost credibility for saying "no," resulting in a new status quo that is perhaps more favorable to men than that which had previously existed. These tensions lead to the assumption that women put up a show of refusing sexual advances and that it is the man's job to overcome this feigned protest. Norris and colleagues (1996) discuss what they call the *cognitive tightrope,* which is women's difficult task of pursuing simultaneously the conflicting goals of affiliation and safety while facing the strain of expressing their sexuality under the dictates of a double standard. Alcohol consumption by women may provide a means of decreasing their sense of conflict, but this strategy leads to adverse effects, as we will discuss shortly.

Based on these traditional scripts, many men believe that women frequently say "no" to sexual advances when in fact they mean "yes." This putative behavior by women has been labeled *token resistance,* acknowledging the assumed intentions of women to manipulate men's impressions of them while performing their prescribed roles as sexual gatekeepers. Initial studies confirmed men's assumptions that women frequently engaged in token resistance (Muehlenhard & Hollabough, 1988). Recently, by combining numerical and narrative analyses, Muehlenhard and Rogers (1993) revisited these assumptions. They found that 34% of women surveyed agreed they had participated in behaviors matching a scenario in which a woman was depicted as having said "no" and meant "yes" with regard to engaging in sexual intercourse with a new partner. However, an examination of narratives from this sample revealed that only a small percentage (<2%) of them had actually interpreted the scenario in the fashion intended by investigators. Instead, respondents described being concerned that their partners were only interested in them for sex, and said "no" to see how their partners would respond. Others described saying "no" and meaning "maybe" or "no," even though "in some ways they wanted to have sex." Of those behaviors that fit the stereotype most closely, it seemed that many occurred as part of playful interaction with an established partner in the context of a long-term formal relationship. Similarly, Shotland and Hunter (1992) found that 80% of the acts classified as token resistance arose from women actually changing their intentions or expressing their uncertainty as "no" rather than from conscious manipulation. A tendency for women to use "no" as an initial response is likely a recognition on their part that not saying "no" invites sexual initiation.

DENIAL AND NORMALIZATION OF SEXUAL AGGRESSION

One of the central criticisms of date rape research has been that it extends the boundary of what is considered traumatic toward the trivial. From this perspective, harm from date rape is reframed as whining and those claiming to be assaulted are stigmatized as aspirants to a victimhood cult (e.g., Gilbert, 1993). The irony of these charges is that women demonstrate remarkable reluctance to admit vulnerability to rape and to acknowledge experiences of unwanted sex as rape. For example, in one recent survey, college women estimated their personal risk of sexual aggression as quite unlikely ($M = 2.27$ on a 7-point scale; Norris et al., 1996). Many did not consider themselves "dumb enough" to be raped, believing that they are good judges of character, could tell if a man were a rapist, and would just "walk out" if faced with rape. Furthermore, they still perceived a greater vulnerability to rape by strangers than by acquaintances, even after extensive dissemination of information about date rape on campuses. Only those previously victimized by acquaintances accurately estimated the likelihood of being sexually assaulted by someone they might know.

Women who have had experiences that contain the legal elements of rape often don't accept that their experience constituted rape. This does not mean that their experience was pleasant or even neutral, but only that they did not believe the event met their understanding of the crime of "rape." The likelihood that a woman will apply the word *rape* depends on her age and her relationship to the perpetrator. Younger women and women whose perpetrator was a date or acquaintance are the least likely to label forced sex as rape. For example, among college students, 55% of women assaulted by a stranger and 23% assaulted by an acquaintance labeled themselves victims of rape (Koss, 1988). Among adult working women who reported unwanted, forced sexual intercourse, 41% considered the incident rape (Koss, Figueredo, Bell, Tharan, & Tromp, in press; Tromp, Koss, Bell, Figueredo, & Tharan, 1995), compared to an overall figure of 27% of college students. These findings suggest that women are more likely to label unwanted sex as rape as they develop and become more sexually knowledgeable. Nevertheless, even among mature women, there still exists a reluctance to admit being raped, even when the incident fits stereotypes involving strangers.

Perhaps the hesitancy to admit to being raped is related to the common practice of victims to minimize their experience. Such minimization can be accomplished by referring to even worse experiences the individual has suffered or by imagining how much more awful the assault could have been. These cognitions form a common coping strategy in the face of trauma. However, sexual victimization is perhaps unique among forms of intentional harm in that victims point to the ubiquity of sexual aggression to minimize their trauma. These women seem to engage in a form of the naturalistic fallacy by reasoning that unwanted sexual experiences are too common to be harmful (Stanko, 1990). For example, a woman interviewed by Kelly (1988) said, ". . . I didn't see them as demands in the sense of pressure, now I do. But then, I just thought it was part and parcel . . . of men" (p. 152). College women appear to believe that sexual aggression is common and therefore harmless, whereas rape is rare and traumatic. Once raped, women tend to avoid the full implications of their experience by confining their cognitive appraisal to what they perceive as relatively normal sexual aggression. However, it has been demonstrated that rape leads to memory characteristics that are discriminable from the memories created by other unpleasant experiences and that these effects occur even in the absence of the victim appraising the incident as a rape (Koss et al., in press).

Critics of date rape have asked, "If you have to convince a woman that she has been raped, how meaningful is that conclusion?" (Guttman, 1991, p. 219). "This implies that women don't know when they're being raped until a researcher tells them. . . . This is insulting." Women's definitions of rape are based partly on legal definitions that have been largely written by men and that have their origins in efforts to protect men's property. Definitions of rape are also influenced by dirty jokes, movies, rock videos, and sometimes by pornography. None of these sources of information are noted for their feminist slant. They promote labeling only a narrow set of events as real rape (Estrich, 1987). Narrow definitions serve the interests of men because both perpetrator and victim will define the interaction as outside the boundaries of rape (MacKinnon, 1993).

When wider definitions of rape are used, they do not necessarily benefit female victims. For example, a growing body of research focuses on the sexual coercion of men by women (Muehlenhard & Cook, 1988; Struckman-Johnson, 1988; Waldner-Haugrud, 1995). Noting that rape laws are gender-neutral, these researchers have extended the idea that men, in addition to women, can be victims of the full spectrum of sexual victimization. The use of these legal reformations as a justification for flipping the victimization from women to men is invalid for several reasons. First, although victims of rape can be either sex, 99% of rape perpetrators are men, according to the

FBI (Federal Bureau of Investigation, 1994). As a result, it seems likely that legal reform was motivated by concern for male-to-male rape, not female-to-male rape. Second, it has been shown that the events men and women are referring to when they respond affirmatively to inquiries about being raped involve very different experiences (Waldner-Haugrud & Magruder, 1995). Third, assuming that victimization questions can just be flipped to study men ignores the social contexts in which men and women interact. Are the sexual scripts prescribing the roles to be played identical? Is there equal power to be communicated and listened to? Is physical strength similar? Are the consequences of unwanted sex, including losing virginity, equal? Because the answers to all these questions are "no," we argue that this research is conceptually flawed and internally invalid. This research trivializes the rape of women by placing it in a context where it is demonstrated that women use coercive sexual tactics just like men, although it is noted that women stop short of physical force. The research has the potential to feed the anger of vulnerable men, for whom it confirms their perceptions of hostility toward women and feelings of being manipulated by them. Moreover, the findings fuel women's beliefs that sexual aggression is so common that it must be considered a natural part of dating. In these ways, research that aimed to be "gender neutral" ends up supporting the status quo.

STEREOTYPES OF DESERVING VICTIMS

Rape has less victim precipitation than other violent crimes, according to the National Commission on the Causes and Prevention of Violence. In contrast to homicide (22%), nonsexual assault (14%), or armed robbery (11%), only 4.4% of rapes were judged to be precipitated by the victim, according to the commission's definition, which was "when the victim agreed to sexual relations but retracted before to actual act or when she clearly invited sexual relations through language, gestures, etc." (Bryden & Lengnick, 1996). However, in spite of low levels of "victim precipitation," society continues to blame the victim of acquaintance rape. This is true for both men and women. For example, women may share with men beliefs that some women make themselves fair targets for rape. They may disapprove of the behavior of the victim, which is interpreted as asking for or deserving rape. For example, following the New Bedford gang rape, community women attacked the right of the victim to claim she had been wrongfully attacked (Chancer, 1987). These women emphasized that the New Bedford rape victim was in the wrong place at the wrong time—she was hanging out at a bar while those who judged her believed she should have been at home taking care of her children (Chancer, 1987).

The belief that victims precipitate rape is not isolated to the lay public. If a victim reports a rape to the authorities, she can expect to see the same attitude reflected in the institutionalized sexism often exhibited by the police and legal systems (Galton, 1975–1976). For example, police asked one reporting victim if she had ever attempted suicide, run away from home, or taken drugs (Holmstrom & Burgess, 1978). Unfortunately, this traditional view and associated censure of rape are not limited to the police and legal systems. These beliefs that victims precipitate rape seem to be common in the mental health field as well. One study of psychotherapists found that 64% reported they would work with a victim to reduce her inappropriate and seductive behaviors, and 56% claimed they would discuss ways in which the victim unconsciously desired or enjoyed the sexual assault (Dye & Roth, 1990).

Several studies have found that rape victims date more frequently and have a larger number of sexual partners than women who have not been raped. At first glance these findings seem to confirm stereotypes about deserving victims, but that is a misinterpretation of the data. Many of the studies fail to establish that these victims' dating practices preceded all sexual victimization. Those few prospective studies that exist have shown that risk behaviors are aftereffects caused by earlier victimizations (Gidycz, Coble, Latham, & Layman, 1993; Gidycz, Hanson, & Layman, 1995; Himelein, 1995). Furthermore, researchers uniformly note the minimal predictive power of these variables in differentiating between women who have been raped and women who have not. For example, Abbey and colleagues (1996) used characteristics of women, including number of dating partners, number of sexual encounters, number of times that a woman's intentions have been misperceived, and frequency of drinking during consensual sex, to predict occurrences of nonconsensual sex. Using these variables, 59% of the women who had been raped were correctly classified by the discriminatory function. Although 59% is not an outstanding result for this discriminatory procedure, it is substantially greater than the 32% who were classified correctly by chance alone. Abbey and colleagues (1996) were much more successful in predicting women who had never been sexually victimized than women who were. This suggests that in spite of the public sentiment that continues to cling to victim-blaming stereotypes, the primary predictor of whether a woman is raped is whether she has had the misfortune of encountering a sexually aggressive man in a location that precludes assistance or escape.

Once victimized, the social context in which women live conspires to create a strong disincentive to report rape to authorities. First, victimized women may feel responsible because they perceive that they have failed in their role as sexual gatekeeper. Second, they may feel they deserved the assault because they participated in activities that they believed put them at risk. Normal behaviors among college students, such as social drinking, are widely understood to render the woman a deserving victim, although the perpetrator's behavior may be excused on the same grounds (Norris et al., 1996). Third, women may fear the stigma of rape for herself and those close to her. For example, sorority women report fearing embarrassment not only to themselves but to the reputation of their sorority and to the Greek system as a whole if they reported rape (Norris et al., 1996). Fourth, in the immediate aftermath of the assault, the victim may convince herself that what happened is common, that it won't be really harmful, and that she will get over it, if she just goes on with her life. Fifth, women are likely to be aware that they live in a society that fails to take sexual assault very seriously.

The net result is that college women rarely report rape to the police. Koss and colleagues found that 8% of the women who had been raped reported to police (Koss, 1988). The rates of reporting were higher (29%) among women raped by strangers than among those raped by acquaintances (3%; Koss et al., 1988). Crimes lacking the stigma of rape, such as physical assault, were much more likely to be reported to police (76%) than rape (27%), among a sample of urban adult working women (Koss et al., 1991).

Ecological Interdependence and Intractability

Evidence reviewed in this chapter shows multiple levels of environmental influences that encourage male sexual aggression and discourage female outrage over victimization. Just as important, clear associations are evident between the behaviors of each sex and the surrounding environments and behaviors of the other sex. No matter which component of the sexually coercive environment one considers, it can be viewed as a probable outcome of the remaining components. When considered in sum, what emerges is a web of mutually dependent relationships between male behavior, female responses, societal reactions, peer support, and system response. For example, the rate of women's reporting of men's coercive behaviors is likely to be associated with the frequency of coercion by men, the acceptance of coercion by society, the low likelihood of punishment, and the unsupportive treatment that women who seek justice can expect. Similarly, the rate of men's sexual coercion is likely to be related to peer support, access to facilitative environments, low rates of women's reporting, and lack of any direct feedback about their behavior by the victim or others. This mutual dependence limits the independent tractability of any given component of the sexually coercive environment.

Intervention efforts must confront this ecological interdependence. The sexually coercive man is supported by his peers, is often successful in his aggressive behavior, and is rarely if ever punished or even reported. Similarly, the female victim is surrounded by male coercion, high levels of male aggression, and the likelihood that she will not be supported if she chooses to report her victimization. Given these realities, it is little wonder that sexually coercive behaviors exist as they do. Unless changes are made to the current payoffs for men's sexually coercive behaviors and women's reporting of the same, sexually aggressive men will continue to maximize sexual conquests regardless of consent, and women will avoid censure from peers and social institutions by hiding sexual victimization.

Interventions must aim to change the currently available payoffs for these behaviors. Peer-group support for sexual aggression can be addressed through proper institutional guidance of campus organizations and education aimed at masculinity and sexuality development. Evidence that sexual aggression shows a naturally developmental course suggests education could speed up the process of change. The next critical intervention is the education of women. Clearly, college women separate their ongoing experiences with men from the idea of rape, accepting a great deal of sexual aggression in the process. A focus on female sexuality as an adjunct to more traditional rape prevention might provide a forum for women to confront the cognitive stress they experience from double-standard expectations and consider methods for addressing it that are more productive than drinking to excess. Young women would benefit from education focused on the development of a better sense of what constitutes equality in the context of a sexual relationship. Other important items for this forum include stereotypes of what constitutes rape and whether there are deserving victims. This strategy might be more effective than an approach focused overtly on rape, which is a message many women appear to tune out. Institutional changes are then needed that assure women they will not be censured and, after paying respect to due process and the rights to privacy, that adjudication will confront a guilty party with genuine sanctions. Finally, women have to make use of the system so that men may reevaluate the costs of sexual aggression in terms of increased chances of retribution. Without these types of change, date rape will continue an enduring feature of the college experience.

If rape were a problem caused by a pathological few, it would pose no threat to our culture's understanding of sexuality. Instead, the force and virulence of attacks against these findings make it clear that the research has struck a central nerve. Not only is sexual aggression more frequent than previously suspected, but it is consistent with and supported by a dominant cultural understanding of sexual relations that endorses sexual coercion. Moreover, research on date rape is an example of scholarship that has influenced social policy. One could create a list of real changes that have occurred on college campuses to minimize sexual assault, such as rewritten student conduct codes, mandatory education sessions, tighter alcohol restrictions, policies regulating the conduct of rush within the Greek system, and oversight of programs and parties. In addition, there have been changes in federal law, including national reporting of crime on campuses, and allocation of funding directed at education and training for campus rape prevention.

These responses all represent deviations from the status quo, with the status quo being a system that benefits that group of college men past and present who pursue the largest possible number of sexual partners with the minimum effort. The responses called for to address the intractability of rape threaten the stakeholders in the current system. Deliberate efforts to alter the scripts that govern the roles of men and women in sexual relationships are undesired by those currently advantaged. Thus, the politicization of date rape was inevitable and, at the same time, is a tribute to social science scholarship that we have investigated so closely something in which people are so deeply invested.

CHAPTER

2

A Longitudinal Approach to the Study of Sexual Assault

Theoretical and Methodological Considerations

JACQUELYN W. WHITE
JOHN A. HUMPHREY

Much of life is played out in our relations with others. Life becomes meaningful, in large part, as a result of our enduring emotional ties with persons important to us. Our relations with others are psychologically rewarding to the extent that we can trust others to hold our well-being important to them. Yet much of social interaction—particularly among people who stand in close relation with one another—is marred by aggres-

AUTHORS' NOTE: The research described in this chapter was supported by Grant No. MH5083 from the National Institute of Mental Health.

sion. This aggression extends from verbal harassment to physical assault and sexual coercion. Ironically, as affective relations between girls and boys begin to form, so too does the combative nature of their interactions (White & Bondurant, 1996).

Culturally influenced aggression in the relations between the sexes begins early in life, becomes patterned and repetitive, and may well escalate into seriously assaultive behavior. The media have been replete with accounts of relationship violence. Considerable empirical evidence supports the pervasiveness of these media depictions. The term *acquaintance assault* has entered our language to refer to a range of aggressive behaviors in relationships.

In recent years, there has been increasing national recognition that relationship violence, largely hidden from public view, is widespread and cuts across regional, socioeconomic, ethnic, and racial lines (Koss et al., 1994).

Kilpatrick's National Women's Study (Crime Victims Research and Treatment Center, 1992), using a national probability sample of 4,008 adult women, has shown acquaintance rape rates strikingly higher than those officially recorded by law enforcement agencies across the country or in previous victimization surveys. He further found that the onset of rape and other sexual assaults tends to occur in childhood and early adolescence. Most rapes occurred prior to age 29, with 54% occurring between the ages of 11 and 24. An additional 29% occurred before the age of 11.

Similarly, Koss and her colleagues, in the only U.S. national survey of sexual and physical assault among college and university students, have provided evidence of the striking magnitude of relationship violence among young adults (Koss, Gidycz, & Wisniewski, 1987). In their survey of 6,200 college and university students on 32 campuses across the country, they found that 53.8% of undergraduate women reported having been sexually victimized. Of these women, 15.4% were raped, 12.1% experienced an attempted rape, 11.9% were verbally coerced into sexual intercourse, and 14.4% were verbally intimidated into other forms of sexual contact. Young women have reported most often being sexually assaulted by their boyfriends, dates, or close acquaintances (Koss, 1985; Mandoki & Burkhart, 1989; Russell, 1984). Other more recent studies have confirmed these patterns, lending support to their credibility (see Koss et al., 1994, especially chapter 9).

The Koss et al. survey (1987) also included approximately 3,000 college and university men. Of this sample, 4.4% admitted to engaging in behaviors that legally constitute forcible rape, with an additional 3.3% reporting attempting forced sexual intercourse. Other forms of sexual victimization were admitted by 17.4% of undergraduate men. College men, in other studies, have reported considerably greater involvement in attempted rape (26%) and rape (15%–17%; Kanin & Parcell, 1977; Mills & Granoff, 1992; Rapaport & Burkhart, 1984). Malamuth (1989) found that 35% of college men report being willing to rape if they were sure they would not be apprehended. Furthermore, the FBI (1994) found that men under the age of 25 constitute 43% of all individuals arrested for rape.

There is mounting evidence that the onset of serious relationship violence begins in early adolescence and tends to persist into adulthood. Both victimization by and perpetration of physical and sexual assault mark the lives of a significant segment of American teenagers and young adults (see Koss, 1993, for an excellent review of prevalence studies). Early victimization, either by a family member, other adult, or peer, tends to lead to repeated victimization later in life. Also, the younger the perpetrator of sexual or physical assault, the more likely the offender is to become a recidivist in early adulthood.

Yet little is known about the beginnings of acquaintance violence—the formation of patterns of victimization and perpetration, the risk and protective factors that influence the trajectory of acquaintance violence, and its adverse consequences. Although the prevalence of forced sexual relations is well documented, its precipitants are less well understood. What is known about the precipitants of acquaintance violence is largely derived from cross-sectional analyses.

Theoretical Considerations

In recent years, there has been a proliferation of analyses of sexually assaultive behavior, particularly among adolescents and college-aged students. These studies of sexual and physical victimization and perpetration tend to fall into one of four theoretical categories: (a) psychiatric and psychological models, (b) cultural norms of violence and sexism, (c) social context, and (d) developmental models. Following a brief overview of each of these approaches, we describe an integrative model and a research program designed to test the model.

PSYCHIATRIC AND PSYCHOLOGICAL MODELS

Psychiatric and psychological models emphasize the personal characteristics of victims and offenders. Specifically, victim-precipitation models (Amir, 1971; Blum, 1982; Selkin, 1978; Shainess, 1979) hold the victim responsible for the victimization. Support for this view has come primarily from differences observed by police or rape crisis centers between rape victims and rape resistors on various personality measures, assailants' comments about provocative behaviors on the victims' part, and observations of victim characteristics found in police reports.

In addition, psychiatric models of sexual aggression focus on the personal attributes of rapist—anger, sadism, and need for power and revenge. For example, Malamuth and colleagues (Malamuth, 1986; Malamuth, Sockloskie, Koss, & Tanaka, 1991) have reported that antisocial tendencies and dominance contributed significantly to aggressors' self-reported sexual victimization of women.

CULTURAL NORMS OF VIOLENCE AND SEXISM

Cultural norms of violence and sexist attitudes contribute to sexual victimization. Women are socialized to accept various rape-supportive beliefs and to blame themselves for their victimization (Morokoff, 1983; Walker & Browne, 1985). Men are socialized to be perpetrators of violence and to see sexual exploitation as a legitimate part of the masculine sex role (Curtis, 1976; Deitz, 1978; Kanin & Parcell, 1977). Sex-role socialization may lead to the development of beliefs and expectations conducive to acquaintance rape (Weis & Borges, 1973). Differences in attitudes toward women, interpersonal violence, and rape-supportive myths have also been associated with sexually assaultive behavior (see White & Humphrey, 1991, for a review).

SOCIAL CONTEXT

Situational models emphasize environmental and situational factors conducive to acquaintance rape. These include victim and perpetrator behaviors such as the woman initiating the date, the man paying for the date, their use of alcohol and drugs, and the woman going to the man's residence (see Koss, 1985; Koss et al., 1987; Muehlenhard, Friedman, & Thomas, 1985; Muehlenhard & Linton, 1987).

DEVELOPMENTAL MODELS

The most clearly articulated developmental model of violence and victimization is the intergenerational transmission of violence (Straus, Gelles, & Steinmetz, 1981). The basic premise is that violence learned in the home will manifest itself in later relationships. Koss et al. (1987) and Koss and Dinero (1989b) report significant differences in the amount of family violence and early sexual experiences of sexually victimized and nonvictimized women. These factors have also been linked to male sexual aggression against women (Koss et al., 1987). This model has been applied to courtship violence in general (Bernard & Bernard, 1983; Makepeace, 1981; Plass & Gessner, 1983) and to date rape in particular (Murphy, 1984).

Each of these theoretical perspectives draws attention to specific risk factors in the etiology of acquaintance violence. Yet no one formulation can account for the range of forced sexual relations. With few exceptions (Koss et al., 1987; Koss & Dinero, 1989b), the four theoretical perspectives have been considered apart from one another. In addition, retrospective designs have dominated previous analyses of acquaintance violence.

To remedy the major drawbacks of previous research, we have undertaken a comprehensive 5-year longitudinal study that uses an interactive model of sexual victimization that draws together the central components of the four major theoretical perspectives and a longitudinal design, the optimum method for analyses of precursors and consequences of sexually assaultive relationships.

The Theoretical Model

Only longitudinal research—the investigation of the same individuals over time—can adequately address the central issues of acquaintance violence. This study marks the first time an integrated sociological and psychological theoretical approach has guided the analysis of the risk for relationship violence. The underlying theoretical model guiding this work assumes that relationship violence is not random but that various victim, perpetrator, and situational factors interact to produce victimization.

The four major theoretical perspectives, previously discussed, guided the development of the model used in the present study of sexual victimization and its perpetration. Although each draws attention to specific risk factors,

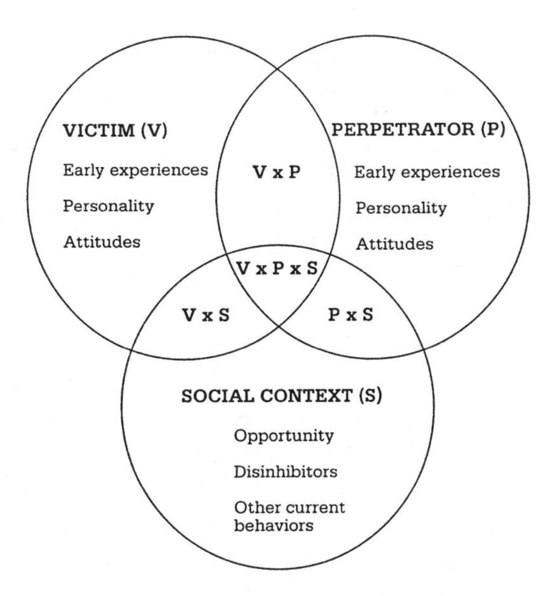

Figure 2.1. Interactional Model of Sexual Victimization

no single formulation can account for the range of forced sexual relations. The significant deficiencies of previous analyses mar our understanding of sexual victimization and assault. With few exceptions (Koss et al., 1987; Koss & Dinero, 1989b; and since the beginning of this project, Malamuth, Linz, Heavey, Barnes, & Acker, 1995), the four theoretical perspectives have been considered separately, and previous analyses have been limited to retrospective research designs. As a consequence, we do not know the causal ordering of the risk factors identified by each perspective or the main and interaction effects of these risk factors over time. Without this basic information, it is impossible to predict sexual assault and its perpetration.

The theoretical model that has guided our analyses integrates the central psychological and sociological risk factors for involvement in sexual and physical relationship violence. This model, which is seen in Figure 2.1, includes characteristics of the victim (V), characteristics of the perpetrator (P), and the social context (S) of the offense itself.

The risk of assault (either as a perpetrator or victim) is influenced by the extent of convergence of a vulnerable victim, a motivated offender, and a situation that provides a suitable opportunity for an assault. The risk of involvement in a sexually aggressive encounter among collegians is increased by the interaction of three components:

1. the sociocultural and psychological characteristics of the victim;
2. the sociocultural and psychological characteristics of the offender; and
3. the social context of the offense itself.

In our project, we focused on experiences with interpersonal violence at three stages in the life course: childhood, adolescence, and early adulthood. Therefore, we have been able to test the model in two ways: separately, at each life stage (childhood, adolescence, and early adulthood), and developmentally. By testing the model developmentally, we can assess the influence of risk factors at an earlier life stage on involvement in relationship violence at a later life stage.

Our design and measures lend themselves well to using a developmental model that treats early childhood experiences with family violence and coercive sex as precursors of adolescent experiences that shape values and attitudes and affect one's mental health status. These factors in turn serve as causal factors in involvement in coercive sexual experiences during the collegiate years. In addition to these developmental antecedents, our model proposes that the social context of the assault (e.g., nature of the relationship between the victim and perpetrator and the use of alcohol and drugs) also affects the likelihood of a sexual assault occurring.

In addition, a longitudinal design permits analysis of each of the component parts and the interactions between them. The potential causal relationships between these risk factors and subsequent sexual and nonsexual relationship violence are analyzed.

To carry out this research, it was necessary to do the following:

1. Establish a baseline for a longitudinal investigation of sexual victimization and perpetration occurring among university undergraduates by analyzing

   a. the prevalence of sexual victimization and perpetration prior to college entrance and
   b. the main and interaction effects of major risk factors that predict retrospectively the probability of precollegiate sexual victimization and perpetration.

2. Prospectively analyze the effect of prior risk factors, including previous victimizations and assaultive behaviors, on the probability of subsequent involvement in such violence by providing

   a. an ongoing analysis of the changes in the main and interaction effects of risk factors over the 4 undergraduate years and
   b. analyses of the prevalence and incidence of sexual victimization and perpetration over the course of a 4-year undergraduate career.

3. Conduct yearly analyses to examine the robustness of the predictive model across 4 years; in other words, do the same models that predict victimization and perpetration during the freshman year predict victimization and perpetration during the senior year?
4. Undertake subanalyses of factors that increase the probability of multiple victimizations and assaultive behavior.

VARIABLES ASSESSED

Three clusters of risk factors were identified. The first was the *Individual Experiences* factor, which contained variables related to one's past experiences, attitudes, and personality (including mental health status). The second was the *Contextual* factor, which contained measures related to the immediate circumstances of the victimization and perpetration. The third cluster of risk factors focused on *Change.* For each cluster of variables, reliability and validity were assessed before inclusion in subsequent analyses.

In the *Individual Experiences* cluster, three groups of items were assessed. The first dealt with early childhood experiences with sex and violence. Two questions about family violence before age 14 inquired about observing and experiencing parental aggression (from Koss et al., 1987). Straus's (1979) Conflict Tactics Scale (CTS) was used to obtain additional details about family violence. Seven additional questions assessed early sexual experiences, including abuse, and were based on Finkelhor (1984).

In the second group, questions about high school experiences with sex and violence were asked. To measure experience with courtship violence, Straus's CTS, as it applies to a dating context, was used. The Koss et al. (1987) Sexual Experience Survey was used to assess sexual experiences. On the first survey, students were asked about adolescent experiences since the age of 14. On follow-up surveys, they were asked the same questions with regard to experiences during only the prior year.

The final group of items in this cluster assessed attitudes and personality variables theoretically predictive of victimization and perpetration and sensitive to change as a consequence of a victimization or perpetration experience. A measure of general sex-role attitudes was based on four subscales of the Multicomponent Female-Male Relations Attitude Inventory (Ashmore & DelBoca, 1987): Acceptance of Traditional Gender Stereotypes, Women Taking Initiative in Dating and Sexual Relationships, Endorsement of Chivalry, and Acceptance of Male Heterosexual Violence. As a general index of mental health, the Mental Health Index reported by Veit and Ware (1983) was used. This yields five highly reliable and valid subscale scores appropriate for assessing mental health in the general population: Anxiety, Depression, Loss of Behavioral/Emotional Control, General Positive Affect, and Emotional Ties. Survey participants also completed the Spence, Helmreich, and Holahan (1979) Extended Personal Attributes Questionnaire to assess positive and negative aspects of masculinity and femininity. Elliott and Ageton's (1980) Self-Report Delinquency Survey was included to assess antisocial tendencies and engagement in antisocial behaviors.

The *Contextual* factors cluster consisted of items assessing the social climate for students. This included the immediate circumstances of a sexual assault, such as when and where the event occurred, and the interpersonal context (i.e., nature of the relationship). This cluster assessed how well the participants knew each other, whether both were students, who initiated the encounter, and whether alcohol or drugs were used, and if so, how much. Peer group characteristics were also assessed.

The *Change* cluster consisted of variables defined in terms of changes in attitudes, personality, and mental health status during the collegiate years, prior to the victimization. This cluster of factors takes into account the possibility that with time some of the variables may change independently of any victimization or perpetration experience and that one's status on these measures just prior to the victimization may be more predictive than one's status on entry into college.

Additional control variables were included in the follow-up surveys and included changes in relationship status (i.e., engaged, married, divorced, etc.), participation in therapy or counseling, and other potential stressful experiences. Additional measures assessing family violence and alcohol and drug use also were added to follow-up surveys.

Rationale for Longitudinal Studies

A debate goes on as to whether all young women are at risk for sexual assault or whether some women are uniquely vulnerable because of personal characteristics or behavioral styles. Part of this debate concerns the issue of blaming the victim, a practice soundly rejected by feminists. There is an inherent danger in studying the characteristics of victims, especially in the search of predictors (see Wieder's 1985 critique of Myers, Templer, & Brown, 1984). Some choose to avoid the topic because findings of differences between victims and nonvictims can be used to blame victims—the usual rhetoric of "you shouldn't have been there; you shouldn't have worn that; you shouldn't have been drinking; you should have know better." However, it seems reasonable to presume that women will benefit more by researchers facing the question and conducting rigorous research. Unfortunately, the typical research design retrospectively compares victims and nonvictims. Retrospective designs also allow for confounds due to different time frames for recall and the possibility that earlier experiences either prime the recall of later experiences or lead to selective forgetting of later experiences (Russell, 1984). With retrospective designs, it is difficult to determine whether observed differences are causes, correlates, or consequences of the victimization experience. Longitudinal research conducted with a contextualist perspective is an ideal approach.

Similarly, numerous questions abound regarding perpetration and reperpetration. Some researchers have concluded that date rapes are committed by relatively normal young men who simply misunderstood their partners' intentions. Such reasoning suggests that sexually assaultive actions could be committed by almost any man, given the right circumstances. This logic suggests that a date rapist is not likely to be a "repeat offender" and that few factors would distinguish an acquaintance rapist from a nonrapist. However, this is an empirical question. Estimates of self-reported rape perpetrated by college men range from 4% to 7%, and estimates of attempted rape are consistently approximately 4%. However, rates of self-reported rape experiences for women hover around 15%. Data such as these suggest that sexually assaultive acts by young men are not uncommon but that not all men are involved in such acts. When the magnitude of these numbers is contrasted with the high percentage of young women who report being victims of sexual assault, a discrepancy becomes apparent. Either women are overreporting and men are underreporting their involvement in sexual assault, or a relatively small proportion of men are responsible for sexual assaults. This latter possibility suggests that a sexually aggressive man probably has multiple victims. There are two approaches to answering this question. One is to ask men how many times and with how many different women they have engaged in various sexually aggressive behaviors. The second approach is to reassess men on multiple occasions across time.

Most research on the perpetration of sexual assault has been retrospective, relying on a one-time assessment of men's involvement in sexual aggression without asking about numbers of victims. The only longitudinal investigation of sexual assault among adolescents to date did not examine the question of perpetration and reperpetration (Ageton, 1983). Rather, Ageton examined engagement in delinquent behaviors in general as a predictor of later sexual aggression among adolescent boys. She found that, compared to their nonviolent peers, sexually assaultive adolescent boys were significantly more likely to engage in index offenses, particularly felonious assault, other crimes against the person, larceny, and public disorder.

That aggressive behavior at a younger age is one of the best predictors of later aggressive behavior is a well-established finding (Huesmann & Eron, 1992; Olweus, 1993). Most of this work on the stability of aggression has focused on acts of physical aggression directed toward peers during childhood as predictors of later involvement with the criminal justice system. However, this work has not looked at sexual aggression. Little is known about the stability of heterosexual aggression in general and sexual aggression in particular.

A longitudinal design permits the assessment of psychosocial and behavioral characteristics at various points in time, and the occurrence of sexual assault status (either as a victim or perpetrator) between each of these points. Typically, such designs are premised on the assumption that all participants are "the same" at time one. However, when this assumption is not justifiable (which it usually is not, except in true experimental designs with random assignment of participants to conditions), the design needs elaboration. Built into it must be a consideration of experiences that occurred prior to the first assessment and a control for preexisting differences, especially earlier victimization or perpetration experiences. If victimized and nonvictimized women do not differ at time one, after controlling for all preexisting differences, but do differ on certain characteristics at time two following a victimization, then these characteristics may be considered outcomes rather than predictors or causes of the victimization. Similarly, distinguishing between perpetrators and nonperpetrators prior to a perpetration experience can help establish which factors are predictors rather than consequences of the offending act.

Furthermore, a longitudinal design is well suited to test hypotheses derived from retrospective studies. Because any single study or any single measure has both strengths and weaknesses (Fromuth & Burkhart, 1996; White & Farmer, 1992), a longitudinal study can aid in providing evidence supportive of hypotheses derived from retrospective studies. A large-scale study that examines a large number of cases over a lengthy period of time with multiple measures tends to mitigate criticisms that results are spurious or due to a misinterpretation of any particular question. Phenomena that in theory should relate across time and that actually do are unlikely to be due to chance. The validity of the theoretical constructs is strengthened.

Thus, being convinced of the soundness of a longitudinal design, we directed our attention to a number of design questions to ensure proper implementation of the study. Specific issues associated with each major step of our research project are discussed in the following sections.

Methodological Issues

An examination of sexual assault experiences across time allows us to examine the predictors, correlates, and consequences of these experiences. The progression of factors across time can be determined, and interrelationships between various affective, cognitive, behavioral, and contextual factors can be assessed. However, a number of methodological issues arise when adopting this approach. Resolution of certain issues, such as definition of variables, is guided by the theoretical model adopted. Other issues stem from practical considerations and cover the gamut of methodological decisions, ranging from design selection to research participant selection to data analysis.

DESIGN SELECTION

A number of designs are potentially available to test longitudinal hypotheses. Because it is commonly recognized that all such designs contain some type of age × cohort × time of measurement confounds, a researcher's choice of design must be governed by conceptual considerations and assumptions about the likelihood and seriousness of potential confounds (Appelbaum & McCall, 1983). Thus, in a study of sexual assault experiences, it is reasonable to assume that cohort effects and time of measurement are critical; for example, results of a survey given in 1990 comparing self-reported sexual assault experiences of people who were at that time 18 or 35 years of age would be very difficult to interpret. Would differences in experiences be due to age, to the older people having had more opportunities to have been assaulted, or to cohort effects related to attitudes and values regarding self-disclosure of such experiences? Thus, a cross-sectional design that includes people of different ages at a particular time of measurement would confound cohort with the age × time of measurement interaction and would be appropriate only if one could assume no cohort or cumulative historical effects. In contrast, a classic longitudinal design, replicated over cohorts, would permit one to look at age changes, cohort, and historical factors. Although this design confounds time of measurement with the age × cohort interaction, a time-of-measurement confound is probably a less serious problem than an age or cohort confound, at least for the study of sexual assault. For example, surveys conducted in the 1950s might yield different results than those in the 1990s; however, any age-related changes observed during each of those time periods would be interpretable, even if not generalizable to other time periods. Thus, we opted for a classic longitudinal design, limiting ourselves to two cohorts (those born in 1972 and 1973), each assessed first when 18 years old and again when 19, 20, 21, and 22 years old. We assumed that there would be no significant time-of-measurement effects.

Another issue related to design is possible sensitization due to repeated exposure to the survey instrument. One solution is to combine several designs so that both between-group and within-group analyses can be conducted. However, this approach proves to be prohibitively expensive in terms of sample size needed, time needed to complete the study, and actual dollars spent. Repeated assessments may threaten external validity by sensitization, fatigue, carryover, or practice effects (Greenwald, 1976). However, many of these effects are most apparent in studies of learning and performance, when sessions are close together in time. In the present work, fatigue and carryover effects were unlikely, given the 12-month interval between assessment sessions. Niles and White (1989) have observed that men responding to the Sexual Experiences Survey (SES; Koss et al., 1987) and other sexual attitude items reported little memory for item content on a second testing occurring 2 to 3 months later. Also, in the present project each survey covered a nonoverlapping year in the student's life. Students were given a fixed reference point that limited the recall interval to the previous year. Furthermore, the attitude and personality measures asked students to report how they felt at the time of response. A further discussion about memory issues can be found in a subsequent section.

PARTICIPANT SELECTION AND SAMPLE SIZE

A critical consideration is who to study. We were interested in studying sexual assault during the collegiate years. However, decisions had to be made regarding which students to select and how to sample them. Depending on volunteers, for example, would introduce biases in the sample. A random sample is ideal, but because participation can never be required, a representative, if not random, sample was the desirable alternative. In addition, a representative sample allows better estimates of incidence and prevalence. We gathered our sample by identifying two incoming classes of students and inviting all to participate. We had worked with the university administration to gain permission to survey students in groups during the first day of student orientation, and we were able to train student orientation leaders to administer the survey, thus making participation in the study an integral part of the student orientation activities. This ensured almost 100% compliance (approximately 50% of all incoming students attended orientation). Students who did not attend orientation, which was not required, were contacted by phone. This process resulted in over 80% of the entering students participating in the initial survey. Demographic information was collected from the sample to ensure representativeness of the sample to the student body.

TRACKING AND ATTRITION

In a longitudinal study, it is critical to maintain sufficient information on each participant to ensure accurate matching of data from time to time. Given the sensitive nature of the questions asked in our project, we also had to ensure the confidentiality of responses.

Before the initial survey was administered, its purpose and methods were explained, and informed consent was obtained via a signature. Students also completed contact sheets for follow-up purposes. These sheets requested information on the student's name, local address, and phone number, along with the name, address, and phone number of a person who would be most likely to know the whereabouts of the student during the next year and who could be contacted if we had difficulty locating the student. To ensure confidentiality and still permit the matching of surveys across time, each survey and corresponding contact sheet was assigned a randomly determined code number and handed in separately. Only code numbers appeared on surveys and answer sheets. Lists of codes and corresponding names were kept in a locked safe to protect the identity of participants; access was limited to the coinvestigators and the data manager. To further ensure confidentiality of the data and to bolster students' confidence in our commitment to protecting confidentiality, we obtained a federal Certificate of Confidentiality from the National Institute of Mental Health.

Toward the end of each spring semester, students were contacted and asked to complete a follow-up survey during one of several sessions held at various locations around campus (i.e., student center, dormitories, classrooms). Postcards were sent to remind students of the follow-up survey and to announce times and locations for the sessions. These sessions were conducted by trained undergraduate psychology majors and graduate students. Students who did not attend one of these sessions were contacted by telephone and invited to participate. They were given the options of attending a session being held on campus or of receiving the survey by mail. This was particularly useful for students who had withdrawn from the university and who were residing out of town. All students who participated in the follow-up surveys received $15 each time they participated.

LENGTH OF THE SURVEY AND SELECTION OF SCALES

Given a comprehensive model, informed by psychological and sociological literature, the options for variables to include in the survey were extensive. However, the reality was that research participants would tire and possibly become bored with a lengthy survey instrument. Developing an instrument that could be completed in less than an hour by most participants was most practical. For forced-choice items, this meant including approximately 200 items. Therefore, it became essential to establish a priority for our hypotheses, and when more than one instrument was available, we selected ones that were most reliable, valid, short, and had established use in the literature. For example, although our overarching interest was in interpersonal violence, this particular project had a specific focus on various forms of sexual aggression, especially those that involved force or the threat of force. Therefore, based on available data and sample size limitations, it was judged theoretically and methodologically appropriate to focus on women as targets of sexual aggression and men as perpetrators of sexual aggression, recognizing that various forms of same-sex sexual aggression and female coercion of men would not be examined. However, we did examine women and men as perpetrators and targets of nonsexual and verbal aggression in romantic relationships because of the parity suggested by the research literature (White & Koss, 1991).

MEMORY/RECALL CONSIDERATIONS

Three related concerns can be raised: problems of retrospective recall, reconstruction of memory in a self-esteem-enhancing manner, and the effect of heavy drinking on memory recall. To deal with self-esteem-enhancing possibilities, we conducted a pilot study to assess the relationship between social desirability and self-reported sexual assault experiences among college men, and we found no relationship (White, Humphrey, & Farmer, 1989). We also designed an interview protocol to be administered to a random sample of participants following the first survey administration to determine reliability of responses on the survey and to assess converging evidence. Furthermore, substantial research conducted by Koss, Malamuth, and colleagues provides sound evidence establishing a relationship between self-reported sexual aggression and a number of theoretically relevant variables in men (Malamuth et al., 1991) and between self-reported sexual victimization and theoretically relevant measures in women (Koss & Dinero, 1989b). In addition, the questions about unwanted, coercive sexual experiences were asked in behaviorally specific terms and judgmental labeling was avoided (e.g., terms such as *assault* and *rape* did not appear in the behavioral descriptions); therefore, we assumed a greater honesty in reporting would result. We do acknowledge that estimates will probably be conservative because our methods could not capture forgotten experiences or those people unwilling to report.

Although we also recognize that extreme intoxication may distort and limit ability to encode information, it is unlikely that people who are extremely intoxicated, to the point of passing out, are able to engage in sexual or physical aggression. However, as a precaution, we plan to exclude from the analyses reports of assault situations involving self-reported levels of extreme intoxication. This decision was supported by evidence that alcohol has its greatest effect on behaviors at moderate levels of consumption. Low levels of alcohol initially suppress inhibitory processes, whereas at higher levels, excitatory processes are inhibited as well (Samson & Grant, 1990). We anticipate losing very little data because of reported extreme intoxication.

To address further potential biases, we took several additional precautions. Eich (1982) has indicated that memory recall depends on three things: content, how well encoded the information to be recalled is, and the circumstances surrounding the retriever (i.e., the cognitive environment of the rememberer). We used instructions and a progression of items that would create a cognitive environment that would facilitate memory recall. We used a clearly specified time frame for each survey. We also used close-ended questions, which essentially turn the memory task into a cued-recall or recognition-recall task. Eich has reported that cued recall and recognition memory procedures produce better recall than free recall procedures, even for events that occurred while under the influence of alcohol. Details are provided in the following sections.

FOLLOW-UP SURVEYS

During the 5 years of study, a number of articles presenting new data, conceptual ideas, and methodological issues were published. This prompted us to consider adding variables to the follow-up surveys. This, of course, necessitated a consideration of omitting some scales so as to maintain a survey of manageable length. Thus, additional measures assessing family composition, family violence, and familial alcohol and drug use were added to follow-up surveys. We also added items related to physical health, additional variables to assess the status relationship between the perpetrators and victims of sexual and physical aggression, posttraumatic stress disorder symptoms, attitudes toward alcohol, peer group characteristics, and plans for the future. All items about childhood and high school experiences were omitted from the follow-up surveys. Several items concerning personality and attitudes were also omitted.

DEFINITIONAL ISSUES AND CONTEXT OF QUESTIONS

Much has been written about definitional problems in sexual assault research (Muehlenhard, Powch, Phelps, & Giusti, 1992) and mechanisms for addressing these problems (Koss, 1992, 1993). Muehlenhard et al. (1992)

has suggested that definitions be clear about the type of behavior specified, and the criteria for nonconsent, including presence of force and consent rendered meaningless due to alcohol or drug intoxication. In addition, Koss (1992, 1993) has discussed the importance of the context of questioning, the time frame used, and confidentiality. Recently, O'Sullivan (1995) has cautioned researchers about the need to distinguish between unwanted but noncoerced, and coerced or forced, sexual activity. A solution is to use behaviorally specific definitions combined with specification of the age of assault to establish whether the assault occurred during childhood, adolescence, or adulthood. We defined sexual assault as follows.

Childhood victimization. Childhood victimization was assessed for both male and female participants. Questions for this portion of the survey were taken from Koss et al. (1987) and were derived from Finkelhor's (1984) method of assessing childhood sexual experiences. The screening context, developed to focus the respondent on the types of incidents we were interested in, stated that, "Many people have sexual experiences as children. The following questions ask about any experience you may have had before you were 14." The first question inquired if, prior to the age of 14, anyone had exposed themselves to the child, fondled the child or had the child fondle them, or attempted or completed sexual intercourse with the child. The second and third questions asked about the perpetrator's age and relationship to the child. The respondent was then asked what tactics the perpetrator had used, including coercion or force. A respondent was categorized as a childhood victim if any kind of sexual act (contact or noncontact) was perpetrated by an adult, regardless of strategy used (e.g., because it felt good; curiosity; made child feel loved or secure; said it was OK or used his or her authority or gave gifts, money, or candy; or threatened to hurt, punish, or use force). An experience perpetrated by a similarly aged other (peer or family member) using physical force, threat of force, or verbal manipulation or coercion (e.g., made child feel loved or secure; said it was OK or used his or her authority or gave gifts, money, or candy) was also categorized as a childhood victimization. Acts involving a similarly aged other engaged in out of curiosity or because it felt good were not included.

Adolescent victimization and perpetration experiences. During the first survey, respondents were asked to indicate how many times since the age of 14 they had engaged in each of the several sexual behaviors on the Koss et al.

(1987) version of the SES. For this group of questions, the context was set by first asking respondents to complete the items on the Straus (1979) Conflict Tactics Scale. They were instructed, "The ways that people can behave when showing anger toward a romantic partner or trying to get their way are listed below. For each of the following behaviors, show how frequently *YOU* have used (use) it with romantic partners and then how frequently romantic partners used it with you." These items were followed by questions about dating behavior during high school (frequency of dating, number of different dating partners), a question about sexual intimacy during dating, and a question about best friends' sexual activity. These were followed by the SES items, introduced with the phrase, "For the next set of questions, answer how often each of the following has occurred from age 14 on." The first question asked, "Have you ever had sexual intercourse with a (opposite sex) when you both wanted to?" The 10 SES questions about unwanted sexual activity followed. Men responded based on what they had done to a female, and women responded based on what had been done to them. We adopted a dimensional view of sexual aggression, which defines sexual aggression on a continuum of seriousness. Thus, men were placed into one of six mutually exclusive categories based on the most serious behavior they endorsed: no sexual experiences, only consensual sexual intercourse, forced contact with a woman, verbally coerced sexual intercourse, attempted rape, or rape. For women, responses were used to place respondents into one of six categories of sexual experience based on the most extreme event they experienced: none, consensual only, unwanted contact, verbal coercion, attempted rape, or rape. For all analyses, only women who had no sexual experiences or only consensual experiences were categorized as nonvictims, and only men who reported no sexual experiences or only consensual experiences were categorized as nonperpetrators. This gave us the option to define victim and perpetrator variously, either as women or men who had any sort of unwanted, coercive sexual experience during adolescence, or as women or men who had experienced attempted or completed sexual intercourse via physical force or threat of physical force. Being able to look precisely at various types of unwanted sexual experiences that were either coerced or forced is a real strength of the SES. Also, by asking respondents to report how many times each event had occurred, we are able to calculate a continuous measure of sexual assault experiences. This method has been used successfully by Malamuth (1986). Similarly, White, Donat, and Humphrey (1996) have reported good psychometric characteristics of this measure, and Kosson, Kelly, and White (in press) have also shown that this continuous measure correlates well with various indices of psychopathy in sexually aggressive men.

Adult victimization and perpetration experiences. Again the Koss et al. (1987) Sexual Experiences Survey was used, but women were asked to indicate how many times during the past year they had each sexual experience, and men were asked how many times they had committed each act (months were listed so they could identify when during the year the event occurred). Categorization as an adult nonvictim or victim, or as a nonperpetrator or perpetrator, was the same as described in the previous section. By specifying the time frame to a particular month within the past year, we were able to ensure that each follow-up survey captured a nonoverlapping time period. In addition, by so specifying a specific time frame, memory for the event was assumed to be enhanced. As stated previously, the behavioral specificity of the SES permits a variety of hypotheses regarding the relationship between various types of unwanted but coerced or forced sexual experiences to be examined. Furthermore, a series of questions about characteristics of the perpetrator, location of the experience, and other situational characteristics allowed better specification of the nature of the event.

DATA ANALYSIS CONSIDERATIONS

Our design and measures lend themselves well to using a developmental model that treats early childhood experiences with family violence and coercive sex as precursors of adolescent experiences that shape values and attitudes and affect one's mental health status. These factors serve in turn as causal factors in involvement in coercive sexual experiences during the collegiate years. In addition to these developmental antecedents, our model proposes that the social context of the assault (e.g., nature of the relationship between the victim and perpetrator and the use of alcohol and drugs) also affects the likelihood of a sexual assault occurring. Analyses can look at prevalence and incidence, using chi-square analyses, logit analyses, and survival analyses. Each analysis permits one to examine different questions regarding the course of victimization and perpetration across time. Analyses can also be conducted to examine the time-ordered nature of various relationships. Specific analyses available are analyses of covariance, multiple regression, and structural equation modeling. Specific analyses permit the testing of different hypotheses. Choice of analysis can also be dictated in part by a particular test's assumptions and the nature of the variables involved (i.e., categorical or continuous; normal or skewed distributions).

Conclusion

Since Koss's groundbreaking work in the mid-1980s, relationship violence, particularly among adolescents and young adults, has drawn the attention of a growing number of researchers. A proliferation of cross-sectional studies has documented consistently the pervasiveness of sexual and physical assault among intimates and acquaintances and that the onset of the sexual and physical victimization and its perpetration tends to occur in early adolescence and to persist into adulthood. Less well understood are the precipitants of relationship violence—the formation of patterns of victimization and perpetration, the risk and protective factors that influence the trajectory of acquaintance violence, and its adverse consequences.

To address adequately issues related to the onset and development of relationship violence, two considerations should inform future research. First, research should be guided by a theoretical model that integrates central psychological, sociological, and cultural precipitants of relationship violence. Risk factors identified in cross-sectional analyses have been suggested by psychiatric/psychological, normative-cultural, social-contextual, and developmental models. To determine the relative merits of each of these perspectives for the prediction of the onset and persistence of relationship violence, they should be integrated into a comprehensive theoretical model.

Second, longitudinal research designs are best suited for testing a predictive theoretical model. Longitudinal analyses permit the testing of hypotheses derived from retrospective studies, the causal nature and the time ordering of the variables assessed, and the control of confounding influences. Our understanding of relationship violence will be advanced significantly by conducting theoretically driven longitudinal analyses.

CHAPTER

3

Measuring Sexual Abuse in Canadian University/College Dating Relationships

The Contribution of a National Representative Sample Survey

WALTER S. DEKESEREDY

According to the sixth annual United Nations (UN) *Human Development Report* (1995), Canada is the best country in the world to live in. In *overall* human development, measured by a combination of indicators such as life

AUTHOR'S NOTE: The research reported in this article was supported by a grant from Health Canada's Family Violence Prevention Division to Walter S. DeKeseredy and Katharine Kelly. I would like to thank the following people for comments, criticisms, and assistance: Martin D. Schwartz, the late Michael D. Smith, Desmond Ellis, John Pollard and his colleagues at the Institute for Social Research, the Ottawa Regional Coordinating Committee to End Violence Against Women, all the students and instructors who participated in this project, and the two anonymous reviewers of this chapter.

expectancy, education, and income, Canada tops 174 nations for the second straight year (Beauchesne, 1995). Furthermore, many outside observers regard Canada as a "peaceable kingdom." For example, compared to members of the U.S. general public, Canadians are much less likely to be physically and sexually assaulted in public settings, such as parks, streets, workplaces, and taverns (Ellis & DeKeseredy, 1996; Silverman, 1992).

However, the UN *Report* also states that Canadian women do not fare as well as men. In fact, Canada is one of four industrial countries that has a "sharply lower" ranking on the "gender-development index" than on the "human development index." Canada is also indicted as a nation where many heterosexual women experience a substantial amount of physical and psychological pain in a variety of intimate and domestic relationships. To support this assertion, the UN cites statistics generated by several major studies, such as those uncovered by DeKeseredy and Kelly's (1993a) Canadian national survey (CNS) on woman abuse in university/college dating relationships.

An alarming number of female undergraduate students who completed DeKeseredy and Kelly's modified version of Koss, Gidycz, and Wisniewski's (1987) Sexual Experiences Survey (SES) were victimized by a broad range of injurious and demeaning male behaviors. These two Canadian sociologists uncovered a rate of completed rape that is consistent with rape data elicited from college/university students who filled out adaptations of the SES in New Zealand, the United Kingdom, the United States, and Seoul, South Korea (Beattie, 1992; Gavey, 1991; Heise, Pitanguy, & Germain, 1994; Koss et al., 1987; Shim, 1992). The main objective of this chapter is twofold: to briefly describe the rationale for the CNS on woman abuse in heterosexual university/college dating and to review some of sexual abuse data generated by this study.

The Need for Reliable Estimates of Sexual Abuse in University/College Dating

Sexual abuse is common on U.S. college/university campuses, and thus, it is no surprise that many female undergraduates do not feel safe in these settings or their immediate surroundings (Bohmer & Parrot, 1993). Similarly, a large number of Canadian female undergraduates worry about their personal safety. For example, of the 1,835 women who participated in the CNS,

- 36.1% felt unsafe and 25.9% felt very unsafe walking alone after dark.
- 35.7% felt unsafe and 12.9% felt very unsafe riding a bus or streetcar alone after dark.
- 34.8% felt unsafe and 38.7% felt very unsafe riding a subway alone after dark.
- 42.5% felt unsafe and 25.7% felt very unsafe walking alone to a car in a parking lot after dark.
- 41% felt unsafe and 31.2% felt very unsafe waiting for public transportation alone after dark.
- 36.3% felt unsafe and 38.9% felt very unsafe walking past men they don't know, while alone after dark (Kelly & DeKeseredy, 1994).

As Currie and MacLean (1993) correctly point out, some conservative scholars and campus administrators contend that these and other female students' fears of being attacked are unfounded because only a handful of women report acts of sexual abuse to the police, campus counseling services, and campus security officers. Several large-scale, government-sponsored victimization surveys conducted in the mid- to late 1980s, such as the Canadian Urban Victimization Survey (CUVS; Solicitor General of Canada, 1985) and the third cycle of the General Social Survey (GSS; Sacco & Johnson, 1990), indirectly and unintentionally supported this conclusion by producing data that show that women's level of fear is substantially higher than men's, even though women's victimization rates are much lower.

However, these fear-of-crime data are misleading because the CUVS, GSS, and other mainstream surveys did not adequately measure the most common types of female victimization in Canada: physical, psychological, and sexual abuse by male intimates (Smith, 1988; Stanko, 1990). What is clearly needed, then, are surveys specifically designed to elicit accurate estimates of woman abuse in Canadian postsecondary school courtship.

Since the late 1980s, several researchers responded to this call for more accurate data, and their surveys are summarized in Table 3.1. Although they used different samples and slightly different measures, the last three of the five surveys described in Table 3.1 reveal that a large number of Canadian female undergraduates are sexually abused by their intimate partners. These studies, it should also be noted in passing, used modified versions of the SES to detect the extent of victimization, a valid, reliable, and widely used measure in both Canada and the United States (Koss & Gidycz, 1985).

For the two surveys that did not employ the SES (Barnes, Greenwood, and Sommer, 1991; DeKeseredy, 1988), it is fair to assume that they obtained

TABLE 3.1 Sexual Abuse in Canadian University/College Dating Surveys

		Description of Surveys			*Abuse Rates*	
Survey	*Survey Location*	*Sample Description*	*Interview Mode*	*Measure(s) of Abuse*	*Incidence Rate(s)*[a]	*Prevalence Rate(s)*[b]
DeKeseredy (1988)	Southern Ontario	308 male university students	Self-administered questionnaires	2 questions	2.6% reported having been sexually abusive	Not examined
Barnes et al. (1991)	Manitoba	245 male university students	Self-administered questionnaires	Students were asked if they had physically forced a woman to have sex	Not examined	0.5% said they did it once, whereas 1% said they did it more than once
DeKeseredy et al. (1992)	Eastern Ontario	179 female and 106 male university/ college students	Self-administered questionnaires	Modified SES	8% of the men stated that they were sexually abusive, and 28% of the women stated that they were abused	12% of the men stated that they were sexually abusive, and 40% of the women stated that they were abused
Elliot et al. (1992)	University of Alberta	1,016 undergraduate students (men and women)	Self-administered questionnaires	Modified SES	Not examined	44% of the students who reported an unwanted sexual experience while registered at the U. of A. stated that the offender was a romantic aquaintance, and 18% said that the perpetrator was a casual or first date
Finkelman (1992)	University of New Brunswick and St. Thomas University	447 undergraduate students (men and women)	Self-administered questionnaires	Modified SES	Approximately 34.4% of the 127 respondents who reported one or more unwanted sexual experiences were victimized by a boyfriend/ girlfriend or date	Not examined

a. *Incidence* refers to the amount of abuse that took place in the past 12 months.
b. *Prevalence* refers to the amount of abuse that took place over a longer time period (e.g., since leaving high school).

markedly lower incidence and prevalence rates because they used single-item measures. Such an approach exacerbates the problem of underreporting because one question cannot cover the full range of unwanted, demeaning, and brutal sexual acts. This is why several woman-abuse researchers now use broad definitions of sexual abuse and multiple measures such as the SES (DeKeseredy, 1995; Smith, 1994). Surveys that employ multiple, behaviorally specific questions generally indicate higher rates of sexual abuse (Koss, 1993).

Although the last three studies described in Table 3.1 indicate that the sexual abuse of heterosexual women in Canadian postsecondary school courtship is a major problem that warrants the development of more effective prevention and control strategies, they have some major limitations that put them "in jeopardy" (Smith, 1994). For example, the incidence and prevalence rates are derived from local, nonprobability samples. Thus, they do not provide accurate information on how many male-to-female sexual assaults take place in the Canadian university/college dating population at large (DeKeseredy & Kelly, 1993a). Furthermore, one of these surveys (Elliot, Odynak, & Krahn, 1992) did not ask participants to identify their abusers' gender. Although this study shows that women (77%) report higher levels of victimization than men, there is no way of knowing the precise number of women who were harmed by lesbian or heterosexual partners because the participants were not told to focus only on heterosexual dating abuse.

Unlike many other methodological problems that continue to plague survey research on sexual abuse in heterosexual dating (see DeKeseredy, 1995; Koss, 1993; Smith, 1994), these two major pitfalls can be either eliminated or minimized by using some of the techniques employed by the CNS. For example, DeKeseredy and Kelly (1993a) obtained SES data from a national representative sample, and they explicitly asked their respondents to report only events that took place in heterosexual courtship.

DeKeseredy and Kelly (1993b) also used a variety of supplementary open- and closed-ended questions to minimize the problem of underreporting.[1] Even though the SES is a valid and reliable instrument, it is necessary to use supplementary questions on sexual abuse and other variants of woman abuse because, as other studies have shown (DeKeseredy, Kelly, & Baklid, 1992; Hanmer & Saunders, 1984; Junger, 1987, 1990; Kelly, 1988; Roberts, 1989; Smith, 1987, 1994), at the outset, people may not report incidents because of embarrassment, fear of reprisal, reluctance to recall traumatic memories, and so forth (Kennedy & Dutton, 1989; Straus, Gelles, & Steinmetz, 1981).

But if people are probed later on in a questionnaire, some reluctant or forgetful participants will reveal abusive experiences (Smith, 1987, 1994). Some of them may also provide data on variants of sexual abuse excluded from the SES, such as their boyfriends' or dating partners' attempts to get them to imitate what they had seen in pornographic media (Schwartz & DeKeseredy, 1994a), an issue to be discussed in a subsequent section of this chapter.

Why are these methodological improvements necessary, and why does Canada need more accurate estimates of sexual abuse in university/college dating? As the late Michael D. Smith (1994) correctly pointed out, survey researchers are obligated to "draw out data that did some justice to the sensitivity and complexity of the subject matter and at the same time attend to the chief concerns of established survey research—getting a representative sample and generating valid and reliable data" (p. 110). Such data can also increase the probability of influencing campus and government officials to devote resources to curb sexual assault in university/college dating relationships (DeKeseredy, 1995).

However, reasonably accurate statistics, such as those presented in a subsequent section of this chapter, often do not motivate policymakers to devote more time, energy, and money to the prevention and control of woman abuse. For example, even though it sponsored the CNS, the federal government did not create new legislation or allocate more funds to make female undergraduates' lives safer (MacIvor, 1995). In addition, the CNS did not command much respect from the media. Based on their analyses of newspaper and television accounts of that research, Currie and MacLean (1993) concluded that the "media responses to findings of the National Survey on Dating Violence were often similarly unsupportive of a woman-centred approach to dating violence and dismissive of the importance in identifying attitudes which support abusive behaviours towards women" (pp. 14-15).

At the time of writing this chapter, the whole Canadian woman abuse discourse is "characterized by a general atmosphere of mistrust and a well-organized backlash against feminism" (Levan, 1996, p. 350). Throughout Canada, many women's shelters, rape crisis centers, and batterers' programs have been or are great risk of being shut down because of funding cuts. Moreover, as in the United States, an enormous Canadian audience exists for people without expertise, experience, or data who mock and taunt female survivors of physical, sexual, and psychological abuse in intimate, heterosexual relationships (Schwartz & DeKeseredy, 1994b).

The Methodology of the CNS

The data presented in this chapter are derived from a national representative sample survey of Canadian community college and university students conducted in the autumn of 1992. A research team administered two questionnaires, one for men and another for women, in 95 undergraduate classes across the country, from the Maritimes to British Columbia. Both French- and English-language versions were administered. Response rates were very high, with less than 1% of the participants refusing to answer.

The sample consisted of 3,142 people, including 1,835 women and 1,307 men. The median age of female respondents was 20, and the median age of males was 21. Although members of many different ethnic groups participated in the survey, most of the respondents identified themselves as either English Canadian or French Canadian, and the majority of them (81.8% of the men and 77.9% of the women) were never married. All respondents were carefully and repeatedly warned, however, that all questions in the survey referred only to events that took place in heterosexual dating (nonmarital relationships). The sample was composed mainly of 1st- and 2nd-year students and a sizable portion (42.2% of the women and 26.9% of the men) were enrolled in arts programs. Approximately 3% of the women were or had been members of sororities, and about 6% of the men were or had been members of fraternities.

The incidence (events that took place 12 months before the survey) and prevalence (events that took place since leaving high school) of sexual abuse were measured using a slightly modified version of Koss et al.'s (1987) Sexual Experiences Survey (SES). The 10 items included in the SES range from unwanted sexual contact to sexual coercion, attempted rape, and rape.

Findings

Because the responses to each of the SES items are described and discussed in great detail elsewhere (see DeKeseredy & Kelly, 1993a, 1993b), this information will not be repeated here. Instead, only the global estimates and key risk factors associated with sexual abuse in Canadian postsecondary school dating that have been identified so far will be briefly described.

Approximately 28% of the female participants stated that they were sexually abused in the year before the survey, whereas 11% of the men reported having victimized a female dating partner in this way during the same time period. As was expected, the prevalence rates are significantly higher than the incidence rates because obtaining estimates of sexual abuse that have taken place over a longer period of time dramatically increases the size of the sample of reported victims/survivors and perpetrators (Sessar, 1990; Smith, 1994). For example, 45.1% of the women stated that they had been sexually abused since leaving high school and 19.5% of the men reported perpetrating at least one abusive act in the same time period.

Despite some methodological differences, the preceding findings are consistent with Koss et al.'s (1987) U.S. national data. In sum, although Canadians can take pride in the fact that their streets are safer than those in the United States, they should take careful note of the fact that their country is a nation where many women experience "the most painful devaluation—physical and psychological violence" (Beauchesne, 1995, p. A2).

Many people regard Canadian universities and community colleges as centers of higher learning, friendly interpersonal socialization, career training, liberal thought, and athletic achievement. Some people also perceive these postsecondary schools as "places . . . where the pursuit of truth and the exercise of reason prevail, and where it is assumed, our daughters will be safe from 'the lion in the streets' " (Pierson, 1991, p. 10). However, the data reported here show that for a large number of women, these institutions and their surroundings (e.g., off-campus houses and apartments) are "hot spots" of male-to-female sexual abuse.

What are the key risk factors associated with sexual abuse in university/college dating? The CNS found that men who report sexually abusing their dating partners are more likely to espouse the ideology of familial patriarchy than those who do not report such behavior (DeKeseredy & Kelly, 1993b). Following DeKeseredy and Schwartz (1993) and Smith (1990), familial patriarchal ideology is defined as a discourse that supports the abuse of women who violate the ideals of male power and control over women in intimate relationships. Relevant themes of this ideology are an insistence on women's obedience, respect, loyalty, dependency, sexual access, and sexual fidelity (Barrett & MacIntosh, 1992; Dobash & Dobash, 1979; Pateman, 1988). These themes were operationalized in the CNS by constructing two indices used by Smith (1990).

The CNS also found that men who espouse the ideology of familial patriarchy are even more likely to sexually abuse their partners when they receive male peer support, a risk factor defined by DeKeseredy (1990) as "the attachments to male peers and their resources that these men provide which encourage and legitimate woman abuse" (p. 130).

If all-male social groups in university/college settings are key sources of the sexual victimization of women, then some people might logically expect that men who admit engaging in such behavior do not have a prior history of sexual abuse. However, Schwartz and DeKeseredy's (1994a) analysis of data generated by the CNS supports the assertion that "many men come to college with the full armory of ideology and behaviours" necessary to engage in sexual abuse (p. 59).

For example, they found that when men who admitted to having been sexually abusive in elementary or secondary school were compared to those who admitted to using force to engage in sexual activities after high school, 8 (32%) of the 25 elementary or secondary-school offenders also disclosed similar forced sexual behavior in postsecondary-school courtship. If one takes a retrospective look, 8 (34.8%) of the 23 men who admitted to using force in university/college also admitted to having used it in elementary or secondary-school dating relationships. In other words, whether one looks retrospectively or prospectively, of the men in the national sample who reported using forced sex in postsecondary-school courtship, about one third of them were engaging in such behavior before they arrived.

A review of the literature reveals that the contribution of pornography to sexual abuse in heterosexual dating is another issue that several theorists relate to male peer support. For example, some men learn to sexually objectify women through their exposure to pornographic media (Jensen, 1995), and they often learn these lessons in groups, such as pornographic film showings at fraternity houses (Sanday, 1990). However, prior to the CNS, there were no empirical attempts to examine whether exposure to pornography is related to sexual abuse in postsecondary-school dating relationships.

Schwartz and DeKeseredy's (1994a) analysis of CNS data shows that 137 (8.4%) women in the sample stated that they were upset by their male dating partners' attempts to get them to do what they had seen in pornographic pictures, movies, or books.[2] Furthermore, of the respondents who were sexually abused since leaving high school,[3] 22.3% had also been upset by attempts to get them to imitate pornographic scenarios. Only 5.8% of the women who were not victimized reported being upset by pornography.

Does pornography cause woman abuse? This is an important question raised by many politicians, feminists, and members of the general public. Certainly this question cannot be answered by correlational data. For example, it may be that the same factors that cause men to sexually assault women also cause them to purchase pornography. In other words, eliminating pornography might not have an effect on the amount of sexual abuse in dating relationships. Even so, according to Harmon and Check (1989), the relationship uncovered by the CNS suggests that attempts to get women to do what their male partners have seen in pornographic media are a component of the overall problem of woman abuse in university/college courtship. Obviously, further research is necessary.

In sum, four key risk factors associated with sexual abuse in Canadian university/college dating relationships have been identified so far. Further analyses of the data generated by the CNS will likely point to other equally, if not more important, factors, such as dating status, age, and so forth. This is not to say that new and better surveys should not be conducted. Despite the fact that those involved with the CNS tried to develop a project that meets the highest disciplinary standards, overcomes the limitations of previous comparable surveys, and takes feminist concerns seriously, several methodological improvements are necessary in future research, such as those pointed out by Koss (1993) and DeKeseredy (1995). After all, the sexual abuse of women in postsecondary-school dating is a "never-ending and constantly evolving issue" (Ledwitz-Rigby, 1993, p. 93).

Conclusions

The data presented here yield several conclusions. Perhaps the most salient one is that a substantial number of Canadian women are sexually abused by their university/college male dating partners. There are, however, large gender differences in reporting the incidence of sexual abuse, and the reporting gap widens for the prevalence data. What accounts for these discrepancies? There is no evidence to support the assertion that "women do often lie about sexual assault, and do so for personal advantage or some other personal reason, which is pretty well why anybody lies" (Fekete, 1994, p. 54). Survey data generated by measures such as the SES do not greatly exaggerate the extent of sexual abuse. On the contrary, they should be read as underestimates for reasons described earlier in this article (e.g., embarrassment, reluctance to recall traumatic memories, etc.).

A more likely explanation for the gender discrepancies in reporting is that social desirability plays a key role in shaping male responses (Arias & Beach,

1987; Dutton & Hemphill, 1992). Eliciting honest and complete responses from male perpetrators is very problematic (Smith, 1987). For example, since the early 1980s, we have witnessed a significant increase in public and legal attention given to sexual assault in North American dating relationships. Many members of the general public now recognize that date rape and other variants of sexual abuse in courtship are criminal or deviant behaviors. Thus, many men will not disclose their abusive behavior for fear of stigmatization or reprisal, even when researchers guarantee anonymity and confidentiality (DeKeseredy, 1988).

Another significant conclusion is that the ideology of familial patriarchy, male peer support, a prior history of sexual abuse, and men's exposure to pornographic media contribute to sexual abuse in Canadian postsecondary-school courtship. However, because a large amount of data gathered by the CNS still need to be examined, it is likely that future analyses will identify several other key risk factors, such as dating status, level of education, and alcohol and drug use.

Finally, U.S. and Canadian survey researchers need to develop better ways of obtaining richer data on the experiences of visible minority students (Koss, 1993). For several reasons described elsewhere (see DeKeseredy, 1995; Ellis & DeKeseredy, 1996), studies such as the one described here include mainly European American or European Canadian students. Thus, ethnic minority "booster samples" are necessary because normal sampling techniques will not generate a sufficient number of ethnic minorities to allow for analyses of the variation in vulnerability to sexual abuse by race/ethnicity (Jones, MacLean, & Young, 1986). Moreover, researchers should translate questionnaires because many foreign students have difficulties reading or speaking either French or English.

Notes

1. See DeKeseredy (1995), DeKeseredy and Kelly (1993a, 1993b, 1995), DeKeseredy and Schwartz (1994), Kelly and DeKeseredy (1994), and Pollard (1993) for more information on the methods used in this study.

2. Schwartz and DeKeseredy used a slightly modified version of a question developed by Russell (1990) to operationalize attempts to make women imitate pornography.

3. For the purpose of their analysis, Schwartz and DeKeseredy operationalized sexual abuse by using four SES items. These items focused on the use or threat of physical force to make a woman engage in various sexual activities.

CHAPTER

4

Acquaintance Rape Is Real Rape

PATRICIA A. FRAZIER
LISA M. SEALES

Several authors have argued recently that the problem of acquaintance rape has been grossly exaggerated to serve a feminist political agenda (Gilbert, 1991, 1992, 1994; Hoff-Sommers, 1994; Paglia, 1993; Podhoretz, 1991; Roiphe, 1993). Most of these authors' criticisms are directly or indirectly aimed at the *Ms.* Magazine Campus Project on Sexual Assault, a large-scale study conducted by Mary Koss regarding the prevalence of rape among women on college campuses throughout the United States (Koss, Gidycz, & Wisniewski, 1987; Warshaw, 1988). In this study, Koss administered the Sexual Experiences Survey (SES), which was designed to identify victims of rape and attempted rape according to legal criteria, to 3,187 college women. Based on their responses to the SES, 15% of the women had been victims of rape and 12% had experienced an attempted rape at least once since age 14. The vast majority of the assailants (89%) were either acquaintances or dates of the respondents.

The *Ms.* study and the resultant prevalence figures have been criticized on several grounds. One criticism is that most (73%) of the women who were identified as rape victims based on their responses to the SES did not identify themselves as having been raped. In other words, although the experiences they described met the legal criteria for rape, the women did not define the experience as rape when asked directly. Critics argue that if a woman does not think she has been raped, then she probably was not raped (see, e.g., Gilbert, 1991, 1992, 1994; Hoff-Sommers, 1994; Podhoretz, 1991; Roiphe, 1993). According to these critics, the experiences that feminist researchers such as Koss now are calling *rape* are more accurately defined as *sexual seduction* (Gilbert, 1991, 1992, 1994; Podhoretz, 1991; Roiphe, 1993). According to Podhoretz, such advocacy statistics instill fear in the minds of young women by creating warped interpretations of normal sexual conduct.

Another aspect of the data that leads these critics to doubt Koss's findings is that approximately one half (42%) of the women identified as rape victims in the *Ms.* study had sex again with the alleged assailant (Warshaw, 1988). According to the critics, if a woman truly had been raped, she would not continue to have sexual relations with the offender (Gilbert, 1992, 1994; Hoff-Sommers, 1994; Podhoretz, 1991; Roiphe, 1993). Koss has countered this argument by hypothesizing that victims may continue to have sexual relations with their assailants because they blame themselves for the assault (Warshaw, 1988).

A final criticism of the *Ms.* study concerns its methodology. For example, one of the three questions assessing rape in one version of the SES is, "Have you had sexual intercourse when you didn't want to because a man gave you alcohol or drugs?" This question, it has been argued, is ambiguous and could elicit an affirmative response based on a broad range of experiences, not all of which qualify as rape (Gilbert, 1992, 1994; Hoff-Sommers, 1994; Roiphe, 1993). Hoff-Sommers noted that the prevalence of rape drops to one in nine women (11%) when women who were classified as rape victims based on this question were omitted from the analyses. Furthermore, when both this group of respondents and the 73% who did not identify themselves as victims of rape were dropped, the prevalence figure is considerably lower.

In summary, according to several critics, many experiences that are being called acquaintance rape by feminist researchers are not actually rape, and these exaggerated figures are being used to support a feminist political agenda. These concerns are based partly on the findings that many women identified as victims by the SES do not define themselves as such and continue to have sexual relations with their alleged assailants.

What kinds of data might be relevant to assessing whether acquaintance rape is a real and serious problem? Two types of studies seem relevant. First are studies that compare the reactions of victims of acquaintance and stranger rape. Presumably, if experiences that are being called rape are really just seduction, then victims of acquaintance rape should report significantly less distress than victims of stranger rape. Second, if researchers are labeling women as victims erroneously, then women who do not define themselves as rape victims should report less distress than those who do identify themselves as rape victims.

We have conducted two studies using different measures and different populations that bear on these issues. The participants in the first study were women seen by the staff of a hospital-based rape crisis program; all of these participants defined themselves as victims of rape. The participants in the second study were female college students who were identified as rape victims via their responses to the SES. Both studies compared victims of acquaintance and stranger rape in terms of postrape symptoms and self-blame. Because the second study used the SES, it also was possible to compare symptom levels among women who described their experiences as rape and women who did not (i.e., acknowledged vs. unacknowledged victims). Results of our research will be described first and then integrated with the results of other studies.

Hospital-Based Study

SAMPLE AND PROCEDURES

Participants in this study were seen by the staff of a hospital-based rape crisis center that provides victims with emergency room assistance and follow-up counseling. Data were collected from 70 female rape victims seen for counseling between 1 and 3 months postrape. Participants who had been raped by a friend, date, boyfriend/husband, or other family member were considered victims of acquaintance rape (55%; $n = 39$), whereas victims who were not previously acquainted with their assailants were categorized as victims of stranger rape (45%; $n = 31$).

MEASURES

Participants completed questionnaires assessing several symptoms found to be common among rape victims (see Resick, 1993, for a review), including depression, anxiety, hostility, and posttraumatic stress disorder (PTSD). Specifically, the Beck Depression Inventory (BDI; Beck, Ward, Mendolsohn, Mock, & Erbaugh, 1961) measured the extent to which victims had experienced depressive symptoms during the week previous to assessment. Two subscales from the Brief Symptom Inventory (BSI; Derogatis, 1977) were used to assess symptoms of anxiety and hostility within the past week. In addition, a 17-item checklist was created from the *DSM-III-R* (APA, 1987) to assess the symptoms of PTSD. Finally, the McPearl Belief Scale—Revision D (MBS; McCann & Pearlman, 1990) was administered to assess disruptions in victims' beliefs about themselves, others, and the world as a result of the trauma. The MBS is an 80-item self-report measure with 10 subscales (i.e., self-trust, other-trust, safety, independence, high power, low power, self-esteem, other-esteem, self-intimacy, other-intimacy).

Internal attributions about the cause of the rape also were assessed. This is important given arguments that victims of acquaintance rape continue to have sexual relations with their alleged assailants partly because they engage in more self-blame than victims of stranger rape. Attributions were assessed via two 7-item scales measuring the extent to which victims blamed the rape on their own behavior (i.e., behavioral self-blame) or character (i.e., characterological self-blame). All measures had adequate internal consistency reliability coefficients ($\alpha s > .71$).

RESULTS

Five *t*-tests were conducted to compare symptom levels among victims of stranger and acquaintance rape. All five tests were nonsignificant (see Table 4.1). That is, women who had experienced acquaintance rape reported levels of depression, anxiety, hostility, PTSD, and disrupted beliefs that were similar to those of women who had been raped by strangers, all $ps > .05$. Moreover, mean scores on the symptom measures indicated that both groups

TABLE 4.1 Comparisons Between Stranger and Acquaintance Rape Victims: Hospital-Based Study

	Stranger *(n = 31)*	*Acquaintance* *(n = 39)*
Symptoms		
BDI—Depression[a]	19.69	22.22
BSI—Anxiety[b]	2.06	1.82
BSI—Hostility[b]	1.80	1.63
PTSD[c]	10.37	9.86
MBS[d]	3.46	3.57
Attributions		
Behavioral self-blame[e]	2.88	3.44*
Characterological self-blame[e]	2.45	2.81

a. Range = 0 to 63; 0-9 = nondepressed; 10-15 = mild; 16-25 = moderate; 26-63 = severe depression.
b. Scale = 0 to 4.
c. Range = 0 to 17.
d. Scale = 1 to 6.
e. Scale = 1 to 5.
*$p < .05$.

of victims in this sample were very distressed. For example, among both stranger and acquaintance rape victims, mean depression scores were in the moderately depressed range and means on the anxiety and hostility scales were more than one standard deviation above norm group means. In addition, both groups endorsed approximately 60% (10 out of 17) of the PTSD symptoms on the checklist.

Two *t*-tests also were conducted to compare victims of stranger and acquaintance rape in terms of the extent to which they blamed themselves for the assault. Results indicated that victims of acquaintance rape engaged in significantly more behavioral self-blame than did victims of stranger rape, $t\ (54) = 2.28$, $p < .02$, whereas the two groups did not engage in differing amounts of characterological self-blame, $p > .05$ (see Table 4.1).

Thus, victims of acquaintance rape did not differ from victims of stranger rape in terms of symptoms; both groups reported similar levels of depression, anxiety, hostility, PTSD, and disruptions in beliefs about themselves, others, and the world. However, victims of acquaintance rape blamed the assault on their behavior significantly more than did those women who had experienced stranger rape.

Campus Study

SAMPLE AND PROCEDURES

Postrape symptomatology and self-blame also were compared among victims of stranger and acquaintance rape in the campus study (see Frazier & Schauben, 1994, for further information). In addition, because the campus sample was composed of women who acknowledged their rape experience and those who did not identify themselves as victims of rape, comparisons could be made between acknowledged and unacknowledged victims.

Participants were 282 female undergraduates at a large Midwestern university. Participants were classified as victims of rape if they reported having experienced at least one of the three experiences on the SES meeting the legal definition of rape (i.e., unwanted penetration through use of threats or physical force) or another question directly asking whether they ever had been raped. This version of the SES did not contain the previously described item regarding unwanted intercourse following consumption of alcohol or drugs that various authors have criticized. Fifty-eight of the 282 women (21%) were defined as rape victims according to these criteria.

Those women classified as rape victims were asked to respond to a number of items assessing their relationship with the assailant and their current psychological functioning. Most of the participants (86%) were categorized as having experienced acquaintance rape because the assailant was an acquaintance, date, boyfriend, or family member. Women who had no prior contact with the assailant prior to the experience were considered victims of stranger rape (14%). The assaults had occurred an average of 8 years previously.

MEASURES

To assess symptomatology, participants completed the entire 53-item BSI (to assess overall distress) and the MBS (to assess disruptions in beliefs). In addition, respondents rated on a 5-point Likert-type scale how stressful the experience was for them (1 = not at all to 5 = extremely). Finally, the extent to which respondents engaged in behavioral and characterological self-blame was assessed using two 1-item scales ("How much do you blame this

TABLE 4.2 Comparisons Between Stranger and Acquaintance Rape Victims: Campus Study

	Stranger (n = 8)	*Acquaintance (n = 50)*
Symptoms		
BSI total[a]	.76	1.13
MBS[b]	2.26	2.89**
Stressfulness of rape[c]	4.88	4.82
Attributions		
Behavioral self-blame[c]	1.38	2.31**
Characterological self-blame[c]	1.50	2.31*

a. Scale = 0 to 4.
b. Scale = 1 to 6.
c. Scale = 1 to 5.
*$p < .06$.
**$p < .05$.

experience on your own behavior [character or personality]"; 1 = do not blame to 5 = completely blame).

RESULTS

Acquaintance versus stranger rape. Three *t*-tests were conducted to assess differences between victims of stranger and acquaintance rape in terms of distress (i.e., overall distress, disrupted beliefs, and the stressfulness of the experience). There were no differences between groups in BSI total scores or stress ratings, both *ps* > .05 (see Table 4.2). However, significant differences were found between stranger and acquaintance victims on the MBS. Specifically, victims of acquaintance rape experienced significantly more overall disruptions in beliefs about themselves and the world than did victims of stranger rape, $t\ (54) = -2.58$, $p < .05$.

Because differences in scores on the total MBS scale were significant, differences in the 10 MBS subscales also were examined. *T*-tests revealed that acquaintance rape victims had more disrupted beliefs than stranger rape victims on 4 of the 10 subscales ($p < .05$). Specifically, they felt less sense of power and control (low power), that other people were less valuable and worthy of respect (other-esteem), less connected with others (other-intimacy), and less comfortable being alone (self-intimacy).

Two additional *t*-tests were conducted to assess differences in behavioral and characterological self-blame between victims of stranger and acquaintance rape. Significant differences were found between groups in behavioral self-blame and marginal differences were found in characterological self-blame. Specifically, victims of acquaintance rape engaged in significantly more behavioral self-blame, $t\ (16.89) = -2.81, p < .05$, and marginally more characterological self-blame, $t\ (13.24) = -2.09, p < .057$, than did those women who had experienced stranger rape.

Acknowledged versus unacknowledged victims. Due to the way in which victimization experiences are assessed on the SES, comparisons also could be made between women who defined their experiences as rape (i.e., acknowledged victims) and women who did not (i.e., unacknowledged victims). The sexual assault experience was considered "acknowledged" if the respondent endorsed the direct question assessing rape and at least one of the three indirect questions ($n = 22$). Unacknowledged victims endorsed at least one of the three indirect questions but not the direct question about rape ($n = 22$). The other 14 victims did not endorse any of the three identified items on the SES but stated that they had been raped. They were not defined as "acknowledged" victims because their experiences did not meet the legal definition of rape. *T*-tests revealed no differences in BSI scores or ratings of the stressfulness of the experience between acknowledged and unacknowledged victims, both *ps* > .05. However, unacknowledged victims had marginally more disruptions in beliefs than did acknowledged victims, $t\ (40) = -1.92, p < .06$.

An additional two *t*-tests assessing behavioral and characterological self-blame revealed significant differences between groups in behavioral self-blame but not characterological self-blame. Specifically, unacknowledged victims blamed their behavior significantly more than did acknowledged victims, $t\ (40) = -2.22, p < .03$ (see Table 4.3).

In summary, victims of acquaintance and stranger rape reported similar overall distress levels and rated the experiences as equally stressful. However, victims of acquaintance rape experienced more disruptions in beliefs about themselves and the world and more self-blame than did victims of stranger rape. Similarly, women who did not define themselves as victims reported as much distress in general and about the incident in particular as women who defined themselves as having been raped. In addition, women who did not define themselves as victims reported more self-blame and

TABLE 4.3 Comparisons Between Acknowledged and Unacknowledged Rape Victims: Campus Study

	Acknowledged (*n* = 22)	*Unacknowledged* (*n* = 22)
Symptoms		
BSI total[a]	1.01	1.29
MBS[b]	2.66	3.05*
Stressfulness of rape[c]	4.86	4.71
Attributions		
Behavioral self-blame[c]	1.81	2.76**
Characterological self-blame[c]	2.14	2.48

a. Scale = 0 to 4.
b. Scale = 1 to 6.
c. Scale = 1 to 5.
*$p < .06$.
**$p < .05$.

somewhat more disrupted beliefs than women who acknowledged their victimization. Interestingly, although 100% of women raped by strangers acknowledged their experiences as rape, only 47% of those raped by an acquaintance did so.

Summary and Integration

Results of both the hospital-based and campus studies suggest that victims of acquaintance rape are as traumatized as victims of stranger rape. For example, victims of acquaintance rape do not differ from women raped by strangers in terms of depression, hostility, anxiety, or PTSD. In fact, some evidence suggests that victims of acquaintance rape are more traumatized than victims of stranger rape. Specifically, acquaintance rape victims tend to blame themselves more for the assault and to report more disrupted beliefs than victims of stranger rape.

These data are consistent with the results of numerous other studies. The majority of studies have found no differences between victims of acquaintance and stranger rape in postrape symptoms, including depression (Becker, Skinner, Abel, Axelrod, & Treacy, 1984; Frank, Turner, & Stewart, 1980; Gidycz & Koss, 1991; Katz, 1991; Koss, Dinero, Seibel, & Cox, 1988; Sales, Baum, & Shore, 1984; Santiago, McCall-Perez, Gorcey, & Beigel, 1985; Siegel, Golding, Stein, Burnam, & Sorenson, 1990; Ullman & Siegel, 1993), fear/anxiety (Frank et al., 1980; Gidycz & Koss, 1991; Girelli, Resick, Marhoefer-Dvorak & Hutter, 1986; Koss et al., 1988; Sales et al., 1984; Santiago et al., 1985; Scheppele & Bart, 1991; Siegel et al., 1990), PTSD symptoms (Kramer & Green, 1991), and overall distress (Katz, 1991; Ruch & Chandler, 1983). A few studies have found victims of stranger rape to be more distressed than victims of acquaintance rape in terms of depression (Ellis, Atkeson, & Calhoun, 1981), fear (Ellis et al., 1981; Ullman & Siegel, 1993), and PTSD symptoms (Bownes, O'Gorman, & Sayers, 1991a, 1991b), although others have found more distress among victims of acquaintance rape (Katz, 1991; Ruch, Amedeo, Leon, & Gartrell, 1991). Nonetheless, the overall trend is that stranger and acquaintance rape victims do not differ in terms of postrape distress and symptomatology.

We located only two studies that compared victims of acquaintance and stranger rape in terms of self-blame. Consistent with our data, Katz (1991) reported that victims of acquaintance rape engaged in more self-blame than did victims of stranger rape. Koss et al. (1988) found that victims of stranger rape attributed more responsibility to the assailant than did victims of acquaintance rape, although the two groups did not differ in terms of the amount of responsibility they attributed to themselves.

Similarly, very little research has examined differences between acknowledged and unacknowledged victims. In one study, Koss (1985) found no differences between women who defined their experience as rape and women who did not, in terms of emotions at the time of the assault (e.g., fear, anger) or the subsequent effects of the assault on their self-esteem, sexuality, relationships with men, or overall adjustment. Another recent study compared acknowledged and unacknowledged victims on several symptom measures an average of about 2 years postassault (Layman, Gidycz, & Lynn, 1996). The two groups did not differ in terms of scores on the BSI, two measures of dissociative experiences, or self-blame. However, acknowledged victims did report more PTSD symptoms on an interview measure. These data suggest that, although a woman may not define an experience as rape, it appears to be as distressing as those experiences that are defined as rape.

One other study addressed why women might not define experiences as rape even though they meet the legal definition. Specifically, Kahn, Mathie, and Torgler (1994) compared "rape scripts" among both acknowledged and unacknowledged rape victims, all but one of whom was raped by an acquaintance. They found that women who did not define their own experiences as rape were more likely to have rape scripts in which the assailant was a stranger and used a great deal of force. Similarly, Layman et al. (1996) found that the assaults of unacknowledged victims involved less force than did those of acknowledged victims. Thus, unacknowledged victims may not define their experience as rape because they have a rape script of a violent, stranger rape that does not match their own experience of being raped in a less violent manner by someone with whom they were acquainted.

Conclusion

Our data and the results of numerous other studies suggest that victims of acquaintance rape are as distressed as women raped by strangers. Specifically, they report equal—and high—levels of depression, anxiety, hostility, and PTSD symptoms. Acquaintance and stranger rape also are rated as equally stressful by victims. If anything, victims of acquaintance rape report more distress in terms of disruptions in their beliefs about themselves and others and in terms of the extent to which they blame themselves for the assault. All of these data suggest that acquaintance rape is a real and serious problem and not merely the fabrication of feminist researchers.

Although women raped by acquaintances are less likely to define themselves as victims, lack of acknowledgment does not mean that the experience is not distressing or not rape. Women who do not define their experience as "rape" do not rate the experience as less stressful than women who do define themselves as rape victims. Unacknowledged victims also generally report as much symptomatology as acknowledged victims. Lack of acknowledgment appears to be related to women's scripts about what constitutes a "real" rape. These findings suggest a continuing need to educate women that they are not responsible for rape and that a rape by an acquaintance is still a rape.

Another consequence of the fact that victims of acquaintance rape are less likely to define the experience as rape is that they are less likely to report the assault to the police (Steketee & Austin, 1989). Furthermore, even if the assault is reported, it is likely to be treated less seriously than stranger rape within the criminal justice system. For example, in one recent study (Frazier & Haney, 1996), defendants in cases involving acquaintance rape were charged with less serious offenses and were less likely to be sentenced to prison if convicted than were defendants in stranger rape cases. Thus, members of the criminal justice system also need to be educated about the severity of acquaintance rape for its victims.

CHAPTER

5

Self-Blame in Hidden Rape Cases

VICTORIA L. PITTS
MARTIN D. SCHWARTZ

Looking at official statistics, one would think that one of America's rarest crimes is rape on college campuses. As other authors have explained in this book, campus victimization surveys have uncovered dramatically more self-reports of victimization than any other source. What this shows is that most campus rape is hidden from view.

One widely cited reason for this is the self-blame that counselors almost universally claim is widespread among victims. In a society widely considered to be rape supportive, the messages that excuse rapists are heard as often and as intensely by women, with the result that women themselves are sometimes unable to affix blame when they voluntarily entered a man's

AUTHORS' NOTE: An earlier and much more complete version of this chapter appeared in *Humanity & Society* (Pitts & Schwartz, 1993). The research reported here was supported by a grant from the Honors Tutorial College at Ohio University.

apartment, when they voluntarily invited him into their apartment, when less physical force was used, or when the woman was drinking.

Interestingly, there is literature in this field that argues that some forms of self-blame are actually good for rape victims. Based on the work of Janoff-Bulman (1979), this literature argues that although it is unhelpful for women to blame themselves after a rape, it is part of the healing process to blame their behavior so that they can focus on avoiding it in the future.

We have critiqued this work on a number of grounds (Pitts & Schwartz, 1993), including the fact that this complex study of how rape victims think did not involve talking to rape victims themselves. Patricia Frazier (1990, 1991), who has an important chapter in this section of the book, is the leading figure in pointing out that much of Janoff-Bulman's theory is incorrect. Victims, she points out, rarely differentiate between different types of self-blame, and there is no evidence that blaming one's own behavior has anything to do with the belief that future rape is avoidable.

One other problem with most of the existing studies of rape victims bothered us. Because most were done in emergency rooms or rape crisis centers, they represented women who had already defined themselves as victims and who had reached out for help. Yet as Mary Koss, Walter DeKeseredy, and many others have pointed out, at least on the college campus, this is a small percentage of the total number of rape victims.

Thus, we began to question the relationship between these two factors: that many women suffer from self-blame and that most rapes on college campuses are hidden from view, unreported, and ignored. It is reasonable to suppose that we have been finding so few women willing to define their experiences as rape and so extraordinarily few women willing to report campus sexual assault because these women have been heavily engaged in self-blame. If this is true, then self-blame is an enormous problem; it prevents women from seeking help.

Methods

Self-report victimization surveys were administered to students in a variety of classes at a large public university, including large lower-division general education classes and senior-level integrative seminars from several colleges. All questionnaires were filled out by students during class time after they were read and given a copy of a human subjects research consent form, which they had to sign before completing the survey. No extra course credit was given, and almost all students signed the form and completed the survey. Although there was a male version of the form, the sample discussed here consists of 288 women, most of whom were at least sophomores (94.1%), white (95.8%), and single (98.6%). They had a mean age of 20.1 years, and almost all (98.3%) had dated males.

To determine the prevalence of sexual assault, the Koss Sexual Experiences Survey (SES) was used, except the question used to elicit information on rape by intoxication was, "Have you ever had sexual intercourse when you didn't want to because you were drunk or high?" Almost one fifth (19.3%) of respondents reported being the victim of *completed* rape by force (3.5%), sexual acts by force (2.4%) (anal or oral intercourse, or rape by instrumentation), or rape during intoxication (17.1%) since entering college. Because some women reported multiple victimizations, these numbers do not add up to 19.3%. However, it is important to note that they do not include attempted rape.

GETTING HELP FROM OTHERS

Two other questions provided the most interesting part of our analysis here. First, in a part of the questionnaire far removed from the SES, we asked, "Has a man ever raped you?" Despite the fact that this question seemingly asks about lifetime experiences and the SES asks only about college experiences, only 27% of the rape survivors ($n = 58$) responded affirmatively. In addition, one out of five survivors was a "hidden victim" in another way: 21% of the survivors said they had told absolutely no one about their experience. Half of those silent women said they did not tell anyone "because I was drunk or high when it happened."

Our interest was in how helpful peer support was for these women. Thus, we looked to those women who had told someone. Most reported that the first person they told was helpful in some way. Few helpful persons suggested that the victim seek counseling or call a hotline (12.5%) or call the police (5%). However, we also asked an open-ended question about the "most helpful response" that these women received to discover what messages these women did receive that they viewed as helpful.

The most common theme used by these women was that of blame. Of the 45 women who could both identify a person as most helpful and who answered this question, 16 discussed blame, or more specifically, the attri-

Response	*Have You Ever Been Raped?*
I. *Told that it "wasn't her fault"*	
"Told me that I wasn't to blame—it's not my fault."	yes
"They did not judge me . . . did not blame me."	yes
"I was not blamed for anything."	yes
"Helped me see that I wasn't at fault for what happened."	yes
II. *Not told that it "wasn't her fault"*	
"Unconditional love"	no
"The person it happened with was a friend because I was drunk and I wasn't thinking clearly."	no
"Helped me to learn from my mistake."	no
"I don't know—I was drunk— really stupid move on my part."	no
"They understood that it was a mistake."	no
"Blamed me partially."	no
"They encouraged me to learn from it. Knowing that she loved me unconditionally and didn't judge me made me let go."	no
"He's my current boyfriend and he doesn't pass judgements (sic) on mistakes or situations I may have gotten into in the past."	no

Figure 5.1. Most Helpful Response to Women Who Were Raped and Whether They Recognize Their Experience as Rape

bution of blame for the victimization. Thirteen of these women had suffered an experience that met the state law definition of completed rape (as opposed to attempted), and these are the responses we looked at further.

In four cases, the women said that the most helpful person told her that she specifically was not to blame. In the other nine cases, they were told that they were at least partially to blame. None of these nine was told that she was not to blame, and most were told some version of how she made a mistake. This blame was still considered to be helpful by the women because they were also given "unconditional love." Still, these answers presume that the woman had done something terribly wrong to bring these consequences on herself. They were not told that they were not at fault; they were loved despite their fault.

How does accepted responsibility for rape affect survivors' definitions of their experiences? As mentioned previously, we asked each of these women (all of whom had been raped) whether they had ever been raped. In every instance in which the "most helpful" person the survivor told either blamed her or encouraged her own self-blame, the victim did not define her experience as rape. She reported to us that she had never been raped. The tentative conclusion to reach here is that women who are blamed by confidants, who accept self-blame, do not accept that they have been raped. Self-blame helps them to accept the responsibility for "mistakes" they made rather than placing the responsibility on the rapist. Some of their comments are summarized in Figure 5.1.

This conclusion is strengthened substantially by looking at the four instances in which the survivor was explicitly told that she was not responsible for what had happened to her. In each of these cases, the woman did define her experience as rape. The women who were not encouraged to self-blame were all able to define their experiences as rape; they were able to blame a rapist for what happened.

Conclusion

Rape survivors clearly are internalizing what others are telling them about who is at fault for unwanted, nonconsensual intercourse (whether it is a generalized, societal other or the specific peers with whom they discuss their experience). Many studies have shown that self-blame is prominent for survivors at rape crisis centers and often leads to increased postrape trauma (Katz & Burt, 1988). Our study suggests that in addition, hidden rape victims —who make up the vast majority of all rape survivors—are greatly affected by self-blame. In the case of the hidden victim, however, the very recognition that she is a victim of crime is the issue.

Much of the literature in this field, following Janoff-Bulman (1979), suggests that properly handled, therapists can encourage certain types of self-blame in rape survivors. If the self-blame is behavioral rather than characterological, these theorists suggest, it may be adaptive and helpful. Our findings suggest instead that the consequences of telling women that they are to blame for rape—even behaviorally—are serious. In addition to increased trauma, blaming the victim ensures that many survivors will be hidden victims. This means that the overwhelming majority of them will not be inclined to seek help, report to the police, or even to seek an explanation for their postrape trauma. This also means that men who use violent or coercive means to obtain intercourse will be able to justify their actions based not only on popular rape myths but also on the behavioral victim blaming of some rape counselors. Fenstermaker (1989, p. 267) argues that under any circumstances acquaintance rape "muddies the normative waters," in that both men and women have great difficulty understanding when a felony crime is being committed. To allow acquaintance rapists to gain the support of rape crisis counselors in their efforts to evade responsibility for their behavior is, in effect, to decriminalize acquaintance rape.

In addition, counseling women to change their behavior to avoid being raped and blaming them for that behavior ignores the fact that women have the right to walk alone at night, the right to go on dates, the right to go to a bar, and the right to drink alcohol. Women have to restrict their lives not because their behavior is wrong or illegal but because men take advantage of the vulnerability of women. In the short run, activity restriction may be the best advice for women who wish to avoid rape, but blaming survivors for the degrading and violent behavior of men not only legitimizes a society in which women are forced to restrict their lives out of fear of rape but takes away their right to be angry about it.

PART

II

Emotion in Researching Violence Against Women

MARTIN D. SCHWARTZ

One of the most interesting areas in sociology in recent years has been the sociology of emotions. This subdiscipline has many derivations and many implications, but the most important one here is the realization that researchers of sexual violence are rarely the pure, disinterested scientists in white lab coats who were described to us in graduate school as the perfect models of good researchers. We were taught that good researchers do not get emotionally involved with research subjects.

There are a number of problems with this formulation. Some arise from arguments in humanist sociology that there is more to being a scientist than just posting lab scores on a bulletin board. From this perspective, research can be used to achieve social goods, to right wrongs, and to make things better for the oppressed and repressed. This does not mean advocacy replaces careful science, of course, but it does mean that research topics and methods may be chosen for personal and political reasons.

Feminist sociology makes a similar set of arguments. Being a feminist does not excuse one from being a good and careful researcher, but it certainly can inform one's research in a great many ways.

The problem outlined by the authors here is that few researchers are trained in how to deal with the demands made on them by the commitments previously outlined. Elizabeth Stanko, in Chapter 6, makes it plain: After you have spent the entire day listening to women describe the horrors inflicted on them, what do you do with your own anger and sorrow? Medical and law enforcement personnel, and even journalists, often develop a cold exterior to keep out the pain. Fine, but is feminist research about turning the researcher into someone who is uncaring by design?

Generally, researchers have not talked about their own anger and pain, except in quiet sessions late at night. Stanko, one of England's highest profile rape researchers, explains what it means to constantly hide your own pain only to find that all advocates for women are degraded as "victim feminists" who exaggerate women's victimization to raise their self-esteem. She recommends that we claim our own emotional responses as a resource.

In Chapter 7, Susan Hippensteele steps away from her carefully constructed scientific work on ethnoviolence to explain how she, as a person, fits into her awkward role at the University of Hawaii. She is the victim advocate for survivors of various types of sexual and ethnic violence there, but at the same time, she is expected to be a careful, disinterested scientist. When I set out to find someone to write this chapter, I was looking for a frontline worker who could talk about the influence of feminist research on her work. What we have here, however, is all of that rolled into one: the important and well-respected feminist researcher who is also the committed frontline worker and activist.

Christine Mattley (Chapter 8) shares with Elizabeth Stanko the notion that it is important to seize your own emotions as a resource, although Mattley expands that concept by suggesting that the reactions of other people to you and your research can also be seized as a data resource. Social psychologists have long talked about a "courtesy stigma," often with approval, as representing the willingness of people with deviant status to allow the researcher to share that status and therefore to gain entry into their world. Mattley talks about what she names a "*dis*courtesy stigma," which is the treatment certain researchers receive from their colleagues and coworkers when they discover that the researcher is working with stigmatized others. In her case, to study a form of what many consider violence against women, the telephone-fantasy sex industry, Mattley gained entry and became a phone sex worker. She talks in her chapter about her own emotions both while doing the work and while dealing with the reactions of the academic community toward her and offers some suggestions for others following in her footsteps.

In Chapter 9, Jennifer Huff addresses a question that is roughly the opposite of all the material in the research literature. There is extensive literature on sexual harassment in the workplace, and many have commented on sexual harassment of people by those with superior power. There is a small amount of literature on contrapower harassment, almost completely limited to a discussion of the harassment of faculty by students. However, students do have some power over faculty—they control student evaluations, which may be taken very seriously in many universities, and they have the power of anonymity. Much student harassment of faculty takes the form of obscene and menacing telephone calls, which accomplish harassment despite differences in formal power.

Huff looks at the problem of sexual harassment of researchers by research subjects in the field. She sets out what, in many ways, is a classic case of sexual harassment in terms of her reactions, self-blame, doubt, consideration of abandoning the project, and so forth. Yet by our standard definitions, she was the one with all of the power. There may be no simple solution here, but Huff takes the position that, at the very least, graduate students should be trained to deal with sexual harassment, to know what to expect, to anticipate their own personal limits, and to know that they are not alone and that their reactions are not isolated or abnormal.

CHAPTER

6

"I Second That Emotion"

Reflections on Feminism, Emotionality, and Research on Sexual Violence

ELIZABETH A. STANKO

Flash: An undergraduate student is preparing her thesis on women's fear of crime. She has insisted on this subject despite the objections of her course directors. She is a medical student, not a social scientist. She feels that understanding women's fear is linked to her questions about the nature of medicine and healing. She wonders why, after exploring the literature, she is beginning to feel more afraid. (December, 1995)

Flash: A postgraduate student audits my session on sexual violence. I watch her face as she responds to what I am saying with nods of agreement. She is silent, speaking only once with the insight of someone who has been to this place I've described and is telling a story from first-person rather than the description of a social scientist. (February, 1996)

Flash: A postgraduate student looks agitated and distressed. His partner has been raped. In today's seminar, we are discussing how the criminal justice system and the wider social context encourage women's silence about sexual assault. When I teach, I know that I am touching raw emotion. (March, 1996)

Emotion and pain are never far from teaching and research on sexual violence. I have wept with my students and my interviewees; I have been so overwhelmed with anger at the treatment of (mostly) women by abusers that I have not known quite how to handle it. After 20 years of academic work as one who has identified (and been identified by others) as a *radical* feminist, I am tired and wonder how all my colleagues have coped with what I now see as inevitable angst accompanying the act of researching sexual violence. The purpose of this brief chapter is to break my own silence about my experiences of harboring anger, frustration, fear, and pain during my own research experiences; my political interventions as an academic activist; and my own personal (but very public) struggles reconciling belief and fact. Indeed, many of my feminist colleagues and friends have talked about similar emotional turmoil, so what I write should be familiar to many readers—whether or not they have shared it with each other.

There is even a name for some of its consequences: burnout. To me, burnout is reached when I wake up wishing I had become a botanist, or better, a tap dancer. However, it is essential that we acknowledge that *doing* work on or about sexual violence—for some of us—involves an account of sexual violence that includes placing into the foreground the still hidden, devastating toll it has for so many. And today, as we find ourselves dealing with the pain of its impact, we are faced with an accusation from other writers and researchers that we have over-egged the pudding, stoked the flames of feminist fury, or whatever metaphor one cares to use. We have been accused of exaggerating our "claims" that sexual assault is widespread (Gilbert, 1991; Roiphe, 1993) and of transforming feminism into "victim feminism" (Wolf, 1993).

A Personal Stake: Sexual Violence Research and Emotional Attachment

As social science researchers, we are expected to be detached from our research and its consequences. Having a personal stake in research, it seems, immediately arouses suspicion about one's research findings and subsequently one's claims. The work on violence against women—as a problem of social science—was tainted from the beginning. The problem was that, as feminists, we cared about the effect of sexual violence on ourselves and our sisters. The fusion of the desire to challenge what many of us saw as a part of oppressive patriarchy with the need to challenge the very manner in which research had overlooked such violence brought a lot of us into disrepute. We had to argue that much of violence against women was hidden *precisely* because women were encouraged to be silent. At the same time, we launched an attack on the institutional processes that abused us for alleging abuse. Eventually, feminist work on violence destabilized some of the criminological discourses on violent crime, which often portray violence as unpredictable, random, and committed by deranged strangers.

In those early days (can it be only 20 to 25 years ago?), feminist research and writing about sexual violence broke many taboos. We questioned the very way social science conceptualized sexual assault as "real crime."[1] The rapist could no longer be portrayed only as the faceless stranger. All too often, he (and still it is overwhelmingly *hes* who rape[2]) is a familiar male; the research demonstrates time and time again that the abuse is typically fostered through kinship, friendship, intimacy, or the abuse of social power. We questioned the capability of social science to define abuse by demanding that women's voices be heard. We accused social science, the law, and the state's institutions of male bias.

Interestingly enough, our research has not altered the patterns of women's silence that we have illustrated. Despite the contribution of a feminist analysis of sexual violence, few of those who experience abuse today tell anyone. Silence reigns as the typical response of those who are sexually assaulted. Women, children, and men who encounter sexual abuse remain steadfastly quiet, despite all the publicity and changes in legal statutes and professional practice over these past 20 years.[3] Of course, we are all much more aware that we are missing information that might more accurately portray the extent of sexual violence. Most of the other chapters in this collection grapple with this problem. But it seems when I am met with a student or a colleague (or sometimes a stranger who writes me an anonymous letter when hearing me as a voice on the radio) who requests that what is said go no further than this conversation, I am reminded how often the so-called subject matter of my academic career is mostly about the individual management of sadness, pain, survival, and courage.

As a woman, I am acutely aware that what is also being discussed is my interconnectedness to *womanhood* (and I am well aware that my womanhood intersects with many features of my life, which include but are not limited to my experiences as a 45-year-old, European American, professional expatriate). Although I am sharply conscious that violence affects men's lives in addition to women's (and I have been one of the few criminologists to discuss actively masculinities and violence), as a woman I *know* that my research and writing are also very much about my own relationship to the social world. I, too, have experienced sexual harassment on the street, at work, and elsewhere; I, too, monitor how safe I feel when traveling; as a mother (and the mother of a girl), I, too, feel the distress of the parent who attempts to shield that child from abuse by those who have legitimate access to her.

My emotional attachment to this subject matter is apparent in my teaching. My approach to sexual violence is best illustrated in my first book, *Intimate Intrusions* (1985). In it, I drew together commonalities in our experiences of various kinds of sexual abuse and made connections between our experiences of the sexual harassment we face on the street with the devastating consequences of rape. Contextualizing a wide variety of sexual violence within what Kelly (1988) named "the continuum of sexual violence" allows us to make sense of some women's responses to what others considered trivial or nuisance encounters with men. Using this approach (and having taught courses on violence against women since 1977) taps directly into students' own emotional reactions to the material. My general observations about the emotional effect of exploring sexual violence as part of the curriculum consistently reproduce themselves. During the first few weeks of the course, there are a number of stages through which the female students pass: disbelief, followed by a rise of acute anxiety, replaced by anger. Some may experience flashbacks. Finally, some form of emotional equilibrium is reached. Sometimes students choose to channel their anger into activism. The male students take various routes: anger at me, shame, overprotectiveness of their female friends, and possibly the sparking of their own memories of abuse. Rarely, though, do the men fear for their own personal safety; the women inevitably do. I describe these emotional reactions to students in the first session of any course that discusses women's safety, fear of crime, or violence. I am careful to include myself in the description; it is not unusual for me to experience a rise of distress when I teach about sexual violence.

Of course, different students react differently, the effect varies, and their levels of emotion diverge. But at the bare minimum, we collectively share the burden of our emotional responses to what is at the best of times disturbing, if not genuinely distressing. Lee (1989) has argued that within a supportive classroom environment, "students feel safe and validated by teachers and each other" (p. 547) when discussing sexual violence. I am sure that many of my colleagues would support this view. But not all students feel supported; not everyone comes out feeling unscathed. The toll that it takes on the lecturer is often hidden. The lecturer may be isolated in her own work site; perhaps she alone demands from her colleagues the creative space to explore violence from a feminist perspective. In doing so, she may also ask uncomfortable questions about her own work context and the quality of the learning environment. Few would be surprised to learn how many times those teaching about sexual violence also confront it: Sexual harassment and abuse of students, fellow colleagues, or even herself are never very far away.[4]

Providing the context for a discussion of sexual violence as an academic subject inevitably invites some students to disclose their own private horrors. Most of the time, such disclosures are very private encounters between lecturer and student. I have coped with many students' tears, quests for therapists, and accounts of sexual and physical violence at the hands of many different kinds of men (and some women). Although the usual advice about always having a box of tissues is helpful, these disclosures also take a toll on the lecturer. Sometimes students tell their stories because it is a way of breaking their own silence; sometimes they seek advice about whether to report their grievances to those in authority, and they agonize about how to proceed. To me, these narratives of abuse bare the structures that encourage silence. The unpredictability of police inquiries, criminal trials, and internal university grievances makes itself visible and *in-your-face,* showing me, time and time again, how the experiences of abuse are rendered invisible through our search for private ways of healing the damage of abuse. Many of us still feel sexual assault is our burden alone, and all of the research demonstrates that making sexual assault public has serious consequences to those who demand public redress.

For me, the most difficult disclosures to cope with are the public disclosures, those that burst forth as part of classroom discussion, reminding all in the room that the "personal is indeed political." After all, I am a lecturer, not a therapist, and it is imperative that we as social scientists do not kid ourselves that we are collectively assuaging women's anxieties and healing students' wounds by providing a safe place "to speak out." All this personal pain that bursts forth in the classroom has an effect on the emotional well-being of the lecturer (assuming, of course, that there was an established well-being in the first place). Sometimes it seems that the catalog of sadness and frustration I hear about when I teach about sexual violence never ends.

But not all is doom and gloom. My motivation for promoting social change is fueled by my personal and political commitment to the study of sexual violence. If I believe—as I do—that sexual violence is indicative of the abuse of gendered social power, then challenging damaging masculinities is one way to minimize the harm of sexual danger (Stanko, 1994). The emotional attachment of many researchers to social change that directly confronts destructive masculinities is a very positive outcome to the study of sexual violence. Such challenges have been accused of being a kind of fundamentalism by the right and by religious conservatives. Some so-called feminist writers have accused other radical, feminist work on sexual violence of encouraging a form of victimism (Wolf, 1993) by suggesting that embracing victimization somehow enhances women's self-esteem. Far from it. Those who make such accusations have not been reading the research carefully (or in the case of Roiphe, 1993, not reading the research at all).

Recognizing the existence of powerful emotions around the study of sexual violence is important for all researchers and for our students as well. Such emotion may be tapped as a resource for expanding our insight into the day-to-day realities of sexual violence. In doing so, some researchers have disclosed their own experiences of sexual abuse and danger; others are less willing to expose themselves; others may be thankful that they have escaped the harrowing situations many women have revealed to us during their classes and research. Nonetheless, recognizing the emotional effect of our work on sexual violence *on us* is important, regardless of the many personal histories we bring to its study.

Emotional Reactions to the Study of Sexual Abuse as Data

In an early and influential book, Kelly (1988) sketches the emotional effect of her study of sexual violence by stating,

> I had anticipated that listening to women's experiences of sexual violence would affect me emotionally. I did not expect to be affected by the discussions of childhood and family relationships that began each interview. (pp. 17-18)

She experienced flashbacks, acute feelings of fear about personal safety, anger, and sorrow and admitted feeling overwhelmed at times. Kelly (1988) acknowledged that her own reactions were "an integral part of the research methodology" (p. 19). In a more recent essay, Moran-Ellis (1996) describes her feelings sparked by her research on child sexual abuse as "pain by proxy" (p. 181). She felt that the emotional upheaval of the research process left an indelible mark:

> In short, researching sexual abuse changed my life to some degree because it changed me, and that was not something I had anticipated happening. (p. 184)

What use can we make of this emotional toil? Can our emotional reactions to the study of sexual violence contribute to the research process?

In my early career, I kept my emotional responses to myself. Yet my recollections of my doctoral research are laced with the lasting memories of great confusion. In conducting an ethnographic study of prosecutorial decision-making in cases of violence, I explored the effect of victim credibility on prosecutors' selection of serious felonies. Many of these cases still remain fixed in my mind. Let me give you one example. A teenage African American woman was being interviewed by the prosecutor about an alleged rape by an acquaintance of her mother. She was only about 14. I remember feeling distressed by the prosecutor's line of questioning, which was trying to detect *what happened* for its possible weaknesses as a felony case (see Stanko, 1981-1982; and, more recently, Frohmann, 1991). After the prosecutor completed his inquiry, I excused myself. In the women's toilet, I began kicking the wall, nearly in tears. I was outraged at what I had just witnessed. I did not know what I should *do* with my reaction. But I certainly *felt* it. I returned to my observation post composed but determined that I would begin to examine the assessment of respectability more closely.[5] Another memorable moment was when a district attorney speculated about a case in which a corrections officer shot his girlfriend in the head. The prosecutor described the success of prosecution as follows:

> If she dies we have manslaughter. If she recovers and remains a vegetable, we have an assault 1 [first degree]. If she recovers with minor complications, we barely have a case. If she fully recovers, she will probably drop the charges. (Stanko, 1982, p. 77)

Witnessing the prosecutors in action enabled me to learn their skills of prediction (see Stanko, 1977, 1981-1982, 1982). These skills are affected by the elasticity of discretion and the need to locate some fault (or its possibility) in the worthiness of those claiming the state's beneficial protection. As

Cooney (1994) has recently suggested, legal evidence itself is embedded in notions of victims' respectability. What I could not do, however, was detach this intellectual interest in the social construction of felony cases from the trauma of those deemed *unrespectable* or *respectable.* Worse, those deemed *unrespectable* were blamed for their pain. And it made me angry.

When I moved to my first academic post in the United States, I applied my ethnographic skills and my knowledge of the criminal justice system to study violence against women. I began to work closely with a local rape crisis center and, in 1977, began the foundational work to start a shelter for battered women (which opened its doors in 1978). Suddenly I found myself in a whirlwind of emotions: anger, fear, outrage, exhilaration (in the challenge of actively participating in feminist community change), and exhaustion all flooded my day-to-day life. I began to question why all that I heard and shared around the kitchen table in battered women's shelters was so absent from criminological discourses about crime, violence, and danger. Women's insights were (and still are) what informed my critique of criminology, and this critique came packed with the emotional baggage of such carnage.

In their short monograph, *Emotions and Fieldwork,* Kleinman and Copp (1993) illustrate how exclusion of uncomfortable topics is often part of fieldwork practice but has an effect on the eventual narrative of the research. I feel now that part of my inability to write about violence against women was my inability to combine the power of emotion with a calm articulation of the damage to women as I was seeing it. I have taken nearly 20 years to channel my emotion into my writing. Somehow, I feel, there must be some way to demonstrate the emotionality of this subject matter. Perhaps this is why I have insisted throughout my academic career that the voices of those interviewed be included in my written work.

Emotional reactions to the research process should give rise to reflection about the published literature in the field of sexual violence. For instance, when I read Roiphe's (1993) diatribe against feminists like myself, it seems to me that she demonstrates clearly her failure to speak with any survivor of sexual assault. She paints feminists as whiners. Roiphe chooses to try to invalidate feminist work on sexual assault by claiming that she is capable of spotting danger and of avoiding harm. And, it seems from our evidence, so are between three quarters to one half of all young women. All the research suggests that for those women who do experience rape and sexual assault, there are very serious consequences. Although these consequences are different for different women, we know about a host of physical, psychological, and practical adjustments that must be made to negotiate physical and psychological well-being. Roiphe's attempts to discredit feminist researchers' accounts of sexual violence center on her mockery of the toll that rape takes on many women's lives. She dismisses our heightened feelings of insecurity, our worry about maintaining our sexual integrity, our more frequent use of avoidance strategies, and our feelings of anger. She ignores countless criminological and sociological studies of women's fear of crime, offering her experience alone as a generalization for all our experiences. She eschews other women's anxieties and fears as if we were all the same or as if these concerns affect us in similar ways. They do not. Whatever the incidence of sexual assault—and by all accounts it is much higher than the incidence of breast cancer, road accidents, and airplane crashes—it has a special effect on our lives *as women.* Take a look at the burgeoning advice industry aimed at women and their concern about personal danger.

Feminist-baiting is, I believe, inevitable. Our struggles against the damage of men's abusive behavior to women bring protest from men who do not wish to be labeled as violent. Sometimes I lose my temper, showing my impatience with having to spend time attending to wounded feelings. Other times I purposely remain calm. For instance, I was once asked to comment on U.K. national radio about a recently released study of the treatment of complainants alleging rape in the criminal justice system. The radio commentator was badgering me to make the clichéd feminist statement, "All men are potential rapists." My reply to him was, "I do not know if all men are rapists. I do know that it cannot be the same 12 guys committing all the rapes." I made the commentator laugh. But had I responded with a cliché, my observations about rape would have been dismissed as coming from an "extremist." Sometimes anger is appropriate, sometimes not. I do not always "get it right."

Feminist practice, explicitly linked to much of the work around sexual assault, is meant to challenge the oppression of women by men. This is not to say that all men are *in essence* and *in nature* rapists. Of course not. Such accusations of essentialism abound—and contribute unhelpfully to a simplistic notion that, as social scientists, we can predict who is dangerous, who is safe, and what action will guarantee the validity of our predictions. But sexual violence, as has been demonstrated by countless theorists, activists, and researchers, is a prime example of such oppression. Some forms of masculinities are damaging to our health *as women.*

Reflection about women's lives in the process of gathering information is not unique to feminist practice or methodology (Kelly, Burton, & Regan,

1994). Reflexivity—the process of standing *outside* and gazing back to see what we can from afar—is a tool, not a blueprint, for developing a sensitivity to what has previously been consigned to silence. Feminist reflexivity about sexual violence ponders the effect of such information on our lives and provides data with which to reflect about sexual violence as a mechanism for maintaining inequality. Moreover, a narrative about sexual violence has a powerful place in popular culture. Is it possible to understand the meaning of its use by the news media as popular tellers of danger (Soothill & Walby, 1991), or the calculated use of rape by war criminals (Brownmiller, 1975), or its systematic use by some individual men to control women (Godenzi, 1994), without placing women's subordination at the center of the analysis? My work taught me to listen to the anxieties and precautionary strategies women use to avoid sexual violence *as* evidence of women's place in society. Resisting the links of such evidence of patriarchy at work, it seems to me, is merely an excuse not to recognize the strength of gender in any act of sexual violence. As Maynard (1994) suggests in her discussion of the debate about feminism and research:

> One of the early driving forces of feminism was to challenge the passivity, subordination and silencing of women, by encouraging them to speak about their own condition and in so doing to confront the experts and dominant males with the limitations of their own knowledge and comprehension. (p. 23)

In many ways, the strength of the opposition to what this information reveals—about our lives, about men's lives, about who is able to claim a stake in the state's system of protection—is testimony to the raw nerves we have hit. As feminists, the evidence amassed over the years on and about sexual violence is itself a call to action. Clearly, we all need to be reflexive about how our knowledge about, and desire for, minimizing the damage of sexual assault and violence could be channeled into productive measures to support those harmed—directly and indirectly. To those of us writing in this collection, nothing short of massive social change will do.

Emotion as Resource

I have suggested that our emotional responses to researching sexual violence are resources. Some of us are still left with uncertainty about the right to be so outraged. Moran-Ellis (1996) wonders,

> I am left, though, with some doubt as to whether I am entitled to have felt the emotions and anxieties I have described. Have I just been indulging in a vicarious type of suffering to which I have no legitimate claim? (p. 184)

As researchers of sexual violence, we should lay claim to these anxieties and emotions. I can say that I have not suffered as much as some of the women I have spoken with over the past 20 years. But this does not invalidate my own anxieties and the anger I feel on my own and others' behalf.

Research and debate about violence against women are rife with high emotion. Cohen (1994) describes feminism as our tutor, which "broke open the convenient, conventional understandings that, blanketed in denial, had masked any meaningful opportunity for knowledge and understanding of the central condition of many women's lives: that they [we] are ruled by male violence" (p. 350). She describes activism and scholarship as informed by "its prime tutelary emotion—anger" (p. 350). Building alliances for social support and for social change is one way to combat the feelings of isolation and frustration many of us working in the field of sexual violence inevitably feel. I would suggest the following strategies as mechanisms to channel one's emotional feelings and to foster personal support.

1. *Share your personal, emotional reactions.* There are many instances in which this simple suggestion is impossible. Some professions expect their staff to handle stress and anxiety as a requirement of the job. Any admission that work on sexual violence causes anxiety may put the individual under suspicion for incompetence. When possible, find a sympathetic support person. Make links with grassroots feminist organizations and sympathetic researchers in the area. Although it may not erase the anxiety, it helps put it into perspective.

2. *As a supervisor, anticipate the need for providing emotional support to fellow researchers, and particularly to students.* We, as researchers, must admit that this work is stressful. We should articulate how we manage to mediate the stress in our own lives. Such admissions—as we found early in the second wave of feminism—helped to establish a collective sensibility about violence. Our students and coresearchers need to know this.

3. *Be prepared to be baited.* Research on sexual violence is in many ways limited by the dominance of the modernist "fix-it" paradigm so prevalent in social science today. The more we isolate the *problem* of rape to the *problem* of men, the more we limit our strategies for change. I do not mean that we stop recognizing the significance of understanding masculinities for under-

standing sexual violence. We must be open to our own blinkers and refuse to simplify the complexities of our findings, even if this means we ask questions that might be uncomfortable. No data set I know of reflects equal proportions of male and female perpetrators. Nonetheless, we should not be afraid to explore all of the gendered dimensions of sexual abuse. Insight about sexual abuse committed by women, one example, will help us put male abusers' actions into perspective. We should insist that we understand the *meaning* of sexual violence for all women—however different they may be and whether they are survivors, offenders, or both.

Simplistic debate leads to further silence (Crenshaw, 1994). There is already too much silence. I do not believe it is unprofessional to reveal one's outrage. To me, it is one step toward expecting the rest of the world to be outraged enough to find ways to stop sexual violence. This is a very positive use of emotion, for we have every right to be angry.

Notes

1. See also Estrich (1987) for an exploration of how the distinction between real and "unreal" rape still holds.
2. Observations about men's contribution to sexual offenses often give rise to an accusation that the researcher is a man-hater. All the social science evidence supports the finding that men are overwhelmingly represented among abusers.
3. For an informative and insightful analysis of legal change, see Roberts and Mohr (1994).
4. My emotionality to my own sexual harassment case is described in Stanko (1996).
5. See also Bumgartner (1993).

CHAPTER

7

Activist Research and Social Narratives

Dialectics of Power, Privilege, and Institutional Change

SUSAN K. HIPPENSTEELE

Prestige and power are institutional phenomena . . .

Like most social scientists, my graduate education taught me to value objectivity in scientific practice. I learned that to acknowledge a personal investment in the outcome of my research was tantamount to admitting a flawed methodology. (I somehow knew better than to ask who might undertake a study of rape, violence, or any other social problem without any personal stake in the results.)

My current role as a victim's advocate does not allow me to position myself as a naive observer when conducting research. However, my role does provide me a measure of freedom most sexual violence researchers on university campuses do not share—freedom to tell stories that challenge the subordinating practices that maintain sexual and racial violence on campus and freedom to challenge rhetorical strategies that have excluded the experiences these stories represent.

As the principal investigator for a multicampus study of ethnoviolence,[1] I am in a unique and perhaps even rare position. My advocacy work allows me to bridge the gap between research and practice. Much less vulnerable to pressures to conform than I was as a graduate student, I have come to agree with Seiber (1993) and others who suggest that the sensitivities and risks researchers of sensitive subjects must learn to recognize are not necessarily those the researcher will consider to be real. I no longer worry that colleagues who criticize my research will leap on the slightest flaw or weakness in my research methods or analyses—most never bother to read my findings (which might prove a diversion from the much more interesting questions about my motivation for studying campus ethnoviolence. "Was she raped by her father?" "What must have happened to her as a child?" "She's just another one of those PC feminists working through her white middle-class guilt," and the all-encompassing, "Of course, it's because she's a lesbian").

Steeped in the heart of the controversy surrounding sexual harassment and other campus ethnoviolence, I do not claim to be dispassionate or objective about my work. I am committed to values that stimulate more than one side of current debates over political correctness, academic freedom, and civil rights on campus, and to exploring the role "activist researchers" (Fine, 1993) play in efforts to mitigate the effect of campus ethnoviolence. I do this by emphasizing the importance of social narratives as evidence in ongoing struggles for social change.

The presence of an advocate on any campus is an uncomfortable reminder of the hundreds of stories they know I hear from women and people of color whose experiences are shameful and embarrassing to the University when told. I often feel like an apparition—haunting efforts to paint the problem of campus violence in empty rhetoric and working within a shadow institution—a campus within a campus, where violence, fear, and intimidation have been normalized by silence—where the shared reality is not academic excellence but the struggle to quietly subvert oppression. Negotiating the territory between the role of advocate and researcher is challenging; my problem-solving strategies as an advocate can easily conflict with my values as a researcher. My work as an advocate is vulnerable to accusations that the alternative reality I claim to be representing is not supported by data. As I struggle to balance my values as an advocate without doing too much damage to my credibility as a researcher, I argue that the terms *is not, will not,* and *cannot* should not be interchangeable. Yet as Fielding (1993) and others have pointed out, practitioners who also conduct research generally find that their field experience dramatically enhances their sensitivity to subtle but important lines of inquiry.

Ethnoviolence research, like other areas of study critically bound by the limits of subjective experience, requires context to be useful. My experiences as a victim of and as an advocate for victims of campus-based violence have had a marked influence on my development as a researcher. I lay claim to an informed rejection of objective inquiry and abstract analysis as a means to increase our collective sophistication in understanding the effects of campus ethnoviolence. I have learned firsthand that when experiences of violence and oppression are lumped together using these types of strategies, all forms of discrimination begin to sound the same (Grillo & Wildman, 1995).

This chapter is about researching campus-based ethnoviolence and about negotiating the political terrain that surrounds applied work in the field. The first section discusses ethnoviolence research as part of a larger social movement and examines the emergence of the campus-based activist researcher as a locus for institutional change. The second section outlines the special circumstances surrounding my own work as an activist researcher and examines how creating a nexus between research and resistance on campus can stimulate opportunities for marked, effective institutional change. The final section explores critical issues I and my colleagues have faced as we attempt to assess and control the application of our research findings, and closes with an argument for urgency in developing site-specific campus ethnoviolence research programs and effectively communicating meaningful results.

My work as an activist researcher draws heavily from narrative theory, a methodology used by critical race theorists to undermine the deterministic hindrances inherent in traditional academic systems used to classify information and knowledge (Delgado & Stefancic, 1995). I argue that social narrative research may provide sexual violence researchers the means to more effectively collaborate with activists, frontline workers, and victims of the violent social reality we would hope to transform. Delgado and Yun (1995) suggest "narrative theory shows that we interpret new stories in terms of old ones we have internalized." Because we draw, in practice, from our own treasury of stories to assess and determine "reality," narratives that deviate too drastically from those we recognize as familiar may be judged as lacking in credibility, false, or even dangerous. The stories of women and minority victims of campus ethnoviolence are currently being questioned in increasingly clever ways. The sophistication of counterattacks that label the victim as the perpetrator—of assaults on truth, free speech, academic freedom, collegiality, professional ethics, institutional integrity, and so forth—requires an unwavering commitment from activist researchers who must develop more effective methods to counter these often outrageous claims.

A social narrative approach to sexual violence research and advocacy emphasizes the story—the context and detail—of victim and advocate encounters with institutionalized forms of oppression. Our inability (or unwillingness) to recognize and understand the fault lines of dissension (Fine, 1993) has limited progress toward meaningful institutional change. Both researchers and advocates help keep women and minorities confined and silenced when we fail to effectively challenge the masquerades of privacy, shame, invisibility, and exclusion that have been so restricting in the past. Narratives not only strengthen and synthesize our efforts to bridge the conceptual and methodological barriers that limit our efforts to prevent campus ethnoviolence, they allow us to expand our understanding of the potential of activist researchers' work as well. In other words, the use of a social narrative method forces us to learn new stories that will enable us to internalize the diverse voices of victims of campus-based violence—across races, ethnic groups, sexualities, classes, disabilities, and political ideologies.

Negotiating the Terrain

Michelle Fine (1993) offers a poignant critique of the conflict between material conditions and scientific ideology that can impede activist researchers working with victims of violence. Fine's analysis clearly marks the point of transition at which the researcher must come to grips with the limits traditional methods pose for academics who work on the "front lines." In one sense, social scientists who study violence and advocates for the victims of that violence work at cross purposes. As researchers, we attempt to investigate the precipitating events, context, correlates, effects, and so forth of violence while influencing the data as little as possible. To be useful as advocates, however, we must influence each of these factors as much as we can. Researchers' actions are based on established lines of thinking (i.e., our methodology), but advocates must intentionally depart from past practice. For the activist researcher engaged in campus ethnoviolence research who must work within an interpretive paradigm (Delgado & Yun, 1995), the social narrative is an antidote with the potential to fundamentally challenge the investigation and interpretation of institutionalized oppression.

The evolution of this new paradigm will find substance in the exacerbation of tensions that exist between research and practice for ethnoviolence researchers. For example, sexual harassment is considered a serious social problem because it is illegal and causes victims psychological harm. But because determining what particular conduct constitutes illegal sexual harassment depends, in large part, on the perceptions of victims, most of our research efforts of the past 15 years have focused on women's individual experiences, sensitivities, responses, attributions, coping strategies, and so forth. Empirical findings from descriptive and correlational studies have decontextualized sexual harassment from its sociopolitical context. Critical issues of racism, classism, patriarchy, homophobia, and related economic variables linked to capitalism that sculpt the conditions of women's work and academic lives have been lost (Fine, 1993).

Nearly two decades of research have relied on victims of violence as the source for information and insight regarding the crimes perpetrated against them and as the site for remedying the illegal acts, as well. Without saying it, we have recognized that research designed to illuminate the social structures and institutional factors that enable perpetrators of campus ethnoviolence to offend and assault is too risky to undertake. Our own stories as victims and researchers is shared in quiet conversation with like-experienced colleagues over drinks toward the end of the conferences we attend. We collectively shudder to imagine that "word might get out" that our interest in our research is more than professional, and our public silence reinforces the victim-blaming we claim to resist.

Many significant questions posed by activist researchers studying sexual or other forms of ethnoviolence have been lost or ignored in the struggle for the legitimacy of the research topic itself. The sexual violence literature is filled with calls for more accurate studies of strategies of resistance, critiques of victim representation, and research efforts addressing the questions advocates need answered (Fine, 1993). But the traditional focus on the individual as a source of explanation for sexual victimization has consistently influenced the research questions researchers have asked. These efforts have done little to weaken the class, race, sex, and ethnic barriers to equal protection under the law, nor have they undermined the limiting effect the institutionalization of victim services has on attempts at reform.

Unfortunately, assessing the effect of ethnoviolence research on social factors that matter to victims is even more difficult than studying the problem itself. The problems are many: Where do we look for results? Do we direct our inquiry toward the number of incidents of sexual violence *reported* on campus in a given academic year? Survey our campus authorities to determine what percentage perceive sexual harassment, rape, race discrimination, and so forth to be serious campus problems? Calculate the amount of money our institution spent on attorney fees and trial or settlement costs paid to victims over the past 5 years? Compare settlement figures with changes in the rate of cases upheld through in-house grievance procedures? Or do we measure effect by examining institutional policies and practices that devalue and constrain women and minorities for signs of revision?

We can, and should, look at each of these variables, along with numerous others, but the politics surrounding a campus response to ethnoviolence are complex. The traditions of the academy that teach that those within the walls of the ivory tower are special and superior also communicate the exclusivity of this privilege. Disdain for members of groups long considered outsiders to academia, women and people of color, continues to be cultivated by practices rooted in the subordination of members of these groups. Because the natural superiority of men is so deeply institutionalized and accepted as normative within academia, we seldom question social practices that secure the entitlements of authority figures within the institutional hierarchy. Like a fraternity, a campus administration will often act as a "brotherhood" of sorts, engaging in practices that effectively shield deviant and violent incidents (often perpetrated by candidates for the advantaged positions) from public scrutiny. The ability to recognize the story of the woman or minority victim of campus ethnoviolence as familiar or at least credible is critical to assessing the effect of ethnoviolence research, because most social narratives evolve to reinforce the status quo.

Many campus ethnoviolence researchers have discovered that maintaining control over the meaning and interpretation of our results so that data are not improperly read can be extremely difficult. The annual reporting figures for rape on campus, for example, are generally gross underrepresentations of the actual number of campus rapes per year, but this single figure remains an item of information most campus administrators want. This one data point can (and will) be used to argue that sexual violence is not a problem on campus, so it is incumbent on the "activist researcher" (Fine, 1993) to report this figure in its appropriate context (i.e., only 5% of rape victims seek victim services, 5% report to police, 42% never mention the rape at all [Koss, Gidycz, & Wisniewski, 1987], etc.). Read this way, annual rape reporting statistics can have a profound positive effect on preventive education and victim-support programming.

The harm of discrimination can easily be compounded by practices that perpetuate the expectation that issues of concern to white researchers are legitimately central to every inquiry (Grillo & Wildman, 1995). Members of dominant groups (to which most academics belong) often impose their interpretation of a problem on its speaker. Although the trend is moving increasingly toward examining questions formerly considered too hot to handle, ethnoviolence research remains ghettoized by factors that will continue to deter efforts to examine important and politically volatile topics. Joan Seiber (1993) describes the ethics and politics of research into sensitive topics as intricately intertwined. For researchers studying campus ethnoviolence, principled research designs that prevent harm and are respectful and fair (i.e., ethical) can collide with the application of established methods and strategies researchers use to leverage power and control. Seiber (1993) also points out that even recognizing ethical and political dilemmas in applied research of this type can be complicated by the motives and perceptions of others whose interests might seem at odds with those of the researcher. A funding proposal to support research examining the intersections of sexual and racial violence, for example, may not be welcomed by campus officials unwilling to risk the inevitable attending charge of institutional racism—the classic example of the conflict that arises when the funding source (the university) has a vested interest in maintaining the antithetical illusion that ethnoviolence research is welcome but unnecessary.

The Nexus Between Research and Practice

Provision for advocacy of victims of campus-based sexual violence did not come easily at the University of Hawai'i (Hippensteele, 1996). In 1989, when a small group of students, faculty, and administrators began arguing that the provision of advocacy for student victims of sexual harassment was consistent with the intent of Title IX, debate surrounding sexual harassment was heated (Hippensteele & Chesney-Lind, 1995). The call for a formal in-house program of advocacy and support for victims of sexual harassment was a measured response to a grievance process perceived as biased in favor of respondent faculty. A committee formed to troubleshoot the grievance process on behalf of complainants and respondents had radically restructured the informal and formal procedures to accommodate the hiring of an in-house advocate. The advocate, it was hoped, would disrupt the balance of power between victims, perpetrators, and the institution by supporting victims' efforts to resist ethnoviolence using these internal procedures.

Since my hire in 1992, between 80 and 100 students, faculty, and staff alleging sexual harassment and related discrimination have come forward each year to challenge the inequities they experience on campus. I quickly learned the limits of piecemeal reform when the advocacy services my program was designed to provide temporarily frustrated previous practice but did little to improve the system's poor track record of resolving individual incidents of campus ethnoviolence. I now realize the more significant role of an in-house advocate is not to disrupt the structural factors that perpetuate campus ethnoviolence but to break the code of silence that has allowed these practices to remain unchallenged for so long.

One of the problems I faced as the first victim's advocate at the University of Hawai'i was figuring out how to assist students who described sexual comments, jokes, gestures, and even direct sexual overtures from professors and other students as acts of racism. Like most institutions, the University of Hawai'i has a sexual harassment policy that is distinct from the policy and procedures used to investigate and resolve other ethnoviolence complaints. I was hired to work exclusively with individuals filing complaints under my university's sexual harassment policy. At that time, the university did not provide advocacy to individuals or groups alleging racial or any other forms of discrimination besides that which was sex-based. Crenshaw (1993) and others have pointed out that emphasizing sex discrimination downplays the interaction of sexism and racism and has the effect of constructing the two as mutually exclusive. I became an unwitting player in a game that excluded most legitimate players. My role had been devised to accommodate the social movement surrounding sexual harassment in the early 1990s—a movement propelled by the actions of women of color—Mechelle Vinson, Kerry Ellison, Anita Hill, and others. Yet policymakers on my campus (and elsewhere) isolated the problem of sexual violence on campus by institutionalizing the link between "victim" and "feminist"—a link with inherent problems of exclusion, rejection, and invisibility for women of color. On my campus, where the student population is composed of eight different race/ethnic groups representing 10% or more of the student body each, the line between incidents of sexual and racial violence are seldom clear.

Institutionalization of campus-based advocacy services inherently limits the forms of protest available to the advocate because "working the system" on behalf of complainants is an implicit part of the job. The addition of an advocate for victims of sexual violence did little to clarify, let alone undermine, the structural inequities that limited women's and minorities' access to options and remedies to ethnoviolence at the University of Hawai'i. Because there is no existing social narrative to accommodate the role, the boundaries and rules of engagement shift constantly. Not only does my position deviate drastically from the "reality" we know and recognize as "tenure-track faculty position at a major research institution," it threatens that reality in innumerable ways. Lacking institutional support for my efforts to privilege the experiences of women of color, my choices seemed to be (a) encouraging complainants to describe their experiences in terms that did not reflect the harm they were experiencing, (b) sending them away from the only source of formal advocacy available through the institution, or (c) violating the explicit instructions of my employer by providing advocacy assistance beyond the scope of my assigned duties.

I sought confirmation of the systemic racial biases I found within my university's response to incidents of ethnoviolence in the social science literature on victimization. Finding very few studies examining the overlap between sexual harassment and other forms of protected class discrimination, I found inspiration and a framework for understanding the stories I heard in critical race theory. I recognized that my first task as a researcher was to develop a method that would enable me to examine and show the commingling of students' experiences of racial and sexual violence. I hoped to use the results of a large survey-format study that would reflect the unacknowledged race and class barriers inherent in my institution's procedures and would help us provide more effective advocacy services with a broader focus. Consistent with Channels's (1993) suggestion that studies of racism are among the most sensitive social problems being studied today, my research associates and I found minimal support for this work even among civil-rights advocates in our own community.

With a small start-up grant and dozens of student volunteer hours, my research group developed an instrument that examined what we now refer to as the "greatest impact" incident of discrimination and surveyed nearly 1,000 students about their most significant direct experience of discrimination, their indirect (covictim) experiences, and their attitudes toward campus ethnoviolence. Our findings clearly indicated that although the University of Hawai'i at Manoa campus is far more ethnically diverse than most U.S. campuses, problems of racism, intersected with sexism and homophobia, were undeniable. We found distinct patterns in the reported experiences of campus ethnoviolence that were disturbingly consistent with the ethnic hierarchy that exists in Hawai'i. First-person narratives showed a dramatic range of participants' personal experiences as victims. Members of racial and ethnic groups (including sexual minorities) most likely to be subjected to economic and employment discrimination in the state also reported the highest rates of ethnoviolence on campus. Pacific Islander, Filipino, and Native Hawaiian students, from among the most economically disadvantaged ethnic and native groups in the state, reported consistently higher overall rates of campus ethnoviolence than Japanese or Chinese students, whose ethnic group membership is often associated with economic and social privilege in Hawai'i. Most compelling to university officials was our conclusion that racism at the University of Hawai'i has many faces—for women, it appeared to be sexual harassment and homophobia; for men, it was physical intimidation, assaults, and homophobic acts that were racially motivated (Hippensteele, Chesney-Lind, & Veniegas, 1996).

Clearly then, the line that had been drawn between race and sex discrimination at the University of Hawai'i was not appropriate, but complainants were still being forced to locate themselves on one side of it or the other. These research findings provided compelling evidence to support our argument that complainants' decisions to file complaints were often based not on the "worst" part of their experience, or even the most salient, but on factors such as the ease and clarity of various grievance options, accessibility of assistance, and even staff familiarity with the various policies. We published articles in nationally recognized journals that critiqued our institution's response to student complaints and cited statistics that suggested students of color often found themselves ghettoized by rigid policies that failed to capture the complexity of their experiences.

Within 2 years, a small but significant change in the language of one of our sexual harassment grievance procedures began moving the university toward broader, more effective institutional responsiveness. The change acknowledges the multiplicity of complainants' experiences of ethnoviolence by allowing them to retain the services of the advocate even if it becomes apparent after they receive "counseling" that their primary allegations are not of sexual harassment. In other words, the procedure now provides for advocacy even when sexual harassment is only one part of the complaint. People of color can now articulate an institutionally cognizable complaint under sexual harassment procedures as a complaint of racism with sexualized overtones—and retain their right to in-house advocacy services.

Obviously, the procedural change did not go far enough—we had argued that our findings supported the creation of a comprehensive program of advocacy services for all victims of discrimination regardless of their protected class status. But it was an improvement. A short time later, though, a series of well-publicized incidents highlighting the university's failure to adequately respond to complaints of discrimination against Native Hawaiians set the stage for the next critical step.

During the early part of the fall semester, 1995, a lecturer in the geography department at the University of Hawai'i called on campus security to forcibly remove two Native Hawaiian undergraduate students from his class. The lecturer, a European-American man from the U.S. mainland, claimed that the two sisters, one of whom was 8 months pregnant, were being "disruptive." I met with the students after they were referred to me by the chair of their department. They refuted the lecturer's characterization of them as disruptive and sought assistance in filing a complaint of race, sex, and national origin discrimination. The students alleged a series of incidents preceding their expulsion from class that included numerous in-class discussions initiated by the lecturer and quoted his misrepresentations of Native Hawaiian history and culture, along with his recitation of racist stereotypes of Native Hawaiians that both women found humiliating and degrading. He had apparently admitted his own ignorance regarding these subjects to the class on several occasions. The students believed they were removed from class because they had challenged the lecturer to provide sources for his statements. Their allegations did not include elements of sexual harassment, so I was instructed not to assist them. The investigation and subsequent finding by the institution offered an ambiguous explanation that supported the lecturer's actions.

The reaction across campus to the finding reflected the earlier reaction to the expulsion itself. The story of this case has become a vivid, tangible symbol at the University of Hawai'i of the institutional racism that privileges white, male culture and disadvantages those who resist it. Fall semester, 1996, found the University of Hawai'i administration, at a time of significant downsizing across campus, expanding advocacy services by hiring a second advocate to provide Native Hawaiian students, faculty, and staff with formal, in-house advocacy assistance. The addition of a second full-time advocate stimulated efforts to create a comprehensive advocacy office that will eventually provide services to *all* students, staff, and faculty who seek assistance. This development is supported by data my colleagues and I had earlier obtained, showing that students and employees experience ethnoviolence at the University, regardless of their protected class status.

The tensions and contradictions inherent in providing in-house advocacy for victims of campus ethnoviolence are significant. The abject failure of most antidiscrimination initiatives to remedy campus ethnoviolence fuels a healthy suspicion of those efforts that become institutionalized. Still, the developments at the University of Hawai'i in the face of angry challenges to the status quo illustrate the growing movement on campuses around the United States that is aimed at altering the balance of power between victims of ethnoviolence, perpetrators of ethnoviolence, and institutions. The expanding body of evidence showing that victims do possess credible, unique perspectives and knowledge that define and mitigate their experiences does not leave room for the continued isolation of these experiences. The power of the social narrative to illuminate campus ethnoviolence lies in its potential to transform what we recognize as "reality." Whether activist researchers can eventually use their work to alter institutionalized practices that enable and support the perpetration of campus ethnoviolence remains to be seen. Certainly, future research efforts must be directed at issues that will lead institutions far beyond piecemeal reforms.

Some Notes on Institutional Change

Researching any form of ethnoviolence carries a tremendous responsibility for the researcher to develop studies and communicate results in ways and to entities that will benefit (or at least not harm) victims. Because ethnoviolence data are so controversial to begin with, they are easily misinterpreted and their broader implications can often be ignored. When data or issues relating to ethnoviolence are misrepresented or misunderstood by campus authorities, social backlash, bad policy, and even harm to the researcher can occur (Seiber, 1993). The principal weakness of survey methodologies—the mainstay of ethnoviolence researchers' efforts to understand the problem—lies in the researchers' inability to contextualize findings in meaningful ways. Without a treasury of stories of ethnoviolence to draw from, the "reality" of the phenomena remains obscure.

Adler and Adler (1993) discuss the significant influence self-censorship has on researchers' examinations of issues and communication of findings relating to sensitive research topics. Activist researchers studying campus ethnoviolence have legitimate cause for concern that the results of their work will not be well-received. The University of Hawai'i's ethnoviolence studies have intentionally reflected incidence (annual) rates rather than prevalence rates of direct and indirect (covictimization) experiences because we felt that the size of lifetime rates might well negate the effect of the data themselves. Adler and Adler (1993) and numerous others admit to censoring the worst cases or features of the stories they hear and of omitting facts or experiences that might reveal particularly sensitive issues of concern to research participants. Thus, activist researchers must balance the advantages and risks whenever they use victim's stories.

Tailored research initiatives at the University of Hawai'i provided empirical evidence of systemic problems of racism that became visible once the availability of in-house advocacy brought victims of campus ethnoviolence "out of the closet." Site-specific research efforts such as these that produce a diverse range of stories of ethnoviolence are far more likely than broad university policies or even Supreme Court decisions to inspire a sense of social responsibility or to revitalize efforts to improve the climate for victims on campus. The resulting dialogue that occurred on our campus once victims began coming forward provided campus officials with unparalleled opportunities to understand the dimensions of ethnoviolence by learning new stories, and it dramatically increased the likelihood that responses to the problem will eventually prove corrective.

Additional studies of the interactions and correlates to campus ethnoviolence are clearly warranted at the University of Hawai'i and elsewhere. The assumption that bias-motivated acts were experienced as a unidimensional phenomenon masked the complexity of the problem of sexual violence at the University of Hawai'i and likely does so on other campuses, as well. Numerous issues of concern to victims, advocates, activist researchers, and campus officials remain unexamined. Most compelling to me are inquiries that offer promise in challenging the institutionalized structures of racism and classism that define the context and experience of sexual violence. The answers to some research questions will be generalizable to other locales, but the results of site-specific studies should be most useful within the context they represent.

Before closing this chapter, I would like to suggest some immediate steps activist researchers interested in breaking the silence surrounding campus ethnoviolence might take. First, conduct a site-specific study of ethnoviolence. Gathering quantitative and qualitative data on the dimensions of the problem as it expresses itself in a particular academic setting will create the foundation for serious, specific, and constructive discussions of the issues. As long as racism, sexism, classism, and other -isms remain theoretical or purely legalistic matters for academics, challenges to the privileges that excuse perpetrators will meet with only limited success.

Second, use the results of the study to review existing procedures and modify them to encourage complaints. Deceptively simple measures such as altering the language of a campus grievance procedure to eliminate legalistic or restrictive-use language can dramatically improve an institution's complaint/resolution process and will serve as an educational tool for the entire campus as well.

Third, use the findings to support and encourage effective resolutions to complaints. Responding promptly and effectively to incidents of campus ethnoviolence requires courage, creativity, and commitment on the part of faculty and campus officials. National publicity surrounding recent incidents on several U.S. campuses suggests that the aftermath of ethnoviolence poorly handled by a university can lead to increased tension and costly litigation. Stories of successful and effective interventions and resolution strategies need to be collected, documented, published, and archived to become visible parts of an institution's collective history.

Fourth, consider expanding conventional preventive education approaches to ethnoviolence. Most preventive education efforts tend to blame the victim by focusing almost exclusively on faculty-student interactions, administrative procedures available to victims, and laws crafted to respond to particular situations. With little or no reference to the social context that serves to keep women and minorities subordinate within the institution, prevention will remain elusive. Finally, broaden the number of groups discussing ethnoviolence on campus. Conventional approaches to campus ethnoviolence tend to emphasize "low"-end prevention through sporadic, superficial education efforts and "high"-end intervention in the form of administrative procedures that are costly and inefficient. Left out of prevention efforts are those whose perspectives and experiences as victims of campus ethnoviolence are integral to the debate and to developing effective solutions to the problem (Hippensteele & Chesney-Lind, 1995).

As our understanding of the dynamics of these social problems develop, we are beginning to recognize the degree to which our own institutions are complicitous in their creation. Narrative theory implies that the structural transformation that might eliminate the social ill of campus ethnoviolence is attainable. Storytelling as a method of conveying new truths can enable activist researchers to confront the exclusion and marginalization that confound our efforts to communicate and collaborate with activists, frontline workers, and those whose social reality of sexual violence we hope to transform.

Note

1. Overt behavior intended to psychologically or physically harm someone because of their ethnic group membership (Ehrlich, 1990, 1992), which includes, among others, race, ethnicity, religion, national origin, sexual orientation, and sex.

CHAPTER

8

Field Research With Phone Sex Workers

Managing the Researcher's Emotions

CHRISTINE MATTLEY

In this chapter, I focus on the difficulty researchers face managing emotion on two levels: first, emotion management in the field during the research process and second, emotion management as part of dealing with other people's reactions toward one during the research process. Specifically, I am concerned with managing emotions that emanate from the application of a stigma that results from researching a marginal or deviant group. A *courtesy stigma* is a stigma that is often applied to an individual on the basis of his or her association with a stigmatized individual or group. In my case, because of the manner in which the courtesy stigma was applied, I have termed it *(dis)courtesy stigma* (Mattley, 1994).

Recently, sociologists have recognized the importance of attending to emotions during the research process rather than holding them in abeyance (see Ellis, 1991; Kleinman & Copp, 1993; Ronai, 1992). Ellis (1991) has argued for an emotional sociology that describes, embodies, and interprets lived emotional experience:

> First, as sociologists we can examine emotions emotionally, feeling for the people we study. Second, reflecting inward as well as observing outward, we can view our own emotional experience as a legitimate sociological object of study and focus on how we feel as researchers as a way of understanding and coping with what is going on emotionally in our research. Third, . . . sociologists can concentrate on studying how emotions feel in the context and by the narrative terms of peoples' everyday lives. (p. 125)

Accordingly, as Ronai (1992) notes, a focus on researchers and their feelings during research situations can be of particular interest. The following is an introspective narrative that relates my emotional experiences during my field research with phone fantasy workers and my experience entering the field.

Just as we cannot ignore participants' feelings and expect to understand the group, we cannot omit our feelings as field researchers. Attending to *our* feelings in the field helps us understand how group members construct meaning and understandings. Researchers who are aware of their feelings in the field and consciously respond to those feelings and feeling norms are what I call *sentient* researchers.

Before turning to my narrative, let me describe how I came to do field research on phone fantasy workers. The research originated from my ongoing interest in the sociology of emotions. The increasing sociological interest in the commercialization of emotion includes the ways in which people are trained to manage their own emotions in addition to the emotions of their customers or clients.

In postindustrial society, the fundamental fact is that most workers talk to other individuals rather than interact with machines. Fewer than 6% of workers now work on assembly lines; voice-to-voice or face-to-face delivery of service has become prominent in our culture. Moreover, service-sector jobs are far more likely to demand emotional labor from employees. A capacity to deal with people rather than with things is required in most jobs (Hochschild, 1983). Scant as it is, virtually all of the literature on the emotion-labor of people in various occupations focuses on traditional occupations such as flight attendants, bill collectors, therapists, missionary wives, or supermarket clerks (Hardesty, 1986; Hochschild, 1983; Romero, 1988; Strickland, 1991; Tolich, 1993).

Consequently, I decided to study work in which the commodity sold *is* emotion-work that is characterized by emotion-labor rather than work in which emotion-labor is just a part. An obvious choice was the selling of fantasy—specifically, the selling of sexual fantasy over the telephone. Callers are not, for instance, buying transportation from one physical location to another but are actually *buying emotions* from a faceless voice, so the issue of emotion-labor is critical to understanding the work and the worker. Likewise, this offered an opportunity to investigate the ways in which workers manage their own emotions and those of the customers.

The data reported here come from field notes written during participant observations conducted over a 9-month period. I spent between 3 and 5 days per week, for a minimum of 6 hours per day, working for an adult phone fantasy telephone line. During that time, I took about 1,890 calls, got to know other workers and the management, and spent many hours talking with all the people working there. Some of the women became friends with whom I occasionally socialized after working hours, whereas others were merely acquaintances.

I kept a field journal recording my own emotions during the entire process—from trying to find such a business, to trying to acquire funding for my project, to trying to gain access—through the time I spent in the field. I was fortunate to have two colleagues who acted as sounding boards for me throughout the entire time, and I included their comments and support in my emotion field journal. I have divided my narrative into three parts. Entering the field is fraught with emotion, so the first section recounts my experience of that. The second section deals with my experience actually working in the field. Finally, I recount dealing with other people's reactions toward me during the entire research process.

Entering the Field

One of the first steps in this research process was, of course, to try to obtain funding to offset the costs of research. I wrote a grant application to try to obtain university funding. One of the reviewers objected to the research site, suggesting that "there must be another occupation to study. . . . Was it chosen simply because it was titillating?" Of course, the implication was that somehow my perverted, voyeuristic tendencies led me to this research topic and site. (Needless to say, I received no funding.) I got trashed by this reviewer, who was a feminist I know well. I wrote in my field journal at the time,

> *I am so disappointed in her, I feel betrayed by her—especially since we have talked about this research and she was supportive face-to-face. Her comments included asking whether I had chosen this research because it is titillating. I guess I expected more from her as a woman and as a feminist. This is obviously part of the sex industry which clearly exploits women. Isn't this a feminist issue? Is she provincial enough to think this research is "dirty"? I feel like my trust in her is shattered. Can I trust anyone about this?*

Field researchers are often questioned about their choice of topics, so although I felt a bit wounded, I didn't take the criticism too seriously. I decided it was probably due to a lack of understanding of the issues involved, and I realized that I would probably face these questions in the future. Such questions would just be part of the territory and should not be taken as reflecting on the worthiness of the project.

I was undaunted. While I was planning my faculty fellowship leave, I happened on a help-wanted ad for a phone fantasy business in a large city nearby.

> *Major breakthrough!! I bought a* Columbus Dispatch *yesterday (Sunday edition) to look for ads for portable CD players and decided to look at the want ads, and BINGO!!! There in the want ads under section 2270 "escorts wanted" was the following ad:*
>
> > TELEPHONE HELP NEEDED—THE STATE'S LARGEST PHONE FANTASY SERVICE IS ABOUT TO DOUBLE IN SIZE. WE ARE HIRING FOR ALL SHIFTS PLUS WEEKENDS. WE ARE LOOKING FOR ONLY SERIOUS PEOPLE WITH A GOOD PHONE VOICE, RELIABLE TRANSPORT, AND GOOD WORK HISTORY. PAY \$300-500 PER WEEK. CALL FOR INTERVIEW MON-FRI 10 AM TO 4 PM (PHONE NUMBER).

I was so excited! The next day I called about 2 p.m. When a man answered, I said that I was calling about the ad in Sunday's *Dispatch.* He said they were interviewing. We set up an interview for 2 days later. In my journal that evening, I wrote,

As I was driving home I saw L walking down the street, so I motioned to him and pulled over and told him what is going on. God, he is so supportive! He is also excited for me and shares the feeling that this is exactly what I am looking for in terms of gathering data. Training, working in a common area, what a perfect setup. I'm happy to have someone to discuss this with, and I appreciate that he is so enthusiastic about this project. His affirmation is so important to me.

Throughout the time I spent doing this research, I came to realize that having a colleague or close friend to use as a sounding board while in the field was critical. For me, using colleagues was preferable because of the sociological imagination they brought to the discussions we had. We sometimes met and discussed how the research was going and what things I should be looking for, and they would listen to my ideas and analyses and respond to them.

Interview Day. I am so nervous about all this. What if I fail the interview? What sorts of things will they ask? Obviously about work history and why I want to do this work. What will I say? Probably that I am wanting to earn some extra money and that I am not sure that I have any other talents, except that I certainly can talk. What if they don't like me or think that I am too snooty or snobby? What will the interviewer be like? What will I say? . . . Should I be truthful? I really don't want to lie and then get tangled in my stories. . . . God, what will I do with my first caller; can I actually do this research?? What if I go blank? On one hand, I think this is great experience just for the interview, but on the other hand I feel like this is a perfect setup and I really hope that it works out. I am nervous—no, beyond nervous!

I was delighted at how easy it was to gain entry. My nervousness and attempts to anticipate possible questions and problems prepared me to successfully complete the interview. Field researchers are routinely cautioned to anticipate and think through as many possible problems as they can, and I believe it is advice worth taking. Yet although my nervousness about gaining entry was assuaged, I was still worried about the work itself.

> *Whew! What a day. As I drove up I realized that I was excited as well as nervous. I got a motel room and drove on to "work." When I walked in Blair (the supervisor) was at her desk, said Hi. She seemed happy to see me, or at least she was very cordial. I sat in a chair next to her desk. When she took a call, I asked if she wanted me to leave (what was I thinking?!?), she chuckled and said no. . . .*
>
> *Finally she asks me if I want to take a call, and I say I have a few questions before I actually do. She says that is ok whenever I feel ready. The phones are busy and at one point she says, "God we're busy I may have to put you to work" but doesn't. A little after 7 pm a call comes through and she asks if I want to do one. I nervously say yes, she says are you nervous? I say yes, but I have to start sometime. She takes down the information and leads me to a cubicle. I have asked her if I can say that I'm new and she says yeah. I sit down and punch the line and say, "Hi, Lawrence, this is Elise. How are you?" I am so nervous, I hope my voice is not quivering. My eyes feel warm and my voice does not seem to be coming from my body, and I feel as though I am listening to someone else say these words. We talk, he asks about me and I about him, then he abruptly says I have to go. Seven minutes have passed, I feel like a failure, I didn't have to moan or anything.*
>
> *I return to where Blair is to find her talking to Richard, the guy who spends about $1,000 per month. When the shift ends we talk about the schedule for the week, and she tells me that I have been the best trainee she has ever worked with, and I laughingly tell her Oh I'm sure you tell that to all the girls!! I say see you tomorrow at 2 and leave. I drive back to the motel and wonder if I can master this stuff, making the right sounds and lose any inhibitions that I have. I keep approaching this as though I can do anything, as though I am unflappable. Am I? It is so much a part of my self image that I refuse to admit that I could be embarrassed. That I can force myself to do anything. Hmmmmm, we'll see tomorrow.*

During my first couple of days at work, I found that the other women were very friendly and helpful. They talked to me about how they felt when they first started working, about feeling embarrassed or nervous, and how they dealt with their feelings. In this way they tried to help allay what they assumed I was feeling. Over time, I realized that although talk was central to the work itself, talk *about* the work was an integral part of how the women dealt with their emotions about the work. Women discussed particular callers, their feelings or thoughts about particular callers, the fantasies they constructed, whether or not they were successful, and how they felt about particular types of fantasies and callers. This joint emotion-work was an ongoing activity throughout the entire time I was in the field. I found it useful not only as an information-gathering strategy but also for dealing with my own feelings. Hearing other women's feelings affirmed my own, thus confirming that my reactions were "normal" or were "in line" with theirs and making interpretations more valid.

Working in the Field

My own feelings changed quickly. I was no longer nervous about whether I would fit in or could do the work. The work became a familiar routine. I became "one of the girls" and found that I was treated and accepted like any of the other workers. The workplace was in many ways like most workplaces. Women were friends, socialized with one another outside of work, sometimes had potlucks at work on Fridays, and shared the details of their lives with one another. Like the others, I joined in these activities, made friends with some of the women, and sometimes socialized with them.

The electricity went off 15 minutes into the shift. Since the electricity was out the building was dark so everyone went outside to the parking lot behind the building. No one was allowed to go home in case the electricity came back on. (However, no one got paid since we weren't on the phones!) We were kind of hanging out listening to one woman's car stereo, some women were dancing, and the rest of us were sitting chatting and we began to talk about the callers. The women agreed that they think four types of guys call. One is the "regular guy." For these men this is just another avenue, not unlike books or movies. As one of the callers told me, "It's a different movie every time I call!" The regular guy also includes men who are first-time callers and simply call out of curiosity. Second is what they termed the "pretty regular guy." This type of man uses the phone lines instead of cheating or because they think they can't tell their wives or girlfriends their

> *fantasies. There seemed to be some disagreement about whether these first two categories were really one category or two—they could be collapsed into one. Third is what the women called the "loser." As they talked about this category they all laughed and described these guys as "butt ugly" and shy. Women assume that for most of these men phone lines may be their only contact with women. These guys are regular callers—have a long history of calling and typically talk 1-3 hours per week. Many of these men form fantasy relationships. Jeremy, one of my regular callers, said, "We fantasize about meeting you. Just like when you pick up a magazine you fantasize that you could have that woman." The fourth category is what the women agreed was the "sick ticket." These men are interested in dominance, torture, and things like pedophilia. The women also agreed that the majority of the callers (about two thirds) fall into the first two categories, another quarter fall into the third, and maybe ten percent fall into the fourth category.*

Women seemed to use this categorization to help label their own feelings about the callers. True, some of the men seemed like "regular guys"—harmless, horny, and maybe curious, with fantasies that were not surprising or different from the media's portrayals of male fantasies. Other men seemed too attached to the women, too desperate, and that seemed pathetic to all of us—although not so pathetic that their calls and money were refused. Still other men seemed "creepy" or "icky," and they were the objects of a lot of jokes. When we got angry at men, including men in our lives, I often heard the phrase, "God, he's such a caller!"

Over the time I worked there, I realized that the workers consistently used these categories when referring to the callers. The categories were a way of distancing themselves from the work and from the callers. They also seemed to be a way of differentiating the callers from the men in their lives.

There were times when women spoke about the effects of the work on their lives and the lives of those around them. One day, I was outside on a break with Devon and Carly, and we were talking. Devon said that the previous night she had been in bed with her husband and had accidentally slipped into character. Her husband "freaked out" and left the room for a while. Carly responded by saying she had experienced several similar incidents with her boyfriend. She said that over time she had become "really good" at "switching out of Carly" so fast he didn't notice. She went on to say that it angered her when it happened. This was a topic that came up several times with other women, and they all agreed that one of the downsides of the work was that their partners were often suspicious of them, wondering if their words were genuine or just part of a "routine." In discussing this phenomenon, workers seemed to be affirming their reactions with one another. They were doing joint emotion-work to deal with their alienation.

Reactions Toward Me

Meanwhile, I was wrestling with my own feelings of alienation. I was having a tough time traversing two lives and never fitting in either place. I felt as though I was caught between two separate lives. I always felt apart from the other women. I was in the field covertly, so there were always things I couldn't say or share. Because I was living in a motel, I felt suspended, as though I had no home. In addition, I was not truly "one of them" because I knew I was there for research. I was not working only for the money, as they were—I had another life and other friends to whom I could retreat. I would drive back to Athens feeling as though I was "driving back into my life." On the other hand, I felt that I no longer fit in my academic life. I was not part of the departmental day-to-day routine. My friends and colleagues were interested in what I was doing, and I was interested in their reactions. From my field journal:

> *I'm fascinated by other people's reactions to this research. T is incredulous. (He thinks that "This is the ticket to Donahue"—that's not the point, I think he misunderstands completely!). J wishes she was going to be a fly on the wall. A is dying to know what happens and wants me to call her immediately. L is also curious and "is dying to know how it goes." I'm not sure if they are really fascinated by the idea of doing something weird, or forbidden or what. They seem to be interested in what I'll say or need to do. It's like they're more interested in the data site than the data. I resolve not to talk to anyone else about this research. Other people's reactions make me uncomfortable and I need to focus on the research itself, not explaining myself and why I'm not a voyeur to everyone!!*

From the day of my interview:

S calls later that night and I tell her about the interview. She is intrigued by it all, but seems not to take it very seriously. She is laughing and teasing me about it, she keeps saying Oooh, baby! R calls on the next day, I talk to her about it and she is amused by it. Likewise, when I talk to D he is amused. Why do all these people think this is funny?

From a couple of days later:

Tonight I talked with B and told her my concerns about this research not being taken seriously, about my fears that I have maybe given off messages about not being serious about this research. She allayed my fears and told me that I have been open about this work and that I have presented this as serious research. She suggested that maybe people think of whether they would be able to talk "dirty." She said that she would not be able to do this work.

In general, people seemed to be interested in my research. I chose not to aggressively pursue conversations about my research with people because I was covert in the field and I simply didn't want to take any chances. However, often a colleague would ask me about my faculty fellowship leave or would introduce the topic around other academics. After this happened a few times, I began to be aware of the pattern of reactions I received. I turn now to that pattern.

First, the reactions to my research were (and are) gendered. After listening to a description of my research into the emotion-work of phone sex workers, always a rather abstract and academic description, men generally first respond by saying (always smiling), "Well, you have a great voice for it!" Then, "So, what do you say? What do you talk about?" I usually reply, "Just exactly what you would think." Undeterred, they continue asking, "Like what?" I never tell them, never describe calls to them, but steer them away from such questions by saying that is not the point of my research. If they persist, I tell them it costs $1.25 a minute to find out.

Callers often told me what a great voice I have, so I have come to know what that phrase means. My identity was a "great voice," a phone worker—nothing else—all else receded. When colleagues say it, I always walk away from the situation feeling as though I am no longer a sociologist but have been reduced to a "great voice." My identity as an academic is leveled. The talk about my research has become talk about talk—meta-talk. Within the department I have also noticed that men who were previously respectful toward me or treated me like "one of the guys" now sometimes giggle, make double entendres, or allude to things such as dirty movies in my presence. I have become sexualized to them. To treat me in such a way is to do me a discourtesy. Consequently, mine is not a courtesy stigma as Goffman (1963) discusses, but a (dis)courtesy stigma. In discussing courtesy stigma, Goffman suggested that when an individual is related through the social structure to a stigmatized individual, that relationship leads the wider society to treat both individuals in some respects as one. A courtesy stigma is then accorded the previously unblemished individual. For example, the parents of handicapped children or the families of alcoholics are stigmatized even though they do not possess the devalued or stigmatized traits. Mine was a (dis)courtesy stigma because of the *manner* in which it was applied to me—in a condescending, discourteous way. Chancer (1993) observed a similar phenomenon when she discusses with colleagues her theoretical piece on prostitution. Her male colleagues reacted with embarrassment or ridicule.

Women, on the other hand, had two types of reactions. Most seemed to be interested in the women I worked with, the people I worked for, and the actual physical site. They generally asked questions about the age of the workers, the social class of the workers, how many women worked there, what the owner was like, whether I felt safe, if I could hear other women on calls, and so forth. They were really curious about the research and the research site.

A second reaction took me totally by surprise. Sometimes, when I was talking to women I know to be feminists, they would listen and ask me the same genre of questions other women asked. Suddenly, it was as though a curtain fell over their faces and they would say, "I could *never* do that sort of work." Or they might ask, "How can you do that? How can you sell something so intimate? Something so private?" Or, "Don't you feel like you're selling part of yourself?" I've even been asked if I got excited doing calls. These questions and comments are usually delivered in such a way as to make it clear to me that although *they* could never do "that sort of work," there must be something about *me* that makes it easy to do the work. Once again I am accorded a (dis)courtesy stigma. Why did this take me by surprise? First, I assumed they understood that my work was research, not some voyeuristic jaunt. Second, I expected more from women and from feminists. This is obviously part of the sex industry that exploits women. I think this is a feminist issue.

Third, this seems like a classist response to me. They could never do this sort of work; the implication is that it is beneath them. Perhaps they have never had to make the choices working-class women have had to make. Chancer (1993) has recognized the class-based nature of sex work—that is, the economic motivation of women who become sex workers. I agree with Chancer in suggesting that feminism must recognize that the marginalization of sex workers is inconsistent with the interests of representing all women.

Although the reactions of men in general and of some women seem to be dissimilar, I think they emanate from the same source. Phone sex is seen as part of the same genre as sex materials. The discourse surrounding sex materials leads people to dichotomize these materials and the people involved into good/bad. Such binary opposition leads to an impasse in discussion, or at least it short-circuits discussion. The logical conclusion to such an opposition is a dichotomous hierarchy of self/Other. My association with sex workers, and ultimately my participation as a sex worker, made me an Other.

In addition, this good/bad dichotomy has implications for what is seen as legitimate research. The dichotomy truncates understanding and restricts space for critical inquiry. An arena of interaction and behavior is ignored, and an entire area of social research is censored.

The fact remains that as sociologists and feminists we can address the sexism, racism, homophobia, and classism manifest in some sex materials, including phone fantasy lines, without using binary oppositions. These images are related to a culturally constructed climate that allows their existence. To construct sex workers as the Other, to discourteously stigmatize them, is to reproduce the climate, not to question it.

Lessons I Have Learned

Attending to my feelings during my fieldwork helped me understand the ways in which other workers experienced the work. Our conversations revealed to me that my feelings about the work and the callers were similar to other workers' feelings. Moreover, the reactions I received from others were similar to what other workers experienced. Workers were well aware of the stigma applied to them. They spoke of choosing to tell some people what they did for a living and not telling other people for fear of being seen "just like whores." This fear was based on the reactions they had already received from men and women who knew what they did for a living. If I had not been consciously aware of my emotions, I would have missed a major component of the emotional effects of this work.

THINGS I WOULD DO OVER AGAIN

Some people have asked me, if I had it to do over, what I would do differently? Many things I would not change; other things I would. First, I would definitely do this research again. I still believe it makes a valuable contribution to our understanding of the commercialization of emotion-work. I also still believe that the context I chose is a great example of selling emotion.

Second, if I were to do this particular research again, I would still do it covertly. I believe that had I tried to do overt fieldwork, I would have failed. I think that I would not have been able to establish rapport with the workers if I had not been "one of them."

Third, I would keep an emotion field journal again. I think it is crucial to keep a field journal that includes the researcher's emotional reactions during the entire research process. The journal proves to be an invaluable source of information. Through my emotional reactions I uncovered, among others, the pattern of reactions I have called (dis)courtesy stigma. Keeping track of my emotional reactions also allowed me to see that my reactions to the callers and the company were virtually identical to the workers around me. Hochschild (1983) suggests that emotion is used as a clue in understanding situations, and clearly researchers can do the same in the field.

Fourth, I would again use friends and colleagues as sounding boards during the entire process, but especially while I was in the field. They listened to my thoughts, my analyses, and sometimes my frustrations. This helped keep me on track, focused, and sane, and I would highly recommend such "sounding boards" to others doing field research.

THINGS I WOULD CHANGE

There are, however, some things I would do differently. First, I would better prepare myself for questions about the legitimacy of the research context. Whenever the research context includes marginal or stigmatized groups, the researcher should prepare to answer tough questions about the choice of research site. At first, these questions caught me off guard, but over time I became used to them. Although I typically explained briefly the concept of emotion-work, how this research would fill a gap in the literature, and how this particular context was a premier example of selling emotion, I sometimes became impatient when the same questions were asked repeatedly. In retrospect, I could have been more patient. Such questions are part of the territory and should not be taken as reflecting on the worthiness of the project. Such questions cannot be ignored or brushed off but should be faced head-on with well-prepared responses so the research cannot be trivialized. Actually, I would recommend that qualitative research training more systematically address this issue. Graduate advisors and senior mentors should make sure that preparation for the field includes "practice" in answering difficult questions about the research site. In the same way we prepare for an interview or lecture, close colleagues or mentors can prepare researchers by asking probing questions in private, to prepare them to navigate these difficult questions in public.

Second, I would have tried to control the talk about my research. There were times that I felt as though my research was the source of gossip. Because I was in the field covertly, I was worried that my research was in danger. One of the women who started working after I did was a student at my university, in a department in which I have several friends. I worried that she would hear gossip about my work and that my cover would be blown. (Eventually I negotiated a "deal" with the owner and manager to do research on the callers, so I no longer worried about my covert status.) A second problem with gossip was that it contributed to constructing my (dis)courtesy-stigmatic identity across campus even among people I did not know. I received reports of a couple of my own colleagues who engaged in such activity with people I did not know. Although I could not have completely controlled the talk, I could have asked people not to talk about my research to others.

Third, although I could not manage others' application of a (dis)courtesy stigma to me, I might have been able to react differently to it. I often left the interaction feeling as though my identity as an academic had been leveled or that I had been somehow diminished. In retrospect, as I saw this pattern emerging, rather than feeling leveled I should have, in the tradition of grounded theory, recognized this behavior as another dimension of my research. Then I could have probed them about their reactions and used that as data on the process of (dis)courtesy stigmatization, thereby greeting each dismissive comment as a welcome data opportunity.

Ronai (1992) suggests that emotional sociology allows readers to incorporate the cognitive/emotional experiences of the researcher into their stock of knowledge and gain a new resource that may be consulted in the future. I hope my experiences and insights will be of use to other researchers.

CHAPTER

9

The Sexual Harassment of Researchers by Research Subjects

Lessons From the Field

JENNIFER K. HUFF

There is no question that the personal characteristics of a researcher influence the research process. Gender, in particular, affects research. For example, some field researchers have attributed their ability to gain acceptance in a setting to their status as women (Gurney, 1985; Warren, 1988; Warren & Rassmussen, 1977). Respondents may stereotypically perceive a woman

AUTHOR'S NOTE: The research discussed in this chapter was funded by a grant from the Ohio Department of Mental Health and Ohio University for the investigation of gender and peer support at a psychosocial rehabilitation center. The opinions presented do not reflect the views of any state agency, including the agency where the author is currently employed.

investigator to be incompetent and powerless. As a result, individuals may consider a female researcher nonthreatening and be quicker to accept her (Easterday, Papademas, Schorr, & Valentine, 1977; Warren & Rassmussen, 1977). Supposedly, then, being female may facilitate access to rich and detailed information.

However, although being seen as incompetent and powerless can be interpreted as an initial advantage, these same characteristics, assigned by respondents, can also hamper women in the field (Gurney, 1985). Once women have "gotten in," they encounter problems, such as not being taken seriously, not being given access to more "masculine" or "serious" kinds of data, sexual "hustling," and the like (Easterday et al., 1977), all of which make research more difficult. Some of the problems that female researchers face, such as hustling, can be conceptualized as sexual harassment.

The issue of sexual harassment and how it interferes with women's ability to do their jobs has received a great deal of attention (Gutek & Koss, 1993). Thus, it seems appropriate to consider sexual harassment as an obstacle to conducting qualitative research. My discussion will center on reflections about my own experiences in the field, including the kinds of sexual harassment I encountered, the difficulty of maintaining rapport while experiencing sexual harassment, and a few suggestions to women who are considering going into the field for the first time.

The Setting

I conducted my research at The Fellowship House,[2] a psychosocial rehabilitation center serving adults with severe mental disabilities. There were essentially three statuses at the agency: staff, volunteer, and member. Those individuals who had mental disabilities joined as "members" of The Fellowship House. Although staff technically also joined as members, they were clearly regarded as separate from "members" and were referred to as "staff" by the other members. I participated essentially as a volunteer, a status made up primarily of young women studying social work, psychology, or music therapy. However, I was also open about my research goals. In my combined role of investigator and volunteer, I participated in activities with members, gave them rides, and often simply sat and talked with them, drinking coffee and smoking cigarettes.

Although I was not aware of it at first, I came to realize that more male members than female members frequented the agency. As a young woman, I was not particularly threatening to the predominantly male membership, which was advantageous with regard to quickly establishing rapport with members. Many members, more often male than female, even sought out my attention. However, some of the attention was undesired and consisted of unwanted romantic overtures, such as touching, hugging, poking, and comments such as "Hey, hotlips." These kinds of behaviors, sexual jokes, and jokes making fun of women not only led to a great deal of discomfort and frustration on my part, but in fact interfered with my work. So, despite the initial advantage my gender seemed to provide, it also made me vulnerable to sexual harassment.

Considering the Setting, Wasn't Inappropriate Behavior Expected?

Individuals with a mental illness are often labeled mentally ill because they breach social norms. Most of the members at The Fellowship House had mental disabilities. Therefore, one might be tempted to point out that I should have expected inappropriate sexual behavior. Perhaps members' disabilities prevented them from knowing appropriate behavior or from being able to read my social cues to know that I found something offensive. Still, this misses the point of this paper, which is not about placing blame. Other men, who are not labeled as mentally ill, behave in ways that are even more inappropriate, with even less ability to read social cues. The goal of this paper is to explore how sexual harassment interferes with fieldwork, discuss special problems responding to harassment as a field researcher, and suggest strategies that women who are going into the field for the first time might want to consider.

Can a Researcher be Harassed by Men in Less Powerful Positions?

Still at issue is whether the behaviors that I encountered at The Fellowship House could be labeled "sexual harassment." The abuse of power is often included as a necessary part of defining behavior as sexual harassment. According to this argument, sexual harassment is exploitation, and an individual in a less powerful position does not have the power to exploit. Thus, a subordinate cannot sexually harass. In my study, the members of the agency were in a subordinate status to staff, whose authority included the power to enforce rules. Similar to staff, volunteers, in some ways, had more power than members. For instance, volunteers were advised to tell staff if members had quit taking their medication, and volunteers reported their activities and conversations with members in a logbook that staff could read.[3] This one-way monitoring of behavior was just one indicator of the power differential between members and volunteers. Because volunteers could exercise power over members, and I conducted my research while I was a volunteer, one might argue that what I experienced at The Fellowship House should not be defined as sexual harassment.

Two things must be considered when addressing this issue. First, although my status in the setting was as a volunteer, I was primarily a researcher, and my power over members as a researcher was questionable. In a very real way, members had power over me. I needed information from them to succeed. Because members, by not talking with me, could jeopardize my research endeavor, I was to some degree at their mercy. Second, being in a position of greater power does not necessarily negate the possibility of sexual harassment. Although a woman may occupy a position of authority, men may still interact with her on the basis of her sex rather than some other status. So, for example, female doctors report sexual harassment by their patients. In a survey by Phillips and Schneider (1993), 75% of female doctors said that they had experienced some kind of sexual harassment, including suggestive looks, sexual remarks, patients brushing or touching them, inappropriate gifts, and pressure for a date. Phillips and Schneider concluded that, although a female doctor's position as a physician is one of power over patients, "the vulnerability inherent in their sex seems in many cases to override their power as doctors, leaving female physicians open to sexual harassment" (p. 1939). If female doctors are not immune to sexual harassment, despite occupying a position of authority and power, then women in many other categories, such as graduate students, would seem to be even more vulnerable.

What Kinds of Behavior Put the "Sexual" in Sexual Harassment?

Another problem is trying to figure out what kinds of behavior can be regarded as sexual harassment. What is nonsexual touching versus sexual touching? I experienced a lot of confusion because I was uncomfortable with touches that were not clearly sexual. Of course, I knew going into the field that someone pinching my buttock or grabbing my breast would be clearly out of line. But what about poking me in the side, hugging me, or brushing my hair out of my eyes during conversation? Is touching sexual only if it involves a certain body part? Or is it the manner in which someone touches?

The context of a particular behavior, it would seem to me, plays an important role in determining whether it is sexual harassment or not. I would not consider a coworker who accidentally brushed my breast on a crowded subway to be making sexual contact. So, figuring out if behavior is sexual harassment seems to call for some understanding of context. To suggest that men who try to hug women are automatically committing sexual harassment would be ludicrous. Rather, I interpreted unwanted hugs and touching (or a member brushing bangs out of my eyes) as sexual harassment because of the nature of that attention, which, as the following examples show, attempted to establish a romantic relationship.

As I tried to make sense of behavior, including touching and hugging, my definition of behavior changed with time. I did not question the first hugs that I received and assumed they were a show of warmth and friendliness. For example, a member, Wayne, would ask me for a hug when I showed up at the agency. At first, I was happy that he was so accepting of me because I had just begun to volunteer there. I simply ignored his frequent comments that I was a "cute girl," which I found embarrassing. Only after I had been in the field for a time did I begin to interpret hugs as potential sexual harassment.

Perhaps some people would not make such an interpretation. But when does it begin? As Wayne's comments and other behaviors continued, I had to redefine them, and I reinterpreted the meanings behind his earlier actions and words. Ignoring his comments or subtly conveying my dislike for them, such as by frowning or telling him that he was embarrassing me, did not stop his bothersome behavior. I became increasingly annoyed. Wayne continued to make comments about my appearance, such as, "Gee, you sure are a pretty girl. If I had a girl like you. . . ." He also attempted to give me gifts of money and cassette tapes. He frequently tried to take pictures of me and once wanted to get his videocamera out to tape me. One day he told me, "Last night I was asleep and something woke me up. If it was you I wouldn't mind." Another afternoon Wayne grabbed my hand and tried to kiss it, to which I responded by jerking my hand away and leaving the room. This was something that I would consider sexual harassment.

Another member, Luke, developed a particularly problematic "crush" on me. At first, I thought I had made it clear that I was unavailable. I thought Luke had accepted that. He even asked me about my boyfriend. But it became obvious several months later that I had done little to prevent Luke's interest. No matter how many hints I dropped, the advances continued. Luke would insist on walking with me when I left the agency. He would ask me to go places with him or to stop by his apartment. Almost always, the first refusal was not enough, and occasionally I had to slip out of the agency unnoticed to avoid his insistence.

Luke began to try to give me gifts: lottery tickets or his scarf, which he laid across my legs as I was sitting next to him. He would let his hands stray, touching my leg, brushing my hair out of my eyes, grabbing my jacket. I would jerk away and frown every time. I also mentioned my boyfriend as frequently as possible, telling Luke that I would be leaving town to be with my boyfriend. But his behavior only became more persistent. Once I was at the agency when Luke called from a drug/alcohol rehabilitation center. While I was talking with him over the phone, he told me how much he missed me and wanted to know what I was wearing.

EFFECTS OF SEXUAL HARASSMENT

Initially, one of the most tormenting problems that I had was trying to determine if I was imagining or misinterpreting some behavior by the men in the setting. But given how some men, such as Wayne, became more aggressive in their attention to me the longer I got to know them, I could not help but be apprehensive about every touch or comment and the meaning behind it. Sometimes female members gave me hugs, and I even enjoyed many of them for the warmth and acceptance I felt from them. But after being in the field several weeks, I was suspicious of hugs that any man gave me. In retrospect, this was merely an unfortunate but logical response to the sexual harassment I was experiencing. The actions of Wayne, Luke, or other members, such as the member who said that he wanted to get me "in bed for one night," created an atmosphere in which I came to suspect all behavior. I became mistrustful and wary of every poke, and even a finger on my earlobe felt like an invasion.

I began to feel incompetent and anxious as I wondered if I had encouraged some of the members' behavior. At times I felt self-loathing, thinking that in my research I had perhaps appeared flirtatious or had failed to discourage the wrong kind of attention. My tendency to search for causes in my own behavior and to blame myself for the harassment may reflect gender socialization in our society. Men are socialized to be sexually aggressive, and it is considered appropriate for them to be so. The responsibility falls on women to avoid or fend off men's attentions. Still, today, the message often conveyed to women is that if a man is sexually aggressive and his actions are unwanted, it is the woman's fault for encouraging him, or at least not working hard enough to discourage him. Women, then, often blame themselves for harassment (Samoluk, Barton, & Pretty, 1994).

This attitude—that it is the woman's fault for aggressive male behavior—was even reflected by staff at The Fellowship House. When I first began to volunteer there, a staff person went over some "basic rules" at the agency, which included advice about how I should dress. The staff person emphasized that I should wear a bra and not wear any short shorts or skirts, or in general any revealing or seductive clothing. I was told later, rather matter of factly, that many of the male members had not "been" with a woman for a long time, so female volunteers should be careful to not go around tempting them or thoughtlessly tormenting them with seductive dress. Such an attitude, which to the staff member was just commonsense understanding, places the responsibility for lewd behavior and the blame for being harassed on the female volunteers. By placing the responsibility to stop harassment on volunteers, the agency did little to actively create an environment that did not permit sexually harassing behavior and did nothing to discourage my feelings of guilt and self-blame.

PROBLEMS OF BEING ASSERTIVE AND MAINTAINING RAPPORT

I had a problem similar to that of many other field researchers: Despite the fact that members behaved in ways that I disliked, I wanted to maintain rapport with respondents (Green, Barbour, Barnard, & Kitzinger, 1993; Gurney, 1985; Warren, 1988). Even if I felt that something was being said or done that I ordinarily would not tolerate, because I was in the setting as a researcher who was trying to establish and maintain rapport, I was not willing to behave as I might elsewhere with other people. When I first went into the field, I thought that I had to cover up the way that I truly felt. I thought that was what researchers were supposed to do, because their goal is to get along with respondents. Goffman (1989) advised enterprising students "to stop making points to show how smartassed you are" (p. 128) and to sacrifice their own ego and comfort for the sake of gaining rapport and acquiring access to data. Lofland and Lofland (1984), citing Charmaz, advise that a successful researcher "who is supportive, cordial, interested, nonargumentative, courteous, understanding, even sympathetic will receive a good deal more information" (p. 38).

But how much is an investigator supposed to tolerate? Believing that I had to suppress my own opinions as a researcher, I assumed that it was best if I said little in response to comments that I found offensive. When men laughed about women who protested a porn star autograph session because "feminists are jealous of big-breasted women," I believed that to be a successful researcher I had to be quiet and keep my "smart-assed" comments to myself. And when a member talked about beating women, I refrained from saying anything because I did not want to appear as an argumentative researcher. I wanted to fade into the background and not stand out by quarreling with members. Similarly, I was hesitant to bluntly tell male members not to touch me or bother me. I believed that I had to worry more about their feelings than my own. So, when a member kept bringing up my appearance or even kissed my hand, I tried to be nice and not create a scene. Even though the longer I was in the field the more I wanted to slap their hands away and yell "quit it," I did not want to risk offending members and then not have them as available sources of information. After all, I had spent a considerable amount of time getting to know some members, such as Luke and Wayne. Without their willingness to talk with me, my research might have been superficial and essentially a failure. Although I tried to convey my dislike for certain behaviors or comments, I was not comfortable with being overly assertive because at the same time I wanted them to like spending time with me. If a researcher is frequently telling individuals not to touch her or that their comments are offensive, will respondents want to spend much time with her? One staff member did not tolerate sexist comments from members, and I knew that Luke regarded her as "bitch" because of that. He explained to me, "When I'm around Cynthia I always seem to put my foot in my mouth. I always say something wrong." Contrasting me to her, Luke told me, "But I can talk to you." So, if I could ignore offensive comments or behavior, I was rewarded by having respondents who felt that they did not have to worry about how I would react to what they did or said.

But how offensive does something have to be before a researcher should not have to overlook it anymore? Part of the stress that I felt came from having to suppress, for my research goal, my desire as an assertive woman to show my dislike for certain comments or behaviors. I could not react as I wanted or simply leave a situation that I did not like, because I had a commitment. I was torn between wanting to be what I considered a successful researcher (who could withstand great discomfort to acquire data) and a strong woman (who was assertive and did not put up with anybody's guff or harassment).

POTENTIAL STRATEGIES

I tried a number of strategies to limit behavior that I did not like. To downplay my femininity, I often pulled back my hair, did not wear much make-up, rarely wore earrings, and dressed down. Yet none of that seemed to help. Besides which, as a strategy, it does little to contradict the idea that it is the woman's fault for attracting unwanted behavior.

Another strategy I used was simply to ignore behavior. Obviously, overlooking behavior was only a short-term solution, because members would often persist with the unwanted behavior and my annoyance with it would fester as I tried to ignore it.

On one of the first days that I visited the agency, a staff person suggested that I make up a boyfriend if I did not have one. Of course, although helpful, it did not work as effectively as I hoped it would. Perhaps a made-up spouse would have been more dissuading? Sometimes I wonder if having a boyfriend did not give me a false sense of security, because I wrongly assumed that male members would not try to establish a romantic relationship with me if they thought I already had a boyfriend.

Even if bringing up a boyfriend or husband works as a strategy, some women may be uncomfortable with using it because it plays into the gender stereotype of a woman needing a man as a protector, even if he is only an abstract man she has made up. By using a boyfriend, real or made up, to prevent direct harassment, a researcher is doing little to challenge beliefs that it is okay to harass an unattached woman.

Of course, a woman may be a lesbian and have a female partner rather than a boyfriend, and she may not want to make up a boyfriend or husband. Mentioning her female partner might also work as a strategy to prevent further advances, but she may also risk rejection or harassment due to intolerance for her sexual orientation. She may even be further sexually harassed if a man perceives her lack of sexual interest in men to be a challenge (Green et al., 1993). Presenting oneself as sexually unavailable, as a strategy in preventing harassment, seems to be more complicated than "just make up a boyfriend."

I also tried to give nonverbal signals to show my aversion to behavior or comments in the hope of stopping them. Sometimes I tried to lightly joke, saying, "you're embarrassing me" or "you're making me uncomfortable." I would feel temporarily that I had done something about my situation that was somewhat satisfactory, but it seemed to do little to prevent similar behavior.

A woman doing research in the field may have to establish relationships with male respondents differently if she were a male investigator, or differently from how she would establish them with another woman. Researchers are encouraged to deemphasize their social distance from respondents and minimize their power as researchers. Yet this may be problematic for a female field researcher because if, in interaction, she attempts to establish intimacy with and be attentive to men, she risks being misinterpreted and sexually harassed (for further discussion on the difficulty of decreasing professional boundaries and risking sexual harassment, see Green et al., 1993).

Going into the field, I wanted to appear friendly and approachable. Certainly, through past experiences, I had come to know that sometimes my signs of friendliness were misinterpreted by men I have met. I had this as part of my stock of knowledge going into the field. But I had also been exposed to methodology literature directed at "anyman" (as Gurney, 1985, describes it), which portrays a field researcher's role as very similar to the traditional female gender role: supportive, interested, nonargumentative, understanding, and sympathetic. So I did not change my behavior in any particular way; I figured that I would do fine if I were just friendly. As it turns out, I would have found it helpful to have been more familiar with the literature surrounding men's misperceptions of women's friendliness.

Female researchers should be aware of how friendliness may be interpreted before they enter the field. Such knowledge might help them prevent feeling self-doubt and guilt when men in the research setting misinterpret their friendliness. We know that men are more likely than women to misperceive a woman's friendly behavior as a sign of sexual interest and availability (Johnson, Stockdale, & Saal, 1991; Saal, Johnson, & Weber, 1989; Stockdale, 1993). With a reading of this literature under her belt, the investigator may be better prepared to connect a man's reaction to her to a problem that many women have, instead of feeling that she individually does not know how to interact with men or is a failure as a researcher. In my own personal relationships, boyfriends have accused me of flirting when I was really only trying to be amicable. After having been accused of this and then having a research informant seemingly misperceive my friendliness, I felt that I had failed, that I had done something wrong, that I did not know how to behave or interact with men without being a "flirt." There was that secret gnawing inside of me, "Oh, my God, I am a flirt and I don't even know it or how." But armed with the knowledge that men are likely to define women's behavior as being sexually motivated when a woman intends only to be friendly, a female researcher would be more likely to see sexual harassment as less her fault and more a problem of male socialization. Misperceptions may not be caused by her lack of good interpersonal skills but rather by sexist and adversarial sexual beliefs. Furthermore, I would also suggest that, because men are more likely to distort a woman's friendly intentions, a woman should be cautious about how she goes about trying to appear approachable and friendly to a research informant.

Another potential strategy would be for the researcher to confront behavior that she is uncomfortable with or finds offensive. In considering the problem of being assertive versus maintaining rapport, I would contend that the female investigator may want to be more assertive. After all, respondents may not even react negatively. Perhaps more saliently, a researcher may gain little by not expressing how she really feels about sexually harassing behavior. I was not usually assertive, instead attempting to convey my dislike more subtly. In retrospect, I am not sure how helpful that was in some of the more bothersome cases. If I had been more blunt about how I really felt, and had offended respondents, would I have ruined my chances of getting information? Perhaps, but the feelings that I experienced after not being more assertive also interfered with my ability to get data. Some days I found it difficult to be around the research setting and resented having to go there. There were times when my stomach would turn and I would forget about everything but avoiding the respondent who made me so uncomfortable. At times, I slipped out of the agency, hoping that a member I wanted to get away from would not notice my leaving. Some women may be able to deal with sexist behavior (Gruber, 1989; Warren, 1988), but if a researcher is very uncomfortable in the beginning, it seems doubtful that she will be able to continue to ignore sexual harassment over a long period of time without becoming even more unhappy, dissatisfied, agitated, or angry. And if, as a result, an investigator ends up trying to avoid a respondent (rather than confront him) because of annoying behavior that makes her uncomfortable or even angry, how much information is she getting anyway?

In future projects, I would even consider avoiding developing a researcher-respondent relationship with men. Although this may sound extremist or antimale, I suggest it for practical reasons. One problem encountered by investigators is that they face time constraints. If they have unlimited time and funds, then they can afford to become involved in relationships with respondents that may fail later. But I would guess that, because of budget and time limitations, most researchers are interested in establishing relationships that are not likely to become problematic just when the respondent begins to open up and share information.

When I began my research, my goal was to establish rapport as quickly as I could. I spent time with those who were willing to talk to me and male members were, for the most part, friendlier and easier to get to know at first. But by establishing relationships with such attentive respondents, I ended up shutting myself off from forming relationships with other women. Researchers cannot get to know everyone and must make choices about with whom they will spend their time, which means they have to sacrifice potential relationships to form relationships with others. By choosing to be with those who were more willing to talk to me at first—the male members—I ended up making it less likely that I would have time to develop relationships with the female members. Some of the relationships that I invested hours in developing ended up being with individuals whom I wanted later to avoid, thus jeopardizing my research. Because it is impossible to predict for certain which men a female investigator will later find uncomfortable to be around, it might make sense for her to establish respondent-researcher relationships primarily with women to ensure that she will be able to finish her research.

No matter what strategies a researcher employs, as Gurney (1985) has suggested, a researcher needs to think about how much harassment she is willing to put up with and how she will respond to it before she ventures out into the field for the first time. Different women have different tolerance levels for harassing behavior. But I would note that when I began my research, I thought I had a considerable amount of patience for members' comments, touches, and sexist jokes.

The sexual harassment that I experienced while doing field research confused me, left me feeling anxious, decreased my feelings of competency, and affected my motivation to finish my study. Considering the effects that it had on me, I think it is important for women who are preparing to go into the field for the first time to familiarize themselves with sexual harassment and to think about the issues that I have brought up here. In addition, those who work with women going into the field, such as senior faculty or thesis and dissertation advisors, should recognize the difficulties women may face, help beginning female researchers become aware of potential problems, and be available to them so they can talk about these issues. As others have noted (Gurney, 1985; Warren, 1988), there are many books to guide beginners in field research, but few address specific concerns related to sexual harassment and women.

Notes

1. I would like to thank the Ohio Department of Mental Health, which funded the research project referred to in this paper.

2. All names, including the agency name, have been changed.

3. However, as a volunteer, I refrained from any behavior, such as these, that I felt would interfere with my role as researcher because I did not want to be perceived as somebody who monitored behavior.

Doing Research on Violence Against Women

MARTIN D. SCHWARTZ

In Part III, four researchers take on four extremely important topics in the study of violence against women. In all four chapters, the authors' main viewpoint is not the research that they did in these areas—each has published that work elsewhere. Rather, here they take the opportunity to discuss the meaning of their research into violence against women and the various issues and problems that this research entailed. In some cases, the problem was practical, whereas in others it was epistemological, but in either case these chapters thoughtfully raise issues that are important for future researchers and readers in this area to consider.

In Chapter 10, Claire Renzetti, editor of *Violence Against Women,* discusses what it means to engage in feminist participatory research. Some of the buzz words from this endeavor have become popular, such as calling research subjects "coresearchers," but Renzetti makes plain here that the feminist act of empowering research subjects is an extraordinarily important and difficult process. She discusses how she rejected much of positivist training, and how her work on lesbian battering should be seen not only as a classic on violence but also as a research classic.

Jody Miller's piece is similar in that she has also published some path-breaking works on violence against prostitutes. Her emphasis in Chapter 11 is not on the results of that research. Rather, she describes her many struggles with feminist ethics and epistemology as she worked with street prostitutes. What does it mean for a nonprostitute to interview prostitutes about their experiences? To what extent does voyeurism play a role in research topic selection? Does this make the relationship exploitative? Miller reviews her own decisions, analyzes how she categorized these women, and discusses how she approached her decisions. She makes it plain that researchers live in a social world where their experiences shape their work, and that ignoring the interplay of these influences with the "data" invariably distorts the project of combating violence against women.

Dawn Currie and Brian MacLean, two of Canada's best-known feminist and critical criminologists, have written an exceptionally important original piece here that makes (among other things) the argument that research is gendered. Despite the common assumption that women will reveal more victimization to women in interview methodologies, they present evidence in Chapter 12 that this may not be the case. The gendered process of interaction is much more complicated than that. For example, they argue, women may be *less* likely to reveal victimization to women, for fear that they will be judged poorly by their peers. There are too many valuable insights in this piece to summarize in a paragraph, but one important conclusion here is that highly trained, well-supervised, and competent researchers are the key to the best research results we can get, rather than the sex of the surveyor.

Finally, in Chapter 13, Kimberly Huisman addresses an important issue. Perhaps the area here in which we have the greatest gaps in our knowledge is violence against women of color. The key question in this chapter is whether middle-class white women (the bulk of the researchers in this area) can adequately conduct research in minority communities. Although there are researchers who claim that only women of color can competently interview other women of color, Huisman documents her experiences in dealing with Asian women who are the survivors of violence and with Asian frontline workers. Much like Currie and MacLean, she makes the argument that prepared, trained researchers with the right attitude can be successful in gaining the rapport needed to gather important information about violence against these women.

CHAPTER

10

Confessions of a Reformed Positivist

Feminist Participatory Research as Good Social Science

CLAIRE M. RENZETTI

I remember well my undergraduate and graduate courses in research methods. My teachers repeatedly impressed on me the importance of objectivity in social science research. I learned how to draw a random sample, how to write "unbiased" survey questions, and how to analyze data using a wide variety of statistical techniques. My education in qualitative methods occurred primarily "on the job," when, in my first and second years in graduate school, I was employed as a research assistant on two nationally funded

AUTHOR'S NOTE: An earlier version of this paper appeared in the *Journal of Gay and Lesbian Social Services, 3,* 29-42. I wish to thank Carol Tully for her helpful comments and suggestions.

studies. Before going out into the field to conduct interviews, I was instructed in how to avoid biasing my subjects' responses through my "presentation of self." I was told in a no-uncertain-terms voice by the project directors never to provide information about myself other than my affiliation with the project and my qualifications to conduct the research. I was never to offer a personal opinion or advice. I can still feel the intense panic that gripped my chest the first time a person I was interviewing asked me what I thought about the subject at hand. I'm not sure of the expression on my face, but I can bet it did not convey cool confidence on my part. I made a quick sort through my mental inventory of "appropriate" responses, generously supplied by my teachers, and said, in as sincere a voice as I could muster, "I haven't formed an opinion on this yet, but I'm very interested in what you think." That caused my respondent to pause for a moment, but soon she fell into line and answered my questions without asking any more of me. As I look back on it, she was probably thinking—as I am now—"This person claims to be an expert on this and she doesn't even have an opinion!" Nevertheless, by the time I graduated I was much smoother in replying to subjects' personal queries; I had become a *trained* social scientist.

Some years passed before I learned that there are alternative methodologies. By then, I had read the radical critiques of the notion of value-free social science (see, e.g., Gouldner, 1970), and I agreed with their position that no researcher could ever be completely objective in her or his work—the act of choosing a problem to study was, after all, a value-based choice. However, I remained committed to the ideal of keeping one's research free from the "contaminating" effects of personal beliefs and sympathies. *I was a positivist.*

This paper is an account of my conversion from positivism to the feminist participatory model of research. Before sharing the details of my conversion experience and what I see as the benefits of using the feminist participatory model in social science research, let me first lay out some of the major differences between these two paradigms.

Feminist and Positivist Methodologies: What's the Difference?

Important to state at the outset is that there is no single, unified feminist methodology. This is due largely to the fact that there is no single, unified feminist theory; there is instead, as Rosalind Delmar (1986) once put it, a "plurality of feminisms" (p. 9). That said, we can nevertheless identify several principles that distinguish feminist from positivist methodologies. Cancian (1992, pp. 626-627), using the work of Cook and Fonow (1984), identifies five elements of feminist methodology: (a) a focus on gender and gender inequality that, in turn, implies a strong political and moral commitment to reducing inequality; (b) the goal of describing or giving voice to personal, everyday experiences, especially those of women and members of other marginalized groups; (c) a commitment to social action with the goal of helping to bring about change that improves the conditions under which women and the marginalized live; (d) a built-in reflexivity that critically examines how factors such as the researcher's sex, race, social class, and sexual orientation, in addition to wider social, political, and economic conditions, may influence the research process; and (e) a rejection of the traditional relationship between researcher and "researched" in favor of an approach that gives research "subjects" more power in the research process (see also Reinharz, 1992).

Perhaps one of the most revolutionary features of feminist methodology is its emphasis on the inclusion of gender as a central category of research. I use the adjective "revolutionary" because, historically, traditional research in the social sciences has typically omitted an explicit examination of gender (e.g., by using all-male samples but generalizing the findings to all people) or has incorporated women into the research as the "other," the "exception" (e.g., by accepting as the norm men's characteristic ways of speaking and acting in particular situations). To paraphrase sociologist Jessie Bernard (1973), practically all social science until relatively recently was a social science of the male world. By promoting the inclusion of gender as a central category of research, feminist methodologists demonstrated that *gender matters,* that our everyday social lives are not only *gendered,* they are also characterized by widespread *gender inequality.* Moreover, this inequality *intersects* with other inequalities: racism, social class inequality, heterosexism, ageism, ableism. Notably, then, feminist researchers "have clarified how the concept of 'women in general' falsely universalizes and privileges the perspective of middle-class, heterosexual white women and denies and devalues the experiences of other women" (Cancian, 1992, p. 627).

At this point, many readers—especially those who, like me, have been steeped in positivism—may be feeling a bit anxious, because in light of what has been said so far, feminist methodology hardly appears to be value-free. Indeed, the notion of value-free research is anathema to feminist social scientists, who point out that although traditional positivist research claims to be value-free and objective, it is actually heavily laden with the values and biases of the researchers (historically, white men) who conduct it (Maguire, 1987; Reinharz, 1992). This doesn't mean, however, that feminist researchers reject scientific standards in their research. Rather, what they seek is open acknowledgment by researchers of the assumptions, beliefs, values, and sympathies that underlie and inform their research. More important, perhaps, feminist methodology calls into question not only the possibility but the *desirability* of value-free social science. Thus, for the feminist researcher, it is not enough to just document a problem; one must also commit oneself to doing something to remedy the problem (Maguire, 1987).

Another significant difference between positivism and feminist methodology revolves around questions concerning the appropriate relationship between researchers and research subjects. Traditionally, positivists have called for a fairly rigid separation or detachment of the researcher from the researched. In this model,

> The researcher is the expert who selects a problem for study, decides how it is to be studied, designs the research instruments, draws a sample, collects and analyzes the data, and presents the findings (usually just to professional colleagues) at conferences or in scholarly publications. Sometimes, but not often, researchers share their findings with those they have studied. Even then, however, this commonly takes the form of the researcher imparting upon them her or his "enlightened" view. (Renzetti, 1992, pp. 7-8)

Indeed, it might make more sense within a positivist framework to refer to the participants in a study as research *objects* rather than research subjects.

Feminist researchers, in contrast, prefer a model of collaboration to the traditional researcher/subjects dichotomy. More specifically, in the feminist methodological framework, researchers are encouraged to "start from their own experience"; to freely share information about themselves, their personal lives, and their opinions with those they are studying; and to adhere to a feminist ethic of care by complying with requests for help and by offering advice and direct assistance when possible (Cook & Fonow, 1984; Oakley, 1981; Reinharz, 1992). Rather than biasing data in a negative sense, feminists maintain that self-disclosure and the establishment of reciprocity between researcher and researched contribute to the success of a project (see, e.g., Bergen, 1993).

Within positivist social science, the emphasis on objectivity and the adoption of the researcher/subjects dichotomy have produced a strong reliance on random-sampling strategies, survey methods, and quantitative analysis. These have come to be seen as the most rigorous and scientifically sound research techniques. The feminist commitment to giving voice to people's personal, everyday experiences—especially the experiences of the marginalized in a society—has instead resulted in a strong bias in favor of convenience and purposive sampling strategies, in addition to qualitative methods, such as in-depth interviews, ethnographies, and life histories. This is not to say that feminist researchers have totally abandoned survey methods and quantitative analysis. To the contrary, there are numerous examples of feminist survey research and quantitative analyses (see, for example, Randall & Haskell, 1995; Russell, 1982a). Rather than rejecting survey research and quantitative analysis per se, feminist methodologists reject the views that these methods are necessarily the most scientifically rigorous and that only statistics provide us with "hard facts" (Reinharz, 1992). Statistics, after all, do not speak for themselves and often have been used against women and other marginalized groups by disguising particular problems, creating erroneous information that carries "statistical authority," and reinforcing stereotypes (Reinharz, 1992). Consequently, feminist researchers often favor the use of multiple methods in a research project, particularly if one of the methods is quantitative or survey-based.

The emphasis on viewing research as a collaborative enterprise has also prompted some feminist researchers to advocate the use of participatory methods. Maguire (1987), whose own work is an exemplar of the feminist participatory model, defines *participatory research* as the combination of three activities: (a) investigation, (b) education, and (c) action.

> It is a method of social *investigation* of problems, involving participation of oppressed and ordinary people in problem posing and solving. It is an *educational* process for the researcher and participants, who analyze the structural causes of named problems through collective discussion and interaction. Finally, it is a way for researchers and oppressed people to join in solidarity to take collective *action,* both short and long term, for radical social change. (p. 35; for other examples of the feminist participatory model, see Kleiber & Light, 1978; Mies, 1983)

In this model, the research relationship is clearly reciprocal rather than hierarchical. The researcher, rather than being a detached expert, engages the participation of community members from the outset, recognizing that both parties bring to a project unique skills, knowledge, and resources. As Maguire (1987) put it, "We both know some things, neither of us knows everything. Working together we will both know more, and we will both learn more about how to know" (p. 40).

In feminist participatory research, the researched are active participants throughout the project. These days it is fashionable to refer to the participants in a study as "co-researchers," but what does that mean in practice? At a minimum, it means that the researched help identify problems to be studied, contribute to the development of research instruments, fully participate in discussions of the data analysis and what the findings mean, and, perhaps most important, decide how the findings will be used. The research experience ultimately should empower those who participate to develop and implement strategies to address specific problems that concern them.

By now you probably realize that adopting the feminist participatory model as the methodological framework for a research project may be daunting. This model is not "quick and dirty," as I've heard some researchers describe attitudinal surveys. Feminist participatory research is time-consuming and requires a substantial investment of personal stock on the part of the researcher and the researched. So why bother? To answer that question, I will turn now to a description of my own experience using the feminist participatory model. Through this discussion I hope to show how such a project may be beneficial to researchers, the researched, various communities, and the social sciences as a whole.

Becoming a Feminist Methodologist: One Researcher's Experience

Because the feminist participatory model requires honesty on the part of the researcher, I must begin my account with a disclaimer: I did not undertake the research project I am about to describe with the conscious intent of using a feminist participatory method. Although I was then—and I remain—a feminist, as are the activists who became my co-researchers, we didn't really know much about this method when the project began. Rather, we "learned by doing" for the most part, and the model evolved as our guiding methodological framework throughout the course of the study. To explain how and why, let me review the history of this project, which was a national study of partner abuse in lesbian relationships.

The project began in spring 1985, when I contacted an activist at a local battered women's service agency in Philadelphia regarding an advertisement I had seen in the *Philadelphia Gay News* for a community forum on lesbian battering. The ad had attracted my attention because of my research interest in domestic violence; I wanted to know more about the problem of violence in lesbian relationships. The activist told me that she would send me the information she had but that it wasn't much because at that point few people had acknowledged the problem, let alone studied it. I asked if the community she represented might be interested in conducting research on this problem, and she agreed to raise the prospect with other activists in the lesbian community.

A few weeks after this initial conversation, a meeting was arranged between myself and a group of lesbian activists concerned about the problem of lesbian battering, several of whom were battered lesbians themselves. From the start, it was obvious that each of us would bring to a research project different talents, skills, and knowledge. I, for example, had access to funding sources, grant-writing experience, and technical skills in research design and data analysis (albeit of the positivist kind). But as a heterosexual woman, I was an outsider to the lesbian community. I had no experience, direct or indirect, with battered lesbians or lesbian batterers, and as the conversation proceeded that day, it became abundantly clear that I knew far less about lesbian relationships than I had originally presumed. In contrast, the activists had years of collective experience in the battered women's movement and experiential knowledge of lesbian relationships, of the lesbian community in Philadelphia and other parts of the country, and, most important, of lesbian battering.

When the meeting concluded, we agreed that an empirical study of lesbian battering would be a useful way of publicly legitimating the problem, of bringing attention to the violence that some lesbians were suffering in their intimate relationships. Such a study would also help us identify potential strategies for reducing the violence and for better meeting the service needs of battered lesbians. Still, there remained a number of unresolved concerns that had to be addressed before a study could be designed. Perhaps the most serious of these revolved around the question of *ownership.*

The question of who would own the project was initially raised at this first meeting by the activists. Would the project belong to the author alone, the activists alone, the funding source, a combination of these three, or someone else altogether? Understandably, there was concern among these women with how a heterosexual social scientist might use the findings. I was more concerned with making sure that the findings, which I saw as potentially having significant implications for the study of domestic violence in general, be made widely available to other researchers, social scientists, and practitioners. At the same time, we were all concerned that the funding source—the Roman Catholic university where I work—might ultimately try to control or censor the findings.[1] This was the first point at which the feminist participatory framework came into play, because the model requires that project ownership be joint. Although we weren't aware at the time that we were using this model, our resolution to the problem of ownership grew from our feminist perspectives of fairness. We decided that I would take responsibility for distributing the findings among academics, social service providers, and practitioners; the activists would be responsible for distributing the findings within the lesbian community.

Lest I give the impression that the question of ownership was thereby settled once and for all, let me emphasize that it resurfaced throughout the life of the project. As time passed, the "boundaries" that we had established at that first meeting became increasingly artificial, and we ended up often working in each other's assigned "territory." What was firmly established at that first meeting, however, was that the principal researcher could not claim sole ownership of the study. This would be a collective/collaborative effort. In short, we were in this together.

The women who attended that first meeting subsequently became the core group that worked on the research, but ours was by no means a closed circle. Throughout the project, new members joined us and participated for as long as they could. We also periodically sought advice and feedback from members of a battered women's group, battered women's advocates, and members of the local lesbian community, including battered lesbians.[2] The primary working group, however, began meeting at least once a week, for 2 hours or more each time, to design and carry out the research. The more we met, the more the meetings also became periods of social activity in addition to work. We each brought food to share, but along with the physical sustenance, we began providing one another with emotional sustenance as well. We shared stories and "news" and relevant information (e.g., jobs that were available, our opinions about a new novel or film). These discussions were often as intense and animated as those about the research, and from them close friendships began to develop. This was unlike any research experience I had ever had.

One of our first challenges was developing a strategy for recruiting study volunteers. Obviously, drawing a random sample would be impossible, but I also resisted the temptation of simply distributing questionnaires at an event, such as a women's music festival, where there might be a large number of participants who were lesbians. The resolution to this problem was again collaborative and drew on our respective skills and knowledge. I suggested advertising for study volunteers; the activists suggested the media. Together we designed the ads and public announcements of the study, but the activists designed a brochure about lesbian partner abuse in which study announcements and self-mailing cards to request questionnaires were inserted.

Yes, I did say questionnaires. Despite the feminist emphasis on qualitative methods, our group decided that a questionnaire would be the best way to at least begin to collect data. Our reasoning was that, given the sensitive nature of the topic, a questionnaire would provide study volunteers with anonymity and thus be less threatening than an interview. In addition, a questionnaire could potentially reach a larger, more diverse group of women.

After considerable group discussion of the issues to cover in the research instrument, I was assigned the task of drafting the questionnaire. I arrived at the next meeting, questionnaire in hand, confident that it would require only minor revisions before it was ready for distribution. Instead, the first draft of the questionnaire was subjected to intense scrutiny within the group, and a lengthy dialogue ensued in which there were pointed disagreements—not only between me and the activists but also among the activists—over virtually every item. Important to emphasize, though, is that our debates were not infused with hostility. In trying to characterize them, I am reminded of Plato's distinction between eristic discussion and dialectic discussion. In the former, debaters argue with the goal of having their individual points of view prevail; in the latter, they argue to arrive at the best answer or solution. Our debates were dialectic. While I shared my knowledge of scaling and other methodological technicalities, the activists patiently sensitized me and one another to issues of language and variations in experience. The questionnaire went through six drafts over a period of 9 months. Although that may seem like an inordinate amount of time to some, the quality of the end product is attested to by the number of respondents who wrote us notes or stated in subsequent interviews that completing the questionnaire actually contributed to their recovery from the trauma of abuse. Apparently, the research project was empowering for many of the 100 study volunteers, a goal noted earlier as central to the feminist participatory model.

On the last page of our 12-page questionnaire, respondents were asked if they would be willing to participate in an interview about their experiences. Despite the advantages of the questionnaire method in this study, our research group also recognized its limitations. We wanted, like other feminist researchers, to give voice to these women's experiences, to let them tell their stories. The development of the interview schedule followed the same collaborative process as the development of the questionnaire, but because we decided that the interview should be largely unstructured, with just a few questions to guide the conversation, and because of the lessons we had learned in writing the questionnaire, we spent less time writing the interview schedule. The interview schedule went through only three revisions.

We decided that I would do all of the interviews alone, either in person or by phone. Of the 100 questionnaire respondents, 77 volunteered to be interviewed, and 40 interviews were actually completed.[3] Each interview typically lasted an hour, and each was tape recorded. Despite my early experiences as an interviewer, in this study I consciously tried to break down any barriers between myself and those I was interviewing. Using a feminist methodology now, I began each interview by introducing myself as a researcher and as a person, and by asking each woman what in particular she would like to know about me. During the interview, I freely offered advice and emotional support as the women recounted what were undoubtedly painful and traumatic experiences. When possible and when asked, I made referrals to specific services, such as support groups for battered lesbians, that had been identified during the course of the project. The interview usually ended with me asking each woman if there was anything else she'd like to ask me or if she would like to give any feedback on the project. A major goal throughout the interview, then, was ensuring the reciprocity of the research relationship.

To preserve the confidentiality of the study volunteers, I personally coded all the questionnaire data and transcribed the taped interviews. Everyone in the group then received copies of the interview transcripts, with all identifying information deleted, along with computer printouts containing the aggregate data analysis. I taught the group how to read and interpret various statistical tests, but the task of explaining the data was once again a collaborative effort. I applied what I had learned from an extensive review of the social sciences literature on domestic violence and lesbian relationships; the activists applied their experiential knowledge as counselors, advocates, and administrators in the battered women's movement and as partners in lesbian relationships, some as formerly battered lesbians.

Together the group discerned what the data meant and then undertook the task of explaining the findings to others. But before any of the findings were published or discussed in a public forum, we prepared a report summarizing the data for the study volunteers, and I mailed it to those for whom I had addresses. As a group we felt we had a responsibility to give the data back to those who had provided it and also to allow the study volunteers additional opportunities to "talk back" to us about the project and how we should use the results. Again, our hope was that the project would be empowering to those who participated.

Once we began to distribute the research findings publicly, our meetings as a group became less frequent. For a variety of reasons, a number of the activists could no longer participate in the group formally (e.g., a change in jobs, a move), but some of us continued to meet periodically to share new ideas, to bring each other up to date on our individual writing and education projects based on the research, and to comment on each other's written work or community activity. Two members of the original group have reviewed nearly all of what I've written of the research, continuing the collaboration we began more than 10 years ago. Most important perhaps, we have remained friends and have provided one another with support through a number of major life events (new house purchases, the birth of a child and the adoption of two others, the deaths of relatives and loved ones).[4]

More specific details about this research and the findings are discussed in my book, *Violent Betrayal: Partner Abuse in Lesbian Relationships* (Renzetti, 1992), where readers may better evaluate the quality of the project. However, it is doubtful that one can gauge the significance of the kind of collaboration I have described, or the transformative effects it had on those who participated, by any "objective" scientific standards.

Feminist Participatory Research as Good Social Science

I do not assume that my personal experience is generalizable to all researchers who have used or attempted to use the feminist participatory model, nor that the model itself is applicable to all research problems or settings. The feminist participatory model emerged as the guiding framework for this project largely for two reasons. First, each person involved in planning and designing the study was committed to feminist principles of equality, partnership, and democratization. Second, the model meshed well with the goals of the project, which were to increase awareness of a problem that had been hidden and ignored and to identify potential strategies for remedying it, and to give voice and recognition to the experiences of a marginalized group—battered lesbians—thus empowering them. Nevertheless, I do think that my experience illustrates some of the general benefits of the feminist participatory model, which should prompt researchers to carefully consider its applicability to their research projects. Let me conclude this paper, then, by briefly discussing these benefits.

Social scientists have long studied stigmatized and marginalized groups, groups whose members and their experiences have been rendered invisible and ignorable by the dominant society. Social scientists, as I noted at the outset, have undertaken these studies as outside "experts," making little effort to understand what members of the group in question see as the most pressing problem for research and rarely sharing the results of the research with them. In using the feminist participatory model, however, researchers become both teachers and learners. Researchers bring their professional skills and expertise to the project, but the full participation of those being researched means that the study becomes truly an educational process for the researcher. Indeed, the process may be, as it was for me, transformative. The participation of the researched in designing and implementing the project also improves the quality and accuracy of the research because they help to ensure that (a) the most significant issues—from the perspective not only of the researcher but also of the researched—get identified and studied; (b) meaningful (in terms of their lived experiences) and nonalienating research instruments are developed; (c) the data collected are analyzed in the realistic context of their everyday lives; and (d) the project has a practical effect in terms of personal and social change.

The researched also benefit as teachers and learners from participation in a genuinely collaborative research project, particularly if they are members of marginalized or stigmatized groups. For one thing, they may acquire valuable research and organizational skills (e.g., how to read tables, how to write a grant proposal, how to interpret various statistics). Moreover, rather than having an analysis of their experiences imposed on them by "experts" who typically are not members of their group, research participants shape the problems to be studied, how they are studied, and how the research findings are interpreted, distributed, and used. Because they are co-owners of the research, the findings are also theirs to use to bring about personal and social change.

Finally, the benefits of feminist participatory research may spill over into various communities and into the social sciences as a whole. This is because one of the major goals of feminist participatory research is the generation of *usable* knowledge, not the production of knowledge for knowledge's sake. In a feminist participatory research project, the knowledge created should enrich practice and inform public policy making. In a way, then, a research project that uses the feminist participatory model is not completed until the desired social change is accomplished, and this means a long-term commitment on the part of both researchers and researched.

Is this biased social science? Of course it is, but then, all social science is biased. In my view, what sets this type of research apart is that it is also *good* social science; that is, it seeks to give voice to and to improve the life conditions of the marginalized, and it transforms social scientific inquiry from an academic exercise into an instrument of meaningful social change.

Notes

1. This fear eventually proved unfounded. The university administration and most of my colleagues provided extensive financial, intellectual, and emotional support throughout the course of the project and continue to do so.

2. In fact, it was through a meeting with one such advocate that we were introduced to the feminist participatory research model. I wish to thank Barbara Hart for this discussion (and for making me aware of Maguire, 1987) and for the many other discussions she's had with me over the years about my research.

3. Interviews could not be scheduled with 37 study volunteers for a variety of reasons. For example, I couldn't reach them at the phone number they gave on the questionnaire, we couldn't arrive at a mutually convenient time for an interview, when they were called they didn't answer, or they changed their mind about doing the interview.

4. I am grateful to Marie Hegerty and Shawn Towey for their long-term participation in this project and for their continued friendship.

CHAPTER

11

Researching Violence Against Street Prostitutes

Issues of Epistemology, Methodology, and Ethics

JODY MILLER

My research on prostitutes' experiences with violence presents a vivid example of some of the tensions that arise in conducting feminist research and provides a framework from which to explore some of the epistemological, methodological, and ethical issues that arise in trying to produce feminist

AUTHOR'S NOTE: An earlier version of this paper was prepared for presentation at the 1994 annual meeting of the American Society of Criminology, Miami, Florida. I would like to thank Judith Mayne, Ruth Petersen, Lori Reed, Laurel Richardson, and Martin D. Schwartz for their support and encouragement during the research, and Barry Glassner for additional guidance in refining my analyses. I am especially grateful to the women I interviewed, for all they and the experience have taught me.

scholarship with political goals. Feminist research raises a number of epistemological questions that challenge traditional positivist assumptions about social science and the social world: What are appropriate relationships between research subjects and researchers? What counts as evidence and constitutes knowledge? What are the goals of research? (Harding, 1987). An important thread in much of feminism has been to question whether research should be or ever can be "value-free." Several important goals of feminist scholarship include the need to understand and document women's experiences and to generate research from the perspectives of women. In this work, this has meant adopting qualitative interviewing as my strategy for listening to what women have to say about their lives. A characteristic of qualitative interviewing is that it provides us with a means of understanding the social world from the distinct points of view of the research subjects, highlighting the meanings individuals attribute to their experiences (Adler & Adler, 1987; Glassner & Loughlin, 1987; Harding, 1987; Smith, 1987; Strauss, 1987).

Although qualitative work provides important contributions to the study of women's experiences, the choice of this (or any) method is not without dilemmas that must be addressed. In this chapter, I will examine some of the unique issues that arise in qualitative interviewing, particularly when we study sensitive issues such as experiences of violence and victimization, and in my work, problems that result from researching a group of women labeled "deviant" by the larger society. I will address several interrelated issues that arise (though not exclusively) in qualitative research: first, the relationship between research subjects and researchers and how these relationships shape the investigation, and, second, the ways in which we come to define evidence as authentic and thus as a reflection of reality. Many of the topics I discuss are universal for social researchers regardless of the methodologies employed. However, they are particularly important to address in feminist and qualitative work because of our research goals. I will begin with a brief introduction about how I became involved in the research, then will provide an overview of the methodology I employed, and finally will move to the substantive discussion.

My decision to study women's experiences as street prostitutes came from a panel I attended at the 1990 National Women's Studies Association conference. Margaret Prescod, founder of the Los Angeles-based Black Coalition Fighting Back Serial Murders, told of the "southside slayer," a serial killer who murdered women in South-Central Los Angeles beginning in 1983. The coalition was formed to demand police accountability. The majority of the victims were poor African American prostitutes, and the police had deemed their deaths "cheap homicides" (Prescod, 1990). As a result of Prescod's moving discussion, I decided to investigate street prostitutes' experiences with violence in my own community. One goal of my study was to assess the magnitude of violence these women face; the other goal was to examine their perceptions of the extent to which the criminal justice system met or failed to meet their needs as victims of violent crime (see Note 1 for a brief synopsis of these findings).

Methodology

The purpose of my research was to understand violence against street prostitutes and its handling by the criminal justice system from the point of view of the women who are members of this social world. The research was based on semistructured in-depth interviews with 16 prostitutes. The sample was drawn from women who were incarcerated at the county jail in Columbus, Ohio, during December 1990 and January 1991.[2] Jail officials estimated that of the approximately 200 women housed in the jail at any one time, about 10% were incarcerated for prostitution-related charges. Women were included in my sample when they fit one of several circumstances: when they were incarcerated for solicitation for the purpose of prostitution, for loitering for the purpose of prostitution, or for other charges but were self-admitted prostitutes who had recent arrests for prostitution.

The women I interviewed ranged in age from 20 to 38, with the majority in their early or late 20s. Nine of the women were African American; seven were white. Fourteen considered themselves crack addicts. The interviews were semistructured and included several groups of questions. I began by collecting general demographic information, then asked general questions about the women's involvement in prostitution, their perceptions of prostitution, and their commitment to the work. Once we had talked more generally about their involvement in prostitution, I began to ask the women questions about their perceptions of violence and danger on the streets, and finally about their personal experiences with violence. They were asked about a specific list of abuses ranging from verbal insults or threats up to rape and were asked to discuss the contexts of such experiences.

When we engage in social research, we encounter a number of tensions as we proceed in our inquiry. These include (a) the establishment of a relationship between research subjects and researchers and its effect on the information acquired and (b) the ways in which our frames of reference as scholars shape how we define legitimate evidence and how we develop knowledge. Both of these raise ethical and political issues in addition to methodological ones. I will discuss each of these topics in turn.

The Relationship Between Research Subjects and Researchers

In-depth interviewing as an event creates a relationship between the researcher and research subject that is more intimate than that which occurs in more quantitative forms of gathering data. Because of the conversational style of qualitative interviewing, because we are discussing matters in our subjects' lives at length that are often personal, and because we often choose to research topics that we feel some passion for ourselves, emotional issues emerge in the context of in-depth interviewing and other forms of qualitative work (see Johnson, 1983; Kleinman & Copp, 1993; Pollner & Emerson, 1983). These issues include those of connection and detachment and of vulnerability and trust, among others.

Particularly for members of stigmatized groups, such as street prostitutes, it is rare to be taken seriously and to be placed in a position to teach others. In describing my research in purely academic terms, I would say that by taking the role of "acceptable incompetent" (Lofland & Lofland, 1984, pp. 38-39) and exhibiting a nonjudgmental demeanor, I was perceived as nonthreatening and was able to establish rapport with the women I interviewed. Most of the women responded to me as teachers and constructed our relationship as one between an experienced, streetwise individual and a somewhat naive "straight" person. Other researchers have suggested that taking a teacher role can provide interview subjects with a sense of meaning and importance (Dunlap et al., 1990, p. 130).

This summary does not fully describe the relationships we constructed during the interviews, however. The dynamics of our interactions were much more complex and nuanced. One of the most crucial factors structuring our relationships was the circumstance of a nonprostitute interviewing prostitutes about their experiences. Not surprisingly, because I am a woman who has no experience with the streets, the women I interviewed reacted to me differently than they would have reacted to a woman more familiar with their lives. Much of their reaction to me appeared related to their understanding of "straight" people and "straight" life. Blondie, for example, told me:

> If you're not on drugs then you can't relate to people that are on drugs. You can only relate to the people that you're like. You know, if I wasn't on the drugs and wasn't on High Street, I'd be relating to people like you, and you know, straight people.

There was a recognition among the women I interviewed that not only can we not relate to one another, but "straight" people are judgmental of their lives. As she used obscene language, Kay Kay said, "I keep forgetting I'm on tape." When talking about "giving head," she said, making reference to the tape recorder, "they're probably like, 'oh my god, listen to this girl talk!' " When I asked her about the number of tricks she saw per day, she responded, "Oh god, you'd think I'm sick." She also often made reference to the hypocrisy of many straight people, particularly some of the men she dated, whom she described as both stuck up and ashamed of their behavior.

Kay Kay sometimes made specific reference to me during the interview as well. She told me of herself, "I'm really a pretty girl, I could go to school, I could get my GED and then I could go to college. And be just like you." Yet even as she stated this as a possibility, she also caught herself ridiculing people like me. Later in the interview, as she talked about her lack of fear of the police, she said, "Now a lot of them teenyboppers like, I mean, you know, school kids like you, they're scared." Although she seemed to reject traditional femininity for herself, Kay Kay treated me as though I were in need of protection. At one point as we were discussing the area where she worked, which was experiencing gentrification, she asked me if I ever rode down High Street. I responded that I lived around the area. She replied, "Why do you live in the Short North, honey?" When she found out where, she said, "Oh, Buttles is nice, Buttles has changed." In contrast to her presentation of self, Kay Kay's construction of me was as both naive and fragile.

In a similar vein, although clearly more cynical in her approach, Jessie commented on the voyeurism inherent in my research. We had been talking for well over an hour, and she remembered two violent encounters that she had forgotten to tell me about earlier. She then said, "You got time for this?" As I said yes, she responded, "You like hearing these horror stories, don't you?" and without waiting for my response, she proceeded to tell me of an incident in which she was almost raped and killed. Regardless of the *specific* approach the women took in their response to me, they all recognized me as someone whose life and experiences were very distant from their own, whether by their choice to lead a life "on the edge," by necessity, or both.

This is painfully illustrated in the matter of voyeurism, which Jessie so keenly raised during our interview. I would like to believe that I became involved in this research topic to aid in the fight for prostitutes' rights. But there is also always some voyeurism involved in looking at the lives of other people, perhaps even more so when those people are socially labeled as deviants and are stigmatized. During the interview process and afterward, I sometimes found myself driving out of my way to go through the areas where the women I interviewed worked. In part, I was looking for them, but I was also just looking to "see" prostitution going on. I've driven down Main Street and found the corner Jessie described as her spot, hoping to get a glimpse of her; but I did so always from the safety and protection of my car, which shielded me from the reality of experiencing the streets. I never stopped and parked, let alone got out and walked around, but instead maintained the distance of a voyeur.

When I think about my actions and my interest in the research, I'm not very comfortable with this aspect of it. Is it exploitive? Am I? How much does voyeurism play a part in any research? Clearly, it is an indication of the extent of the power relations in social research. What are the implications for our scholarship if we do not recognize and grapple with this aspect of our work? Although we are not dispassionate researchers who distance ourselves from our values and emotions, we continue to objectify our research subjects through the very power we employ as researchers.

Probably one of the most challenging aspects of my research was grappling with my understanding of rape in the lives of the women I interviewed and in my own life and of how the issue played itself out in the interview process. The following is an entry from my journal notes, written during the time that I was conducting interviews. I had spent several days in a row interviewing between two and four women per day, was feeling overwhelmed at the amount and severity of violence I was being told about, and at the advise of an advisor, decided to stop temporarily. I wrote,

> *After these experiences, I really need a break. A little time away from the research. Although that doesn't stop me from thinking about their experiences 24 hours a day, or 24-7, as they would say. I lay in bed at night, for what seems like hours, trying to fall asleep, but with images of these women's stories keeping me awake. On Friday, I was really*

> *jumpy around the house in the morning. It really does make me more aware of my own vulnerability.*

Because I am a woman and therefore live with the threat of rape, I felt as though I related to their discussions of violence and, looking back on it, probably identified some experiences as "rape" that they would not have (for a variety of reasons, not the least of which is self-preservation on their parts). One recent researcher wrote of wife battering that "as a woman in this society, I am vulnerable to such violence. Being aware of this makes a difference in how I understand the problem" (Yllö, 1988, p. 34). Likewise, I think it is telling that I dwelled so much on the violence, to the point that it sometimes enhanced my own fear of being sexually assaulted. Yet, if anything, it should have made me aware of my relative lack of vulnerability in comparison to these women, who bear the brunt of intense social stigma that defines them as "unrapeable" and condones and supports their victimization (Delacoste & Alexander, 1988; Frohmann, 1992; Hatty, 1989; James, Withers, Haft, Theiss, & Owen, 1977; Miller, 1991; Miller & Schwartz, 1995).

Herman (1988) notes that "women live [our] lives according to a rape schedule" (p. 260) that dictates to us the circumstances under which we lead our daily lives—when we go out, with whom, and where we go, for example. But obviously, street prostitutes do not and cannot live according to the same schedule as I do. In many ways, fear of sexual violence seems to be much more monumental in me than in many of them. My response to that fear, in how it constricts my behavior and movement, is also quite different. This is precisely why they adopt a different understanding of the phenomenon than I do; adopting my fear of sexual violence would leave them immobilized, unable to work. To say this is in no way meant to imply that they did not define their experiences as rape or experience rape as a traumatic event. As Blondie told me, "Being prostitutes, we still know the difference between rape and not gettin' raped. Just because we do it for a living doesn't mean we want it, you know." What it is meant to imply, rather, is that my sometimes paralyzing fear of rape, which was intensified during the interviews—in fact, the very ability to live by a rape schedule—is in many ways born of privilege.

This recognition raises broader questions, for my own research and for social research more generally. Even as we purport to "give voice" to the subjects of our research, our understandings of the experiences of these individuals are shaped by our own life histories and by our political and theoretical understandings of the social world. In the next section, I will discuss some of the issues that arise in trying to create knowledge within social research, and the unavoidable ways in which our frames of reference as scholars shape how we accomplish this.

Definitions of Reality: What Constitutes Evidence?

Examining the experiences of a group that has been stigmatized and silenced, it was important to me to structure the research in such a way that it involved my listening to what the women had to say about their lives. However, this is much more complicated in practice than in theory. For a social researcher to create a research project that is not grounded to some extent in that researcher's understanding of the social world and the phenomenon under study is virtually impossible. This has led some scholars to argue that researchers should be members of the groups we study. Collins (1990), for example, argues that to make legitimate knowledge claims, researchers should "have lived or experienced their material in some fashion" (p. 232). In particular, this is of critical importance when the research in question is conducted about an oppressed group.

Other researchers, unwilling to study only themselves, have suggested instead that scholarship should be reflexive, preserving "in it the presence, concerns, and the experience of the [researcher] as knower and discoverer" (Smith, 1987, p. 92; see also Harding, 1987) so that the subjectivity that exists in all social research will be a visible part of the project and thus available to the reader for examination. One means of doing so is to continue to reexamine our work over time. With the passage of time, our perspectives develop in new ways and we can become more explicitly aware of the frames of reference that shaped us previously.

Looking back on my work, a key issue is how I constructed my work around not just experience with violence, but specifically victimization. This is evident in my previous discussion of rape. Going into the project, I was aware that the women I interviewed were not totally victimized, that in many ways they were active agents in their lives, and this was a theoretical framework that I brought with me into the research (Harding, 1987). Yet I wanted to interview them about their experiences with violence. Even as I tried to define them in my mind and my research as both victims and agents, I did so in a problematic way. I defined their work as prostitutes as a form of agency, because, for example, they made economic decisions based on the alternatives available to them. But I defined their experiences with violence totally in terms of victimization. I compartmentalized and categorized their lives in terms of what I saw as victimization and agency rather than recognizing the complexities of victimization and agency, the ways that both are part and parcel of violence, economics, and other dimensions of their lives.

Through the construction of my interview guide, I told the women, at least implicitly, how I defined their experiences. For example, from the outset, I presented my research to them in negative terms. I wasn't interested in finding out about their overall experiences with prostitution but about their "problems," specifically with "violence." Although in most cases we spent at least the first half of the interview talking more generally about their involvement in prostitution, because I had initially brought up "problems" and "violence," this shaped the discourse throughout. But the women I interviewed often resisted my definitions of victimization and talked about their resistance to violence in powerful ways. They did not allow themselves to be viewed only as victims. Perhaps the most exciting aspect of my research is being able to see the ways that the women I spoke with resisted my unconscious categorizations, my unwitting framing of their lives, when it didn't fit with their realities—to the extent that I later wrote an article that focused explicitly on prostitutes' strategies of resistance.[3]

Similarly, I tried to make my recognition of their agency an integral part of my analysis, this time by framing their experiences with prostitution in economic terms and as work. Unfortunately, my notions of work reflect the notions of the dominant culture. I labeled the men they see as "clients," whereas they called them "tricks" or "dates." In trying to apply an economic model to what they did, I asked questions about their "work" schedules, such as how many hours a day they worked, what hours, and so forth. But my notion of work was too rigid, as was my notion of time. I recognize now that their sense of time was not the same as mine. Sometimes they were out on the streets for days and nights on end, and they didn't pay attention to dates and times the way I did. Unfortunately, often definitions of time and reality that are in contrast with the dominant ones are viewed with skepticism, seen as invalid, unreliable, and even unbelievable. This leads to a problem I will discuss in more depth in the following pages; namely, what constitutes legitimate knowledge and who has the power to decide?

In social science, "our training teaches us to ignore the uneasiness at the junctures where transitional work is done—for example, the ordinary problems respondents have of fitting their experiences of the world to the questions in the interview schedule" (Smith, 1987, p. 93). One area in which this became very clear to me when looking back was in my attempt to quantify experiences with violence. To ask how many times during the last year they have been slapped, hit, kicked, raped, stabbed, and so on is to ask what is perhaps unanswerable, due to the frequency of their encounters with violence. For example, Lacy responded to my questions with a variety of answers that indicated the extent to which her experiences were uncountable: "All the time, all the time. It happens to us girls all the time." "I could tell you, we could sit here all day and talk about it." When I asked her if she had ever been stabbed, she held out her arm and said, "Yeah, take your pick," referring to the numerous scars on her hands and arms.

So I found that in this specific research, the quantitative data I attempted to gather were difficult to obtain. That fact itself teaches us about the frequency and severity of the violence these women face, even without the hard numbers as reference. As I noted previously, qualitative research does provide a challenge to traditional positivist research because of its emphasis on the complexities of social worlds. However, it is important not to perpetuate a qualitative/quantitative dichotomy that recognizes qualitative research as valuable and defines quantitative research as inherently flawed or inherently oppressive in its reduction of subjects' experiences into fixed, preformed categories. As my previous discussion reveals, qualitative research is also shaped by researchers' prior understandings of the social world and, as such, is not inherently problem-free in this regard. Furthermore, both forms of research provide valuable and potentially complementary information about the social worlds we want to understand, and our goal as researchers must be to find ways to bring these methods of gaining knowledge together in meaningful ways. This is particularly important for understanding and generating strategies to combat violence against women.

Another issue remains and is perhaps uniquely troublesome for qualitative interviewers (though clearly it is at the core of much quantitative work in different ways). A goal of much qualitative work is to employ an epistemology that recognizes the individuals we interview as being in the most capable position to define their realities. And yet we have and use the power to define what is "truth" in our research, sometimes rejecting subjects' own stories of their lives. In the case of quantitative work, this takes place to a large extent in the construction of methodological tools and measures. In qualitative interviewing, it is interactive and often occurs in the context of gathering data. (For both, it also occurs in assessment and analysis.)

In my research, I exercised the right to exclude an interview that I decided, based on my subjective understanding of what makes information legitimate, was fictitious. During my interview with Kay Kay, she told me of another woman who was preparing for her interview by "writing a list" about prostitution. Kay Kay told me:

> She's a trip. She'll tell you about Main Street. She'll tell you about men . . . pushing her out, beatin' her up. Poor girl. Yeah, she'll tell you. She says she's gonna rock your world when she gets down here tellin' you the stories. She's gonna turn you out.

Later the same day, I interviewed Jazzie, a woman who worked the Main Street area. I have no way of knowing for sure that she was the woman Kay Kay spoke of, but I chose to exclude her interview because it was full of what I considered "tall tales" that I found implausible, inconsistent, and unlikely to have occurred. Jazzie's was the only interview I left out. The others passed my subjective definitions of legitimate knowledge. One of the advisors overseeing the project was highly skeptical of another interview as well, though I disagreed.

Regardless, based on my power as the researcher, I was in the position to choose what was truth or lie. But is anything "truth" or "lie"? That all of the interviews were socially constructed interactions in which we both responded to one another based on categorizations (such as "streetwise" versus "straight") is an unavoidable conclusion. Nevertheless, as social researchers, we are in the position to make decisions about what constitutes legitimate evidence and what does not. We decide for ourselves what is truth and what is fiction, based on our subjective interpretations of what, in our eyes (and from our experience and our frame of reference), is believable. When does this become imposing our reality on our research subjects? Or can it ever be anything else? As Ladner (1987) points out,

> The relationship between the *researcher* and his[/her] *subjects,* by definition, resembles that of the oppressor and the oppressed, because it is the oppressor who defines the problem, the nature of the research, and, to some extent, the quality of interaction between him[/her] and his[/her] subjects. (p. 77)

As researchers, we need to remain cautious and ever-vigilant of our powers to define what constitutes truth and reality, and particularly so when we study groups we do not belong to, and groups who face widespread social stigma, as is frequently the case when women are victims of violence and abuse.

Concluding Remarks

The goal of this chapter has been to explore some of the issues and dilemmas that emerge in conducting feminist qualitative research with the goal of understanding the distinct perspectives of the women interviewed concerning their experiences with violence. Harding (1987) suggests that the best research

> insists that the inquirer her/himself be placed in the same critical plane as the overt subject matter, thereby recovering the entire research process for scrutiny in the results of the research. . . . Thus the researcher appears to us not as an invisible, anonymous voice of authority, but as a real, historical individual with concrete, specific desires and interests. (p. 9)

In this chapter, I have attempted to produce an illustration of this self-reflexivity. Within the social sciences, we are not typically encouraged to be self-reflexive and critical of our work in these ways. Pointing out our flaws and our own understanding of the social world often delegitimizes our studies in the eyes of many scholars. But regardless of whether we discuss the issues, they invariably frame our work, whether it is qualitative or quantitative. As Bograd (1988) notes, "the common social science practice of not discussing one's values leads to biases that often go unrecognized or unacknowledged" (p. 21). We need to create a space in our field that recognizes that as social researchers, we are also people living in the social world, and our lived experiences, values, and beliefs inescapably shape our work. The extent to which we can voice these influences and examine them in our work strengthens our larger goal of building knowledge to combat violence against women.

Looking back on my research, I am keenly aware of the many ways I could have approached it. Lather (1991) argues that we need to "position ourselves less as masters of truth and justice and more as creators of space where those directly involved can act and speak on their own behalf" (p. 137). In writing up my findings for articles and presentations, I have tried to be "multivoiced" in my analyses by putting the women I interviewed in dialogue with one another and trying to remain steadfast in my self-reflexivity. Still, I recognize that my very ability to present my data in such a way comes from the power I have as a researcher—talking about giving marginalized research subjects "voice" glosses over the fact that in our society, not all voices carry equal legitimacy (Lather, 1991, p. 43). So although it remains a laudable goal, it is also a romanticized one. Perhaps the most difficult conclusion I have reached is the recognition that many of these dilemmas remain unresolvable.

Notes

1. The women in this study faced an enormous amount of rape and other violence. For example, 75% had been raped by tricks; 62% had been raped in other contexts on the streets; and 87% had been the victims of physical assaults, which ranged from being punched or kicked (31%), beaten up (61%), stabbed or slashed (31%), or being hit with an object, such as a baseball bat or brick (25%) (see Miller, 1993; Miller & Schwartz, 1995). The existence and use of drugs on the streets contributed to an environment in which the women were vulnerable to attack by men who were under the influence of drugs, and by dealers and users on the streets, for whom they made easy targets for robbery and assault (see Miller, 1995).

In addition, the women highlighted the ways in which rape myths come together around prostitutes to fuel violence against them and the devaluation that allows this violence to be ignored and not taken seriously. The women I interviewed rarely turned to the police when they had been victimized, mostly because their expectations and previous experiences told them they wouldn't be taken seriously. Most reported that when they did turn to the police, they were laughed at or told, "What do you expect?" (see Miller & Schwartz, 1995). Several women did report that some vice officers had been willing to keep an eye out for a particular man who repeatedly attacked women prostituting in the area, but to warn him and scare him off rather than pursue criminal charges.

2. Interviews in jail provided longer periods of uninterrupted time than the streets would have permitted (Agar, 1977). In addition, when prostitutes are on the streets, time is money. I was not in a position to compensate them financially, and the jail setting allowed me to interview them at no cost while providing the women with a release from the boredom of incarceration. In a recent similar study, Boyle and Anglin (1993) report that they were able to offer one cigarette and a candy bar as payment, but jail personnel would not allow me to do even that. Instead, I provided them with a referral list of local hotlines and services such as rape crisis and treatment facilities, and AIDS information and free testing sites.

The choice to interview in an institutional setting is not without costs. Agar (1977) has suggested that out-of-context reports from research subjects are often not completely accurate and may present a more glamorous, exaggerated, or smooth picture than is warranted. In addition, the generalizability of any incarcerated sample is always a concern. This concern was somewhat tempered by extensive research that reveals extremely high rates of arrest for street prostitutes (Diana, 1985; Miller, 1986).

3. The women in this study developed a number of strategies to protect themselves from attack. For example, they developed typologies of clients and avoided dates with categories of men they perceived as dangerous, they shared information about violent dates with one another, and some carried weapons (see Miller, 1993).

CHAPTER

12

Measuring Violence Against Women

The Interview as a Gendered Social Encounter

DAWN H. CURRIE
BRIAN D. MACLEAN

The introduction of the concept of gender during the 1970s has transformed how we think about sociology. Reflected in the growing field of "sociology of gender," considerable research has been directed to new topics, such as sex roles, sexuality, domestic labor, male violence, and so on. The effect of this field is further reflected in the requirement by national funding agencies—such as Social Sciences and Humanities Council of Canada and the Canadian International Development Agency—that all research be sensitive to the gender dynamics of social investigation. The notion of "gender-sensitive" research, however, is typically directed to mapping the social world as gendered; much less attention has been paid to research itself as a gendered process. This omission is glaring in the field of victimization survey research.

Originally designed to capture the "dark figure" of crime, victimization surveys have made important contributions to establishing the frequency and distribution of criminal and noncriminal violence against women. Although there have been moves during the past decade to ensure that these types of surveys are sensitive to the gendered nature of male violence, it is not at all clear how this research can be rendered more adequately sensitive to the gender dynamics of the research. This lack of clarity stems from the fact that more effort has been given to refining the "tools of measurement" (such as better-designed questions), "tools of respondent selection" (such as complex sampling designs), and "tools of data analysis" (such as sophisticated mathematical models). In this paper we argue that many of these technical innovations direct attention away from research as a complex social interaction. Specifically, refinements to techniques of data collection are no guarantee that women will discuss matters of violence with researchers. Although a vast body of work asks, "What are the best techniques to accurately measure violence against women?" this question presupposes that women will disclose experiences of violence. We ask instead, "What are the problems for women to disclose woman abuse?" and "How can these problems be addressed in the interview setting?"

In this chapter we recount how these questions helped to inform the research decisions made in the Islington Crime Survey (ICS; Jones, MacLean, & Young, 1986). The purpose of this discussion is to share the thinking behind the ICS in an attempt to further our knowledge about violence against women through scientific study that meets the needs of both women respondents and researchers. To address both needs, we were required to think about the interview itself as a gendered social encounter. In doing so, the ICS incorporated an experimental design that investigates the use of direct versus indirect questioning of respondents, by male and female interviewers. We discuss the ways in which findings from the ICS raise questions that can further our understanding of the gendered dynamics of the interview setting.

From Nonreporting to Nondisclosure

Victimization surveys first emerged as a way for researchers to estimate the extent of nonrecorded crime. For purposes of this discussion, *nonrecorded crime* refers to incidents of criminal victimization that were not brought to the attention of the police by either the victim or a witness. Because a good deal of crime remains unreported, it is not processed through the criminal justice apparatus and does not end up being reflected in official crime data, such as crimes known to the police. As a result, were criminologists to rely on official crime data to determine how much crime exists and where crime is located, their estimates would not reflect social reality. This is a particularly important issue if we want to know about violence against women. Historically, domestic and sexual assault are the most underreported crimes (see Clark & Lewis, 1977; Dobash & Dobash, 1979; Faith & Currie, 1993; MacLean, 1989). Thus, victimization surveys have received much attention in the specific field of violence against women.

The logic behind the victimization survey is that people's everyday experiences are a good source of information about both crime and policing. Through probability sampling techniques, researchers can select a sample of residents from a population in a specific geographic location, who are then interviewed about their experiences with crime and victimization over a fixed period of time. The goal of the interview is to encourage respondents to disclose incidents to the researcher. From these disclosures, researchers can mathematically estimate how much crime occurred during the period covered by the survey. Once these estimates are constructed, they can be compared to official crime statistics recorded during the same period in the same jurisdiction as the survey. The difference between survey estimates of how much crime occurred and the officially recorded number of crimes serves as an estimate of "the dark figure of unreported crime."

Although the logic behind victimization surveys is impeccable in theory, it assumes that respondents will disclose an incident of victimization to the researcher when asked to do so. Such an assumption may not be warranted, however, particularly when the respondent has already failed to report the incident to the police when it occurred. Thus, one key difficulty for the victimization survey as a way to investigate nonreported crime is to identify methods that improve respondents' willingness to disclose experiences of victimization to the researcher. From this perspective, even though victimization surveys are a promising alternative to official statistics on violence against women, they present researchers with a number of special problems. These arise because experiences of physical and sexual victimization, especially by acquaintances, differ in significant ways from experiences with other crimes such as robbery. As Morris (1987, p. 163) notes, violence against women has five distinctive features:

- Women are victimized primarily by men.
- Women are more likely than men to know the perpetrator.
- Women are more likely than men to be victimized in their home.
- Women are more likely than men to experience long-term emotional stress after victimization.
- Women are more likely than men to shoulder blame and to experience feelings of guilt for their victimization.

As research during the past two decades has shown, one reason why women do not report male violence to police is that they themselves are likely to be seen as having precipitated the incident. Wives reporting domestic violence were seen by police as having "asked for it" by being neglectful, spiteful, or overbearing; women who did not fit the profile of the "rape victim" would be questioned about their own behaviors if their complaints ever went to court (see Chambers & Millar, 1984; Clark & Lewis, 1977; Dobash & Dobash, 1979). In short, historically, social attitudes have not encouraged women to talk about male violence, especially violence by intimates (Currie & MacLean, 1982). Because women are made to feel responsible for male violence, a woman who is beaten or raped may not want to report the crime because she does not want others to know. Why should she now do so to researchers?

A second key difficulty for the victimization survey is its cost. For example, if the researcher is concerned with identifying who is most at risk for a particular kind of crime, it becomes necessary to partition those respondents who have disclosed victimization into different groups by respondent characteristics. The more personal characteristics identified by the survey, the more groups are required for partitioning. More partitioned groups means fewer respondents in each group, and the fewer the cases in any group, the less reliable are the statistical analyses. For this reason, it becomes necessary to select extremely large samples, leading to an exorbitant cost of conducting the research. For example, when the National Crime Survey (NCS) was officially launched in 1972 for a 5-year trial period in the United States, $53 million was allocated to the project (U.S. House of Representatives, 1977). The key reason for this huge expenditure was the fact that the survey aimed to conduct approximately 130,000 interviews in 72,000 households twice per year (Sparks, 1982). The magnitude of resources necessary to carry out such large-scale surveys is prohibitive, and a considerable amount of energy has been expended to determine how to make the victimization survey more cost-effective.

These two difficulties, disclosure and the need for large numbers of completed questionnaires, present a dilemma for researchers. Efforts to improve disclosure increase the cost of the research, whereas labor-efficient methodologies that are cost-effective typically inhibit disclosure. This contradiction emerges because the major costs associated with large-scale survey research can be attributed to fieldwork. When the survey employs face-to-face interviews as the method of data collection, numerous costs are generated as fieldworkers or interviewers are selected, trained, and supervised. A well-trained field staff for a large-scale project requires that hundreds of potential interviewers be selected from an even larger number of applicants for the job. Once selected, these interviewers need to be trained using a series of briefing sessions that include mock interviews and role plays as a way to assess the limitations of the fieldworkers, improve their interviewing skills, and thoroughly familiarize them with the intricacies of the interview schedule. Once trained, interviewers are assigned to a particular location, and the travel costs associated with getting to the field add a further expense to the project. In addition, once in the field, the interviewers must be continually supervised to control for potential interviewer effects and to ensure that the interviewers are completing their task as trained. Another cost is associated with noncontact or noncompletion. Noncontact refers to the interviewer being unable to establish contact with the target respondent after a number of attempts, usually four. Four trips to the field without a completed interview means a fourfold increase in unproductive travel costs. Noncompletion means that the respondent has been contacted but either refused to participate or failed to complete the interview. In both instances, a considerable degree of resources has been expended without a corresponding increase in the number of completed interviews. Although the costs of the research include those associated with uncompleted questionnaires, incomplete interviews diminish overall rates of disclosure.

Given these types of dilemmas, how have researchers coped with the problem of reducing the costs of conducting research? One common strategy is to subcontract the fieldwork to private sector research companies that specialize in data collection. The independent research company carries out the fieldwork for the principal researcher for a set fee. The difficulty with this strategy is that for subcontractors to realize a profit, they often must find ways to reduce the costs associated with data collection. For example, they might cut corners in training interviewers. A fairly standard practice for these companies is to establish an inventory of interviewers who are employed on a variety of projects subcontracted by the company. Whenever a new project is acquired, these interviewers are sent a fieldwork kit and a set of instructions by post. Because these interviewers are experienced, it is assumed that briefing sessions to sensitize them to the nuances of the project are both costly and unnecessary. Thus, the danger with subcontracting is the possibility that the interviewers are not as adept at securing disclosure as are fieldworkers who are well-trained and directly supervised by the research team. If the kind of information sought from the respondent is sensitive in nature, such as disclosure of sexual assault or wife-battering, it is often necessary for the interviewer to expend a good deal of time developing rapport with the respondent so that they feel comfortable enough to discuss painful and socially sensitive events. However, because interviewers typically are paid the same amount for each interview, regardless of whether or not the respondent discloses abuse, the interviewer has an incentive to hurry through an interview with few probing or follow-up questions. Under these conditions, the likelihood that a respondent will disclose woman abuse is diminished.

A second way to reduce the costs of survey research is to employ self-completed questionnaires or telephone interviews instead of face-to-face interviews. Both of these methods are less expensive than face-to-face interviews, although the completion rates are lower for data collected in these ways (Babbie, 1995). Putting the issue of completion rate aside, we still do not know whether women will disclose abuse in these settings. Researchers have argued that respondents are more likely to self-report socially sensitive behaviors when a state of "deindividuation" has been established. In such a state, the respondent is not merely anonymous—as when they are guaranteed confidentiality—but remains personally unknown to the interviewer. This argument suggests that both telephone surveys and self-completed questionnaires would have high rates of disclosure for the sensitive topics of physical and sexual woman abuse. At the same time, however, neither the self-completed questionnaire nor the telephone interview provides the same opportunities for the interviewer to establish rapport or motivate the respondent. The question of whether women are likely to disclose sexual or physical abuse to a stranger on the telephone or anonymously in the depersonalized context of a self-completed questionnaire has not been answered, although it remains a matter of debate. Two surveys show that the impersonal methods of telephone interview and self-completed questionnaires *can* achieve high rates of disclosure. Smith (1994) was able to produce estimates of abuse from a telephone survey that were significantly higher than those gleaned from traditional face-to-face victimization surveys, at a fraction of the cost. One of the key methodological innovations he employed was to provide the respondent with several opportunities throughout the interview to disclose the abuse. DeKeseredy (1995) draws on many of Smith's innovations in a national study of violence in dating relationships among college students. His self-completed questionnaire incorporated multiple measures that go beyond what other researchers in this field have traditionally employed, such as the Conflict Tactics Scale (CTS; Straus, 1979). Also, DeKeseredy supplemented quantitative measures of abuse with qualitative or open-ended questions that would allow the respondent to contextualize disclosed events. Because DeKeseredy was able to employ group completion of questionnaires by using the classroom setting, like Smith he reduced the costs of fieldwork.

In the final analysis, both Smith (1994) and DeKeseredy (1995) were able to improve rates of disclosure in their victimization surveys at reduced costs. However, their results are not necessarily the simple by-product of data collection methods. Unlike previous victimization surveys, these studies employed an approach to the research that paid more attention to the gendered nature of violence against women than have previous victimization surveys. Specifically, researchers approached their studies from the experiential framework of female respondents. As our data suggest, it is likely that the gender-sensitive nature of the research accounts for the higher rates of disclosure on these two surveys. Were these researchers to employ face-to-face interviews in combination with the gender-sensitive innovations they developed, it is likely that they both would have secured even higher rates of disclosure.

In summary, except in the cases of Smith (1994) and DeKeseredy (1995), the move toward cost-effective data collection methods for the study of violence against women has proven to be counterproductive when we consider that our goal is disclosure of woman abuse. Overall, methods of data collection that meet the needs of researchers for questionnaire completion from large probability samples have not been gender sensitive. Their disappointing findings on violence against women have led Chesney-Lind (1995) to complain that criminologists have been so concerned with the development of "macho methods" that they have lost sight of the purpose of victimization surveys. By *macho methods* she refers to the construction of sophisticated but nongendered approaches that are guaranteed to underestimate the extent of violence against women. However, even when these methods address the gender-specific nature of research on woman abuse, as in the cases of Smith and DeKeseredy, the necessity for cost-effective data collection means that researchers cannot always conduct face-to-face interviews.

Improving the Rates of Disclosure

As argued previously, the key challenge for researchers of violence against women is to provide a research design and method of data collection that encourage the respondent to disclose incidents of abuse to the researcher. Clearly, such a task requires methodologies that are sensitive to the gender dynamics of both woman abuse and the interview as a context within which the disclosure of abuse is encouraged. As feminists have argued, these considerations are likely to transform the way in which we approach research. They claim that traditional methodologies silence women and render their experiences invisible because data collection methods are typically seen as an instrument of data collection and an opportunity to manipulate the respondent in a "pseudo-conversation" that serves the researcher's rather than the respondent's needs (Oakley, 1981).

Within criminology, the invisibility of women is reflected in large-scale national victimization surveys that lead to the conclusion that crimes such as domestic violence and sexual assault are infrequent (Currie & MacLean, 1993). This invisibility has fostered two types of feminist critique of victimization surveys. In the first variant, researchers are criticized for being masculinist in their approach, failing to be sensitive to the gender issues that surround violence against women. Although most researchers would agree that violence against women is a gendered phenomenon, few are gender sensitive in their methodological innovation. The work of Diana Russell (1982b) attempts to address this point.

Russell (1982b) conducted an innovative replication study on sexual assault against women for one of the geographic locations and for the same time period as one of the sweeps of the National Crime Survey in the United States. Although she was careful to employ similar indicators and sampling techniques as the NCS, she also incorporated a number of key methodological innovations pertaining to the selection and training of interviewers. These included the following:

- An interview schedule designed to encourage good rapport with the respondent
- Selection of interviewers based on interviewing skills and sensitivity to sexual assault
- Extensive training of interviewers that included education about rape and sexual abuse and desensitization of sexual language used in the interview by the interviewer
- Matching interviewers with respondents on ethnic background
- Paying respondents 10 dollars for participation

The logic of Russell's (1982b) replication strategy is experimental. By controlling for all other variables in the design and the application of her study so that they matched the approach of the NCS, any differences that she might discover between her findings and those of the NCS would have to be the result of the methodological innovations described previously. In fact, Russell found a rate of sexual assault in her study that was 700% higher than that found on the NCS for the same period and geographic location. Her work made it clear that the crafting and use of more gender-sensitive methodologies than those employed on the NCS can yield dramatic increases in rates of disclosure.

The second variant of critique involves criticism of the victimization surveys for using male interviewers. For example, in the first sweep of the British Crime Survey (BCS; Hough & Mayhew, 1983), only one case of attempted rape was identified in 11,000 interviews. Although it may be true that only half of the sample were women, only one case of attempted rape among 5,500 female respondents clearly underestimates the frequency of sexual violence against women. Ruth Hall (1985) criticizes the BCS for using male interviewers and claims that this is the primary reason for its pitiful estimates. In her own study, Hall employed female interviewers, a different kind of sampling design than the BCS, and indicators that measure sexual violence over the respondent's lifetime. This latter innovation differs from the BCS in two important ways. First, the BCS asks respondents about only the previous calendar year, while Hall (1985) asks about lifetime experiences. Second, the target population for the BCS is people aged 16 years or older, whereas Hall's study, because of the lifetime measure, would capture cases of violence that occurred when respondents were under the age of 16.

Although the BCS argues that one woman in 5,500 would be the victim of an attempted rape in the survey year, Hall (1985) finds that about one in five women would be the victim of an attempted rape over a lifetime. In addition, although the BCS finds no other forms of sexual violence, Hall's study estimates that almost one in two women would experience a rape, sexual assault, or attempted rape during their lifetime.

Although it is clear that Hall's (1985) estimates dramatically exceed those of the BCS, we remain unconvinced that the difference is simply caused by the sex of interviewers. Nevertheless, the work of Russell (1982b) and Hall raises an important but neglected question: What role does the sex of the interviewer play in rates of disclosure by victims of violence against women? We address this question more fully in a following section. Before we do, one further problem requires attention: As feminists and researchers, what do we do when a respondent does disclose an incident of violence?

After Disclosure: Now What?

Aside from the measurement issues discussed previously, there are three ethical issues pertaining to the study of violence against women. First, there is the ethical issue of including juveniles in the study. Although it is clear from work such as Hall's (1985) that the mode of the age/risk curve for sexual assault is approximately 14 years of age, to include girls at this age in any survey would mean having to secure parental permission. Researchers have been remiss in this task because it is not clear how this cumbersome requirement would increase disclosure. For example, parents might require that they are present for the interview. A girl would be extremely unlikely to disclose an incident to an interviewer in the presence of a parent to whom the child has not already disclosed. For this reason, researchers such as Hall

(1985) and DeKeseredy (1995) have employed retrospective measures. In this way, the highest risk age-group can be identified without the ethical difficulty of interviewing juvenile girls.

A second ethical issue concerns the effect of the interview on a respondent who discloses a painful and personal incident. Because the primary target group is women who have been abused but who have not reported the abuse, we are often asking women to disclose, perhaps for the first time: This disclosure can have long-term effects. This problem is not an argument against research on violence against women, however. Research that is sensitive to this issue shows that disclosure in such a setting can be a process through which the respondent's experiences are validated. As such, the interview has the potential to be a first step in addressing the abusive situation. However, it means that the interview may be creating a situation in which some form of professional intervention is required. The researcher must be prepared to deal with this kind of problem should it emerge. Interviewers must be well-trained to observe signs of this kind of reaction and be equipped to refer the respondent to appropriate helping agencies such as Women Against Violence Against Women, rape crisis centers, women's aid groups, and so forth. The researcher is obligated by the ethics of conducting research on human subjects to ensure that the respondent's well-being is not jeopardized by the encounter. The respondent must be aware of the potential harm and decide to proceed in spite of this potential. This notion is referred to as informed consent to participate; however, even with informed consent, it is still the responsibility of the researcher to either minimize the potential harm to the respondent or to provide avenues for the debriefing and rehabilitation of the respondent, should that be necessary.

Third, and of most importance to the current discussion, is the ethical problem raised by disclosure in the presence of an abusive spouse or partner. To illustrate this problem, let us paint two scenarios.

In the first scenario, the researcher is interviewing a woman who is being battered on a regular basis by an abusive husband. The interview is taking place in the respondent's kitchen. In the respondent's living room is a husband who is drinking beer, eating popcorn, and watching the football game on television, with one ear tuned into the interview going on in the kitchen. When the interviewer begins the questions about assault, the respondent discloses that her husband is indeed abusive. However, the disclosure is overheard by the husband, who enters the kitchen, terminates the interview, and promptly demands that the interviewer leave. Are the interviewers or researchers prepared to take the responsibility for the respondent's black eye the next morning? If not, then they cannot ethically conduct the interview.

In the second scenario, the respondent is the principal wage-earner in the family, and her husband is unemployed. She works at an office job in a clerical capacity for a low wage, yet her wage is the sole source of income of the household. At her job, she is being continually sexually harassed by her male supervisor, yet she endures the harassment for fear of losing her job. Because her husband is quite possessive and dominant, she dare not disclose to him the problem at work for fear that he may show up at the workplace and take matters into his own hands resulting in the respondent's loss of work. Again, during the interview, the husband overhears the disclosure by his spouse to an interviewer. Are the interviewers or researchers prepared to accept the responsibility for the respondent being terminated from her family's only source of income? If not, then they cannot ethically conduct the interview.

As suggested previously, in the face-to-face interview situation, there are often times when husbands, partners, and so forth may be in a position to overhear the interview, with serious repercussions for the respondent. Researchers must find a way to deal with this ethical problem before going into the field; otherwise, they may be placing respondents in a dangerous situation to collect information from them. The Islington Crime Survey (discussed in the next section) explores some possibilities in coming to terms with this problem.

The Interview as a Gendered Social Encounter

THE ISLINGTON CRIME SURVEY

Financed by the London Borough of Islington, the Islington Crime Survey (Jones et al., 1986) was a cross-sectional survey that measured 550 crime and policing variables in inner-city London. Fieldwork for the study was conducted during spring 1985, with 1,977 respondents interviewed in a face-to-face setting about incidents of household and personal victimization in 1984. A total of 897 respondents were identified as victims of burglary, vandalism, theft from person, assault, and sexual assault. These respondents were interviewed a second time about their experiences as victims of those crimes. For purposes of this discussion, we shall restrict ourselves to the problems associated with the investigation for the sexual assault and domestic assault (a subcategory of assault) victims.

Background to the Fieldwork

In preparing to conduct the ICS, it was important not only to grasp the problems associated with the disclosure of violence against women in incidents such as those enumerated previously but also to develop practical research strategies to overcome these problems to carry out the research. Following from the previous discussion, two important issues were considered in the ICS: Are male or female interviewers more likely to obtain a higher rate of disclosure? How can researchers deal with the ethical problems of disclosure? At the time, the work of both Hall (1985) and Russell (1982b) was seen to indicate that, for violence against women, female interviewers would be more likely to secure the kind of rapport necessary to facilitate disclosure by female respondents. However, a careful review of the methodological innovations employed in those two studies suggested to us that such a conclusion is not necessarily correct. In short, commonsense assumptions are being made about the way gender operates in an interview situation. Although it is true that all people must make assumptions to proceed, assumptions usually refer to notions about the nature of things that cannot be empirically tested. Fortunately, we can test empirically whether or not the sex of the interviewer has an effect on disclosure by the respondent. Rather than leave this important decision to assumption, a good scientist would rather test the idea and then proceed in the way best illustrated by the data.

Because debate surrounding this subject was not empirical, a series of unstructured interviews with woman abuse shelter workers was conducted in the hope of determining how to proceed with the selection of interviewers. We wanted to draw on the experiential knowledge of those who are likely to be sensitive to the needs of victims of male violence. These interviews were important because they challenged the conventional wisdom of the time. Specifically, this wisdom directed us to the conclusion that female interviewers would secure higher rates of disclosure than their male counterparts because they would be most attuned to the needs of women. Against this view, shelter workers were of the opinion that, although women would be more comfortable disclosing incidents of sexual assault to a female interviewer, they would be more likely to disclose domestic violence to a male. The logic behind these perceptions was that, in the case of wife-battery, the respondent would be concerned that a female interviewer would be making clandestine judgments about the respondent's abilities to perform her wifely role. A male interviewer, in contrast, would be seen by the respondent to be more sympathetic and less judgmental of the respondent than a female interviewer. In the case of sexual assault, however, the shelter workers argued that a male interviewer would be associated with the male perpetrator and his presence would serve to silence the respondent. A female interviewer, in contrast, would be seen by the respondent as sympathetic, concerned, and supportive, and she would therefore be more likely to encourage a disclosure.

The information gleaned from the shelter workers led to two very important conclusions. First, it was clear that, although many people working in the field of violence against women have definite beliefs about the way the sex of the interviewer affects disclosure of woman abuse, these ideas are based on conjecture, not empirical evidence. As a consequence, the ICS presented an attractive opportunity to answer the question empirically.

Second, these beliefs about which sex would make a better interviewer are based on a limited understanding of gender dynamics. Specifically, the notion of matching female interviewers with female respondents assumes that processes of gender operate only across genders. In other words, this position advances the notion that, during an interview, gender processes occur between men and women. Yet gender dynamics clearly operate in an all-female setting, in an all-male setting, and in a mixed-gender setting. To match female respondents with interviewers of the same sex does not mean that gender processes are eliminated—only that they take on a different form. Whether or not this variant of gender dynamics is more conducive to disclosure is an empirical, not a theoretical, question.

In terms of the ethical dimension referred to previously, the ICS developed a method, not as yet used elsewhere, that protects the respondent while allowing disclosure when interviews are conducted in the respondent's home. Very simply, the questions pertaining to assault and sexual assault were reproduced identically on separate sheets of paper for self-completion. Rather than ask the respondent these questions directly, interviewers were instructed to use the self-completion sheet in cases where husbands were at home and in approximately 50% of the cases overall that involved a female respondent. We term this approach an indirect method of questioning.

Selection, Training, and Supervision of Interviewers

There are a number of complex methodological concerns raised by the recognition of the interview as a gendered social encounter. Clearly, no single study can adequately deal with such concerns; however, the advancement of knowledge often comes in small steps. For the ICS, it was determined that some key methodological innovations, in part derived from Russell's (1982b) pioneering work, are necessary if research on violence against women is to be gender sensitive while improving rates of disclosure. These innovations included the following:

- An interview schedule designed to encourage good rapport
- Selection of interviewers based on interviewing skills and sensitivity to gendered processes
- Extensive training of interviewers in relation to sexual and physical assaults on women and their investigation in the field, including the effect of gender in the interview situation
- A carefully controlled experimental design that would allow comparisons across different interviewing situations (following)
- Use of an indirect questioning procedure (discussed previously) that would help to reduce embarrassment or difficulty of relating the incident directly to the interviewer

All interviewers were required to attend a series of at least three briefings specifically designed to improve their productivity in the field. Seminars were presented on topics such as interviewing technique, strategy, and tactics, and the role of gender-specific facilitators and inhibitors. These sessions included discussions on topics such as nonverbal communication in the interview, how communication is mediated by gender, and how such knowledge might be used to quickly develop rapport with the respondent. Interviewers were also briefed on the nature of the project, the gender-sensitive issues involved, the contents of both questionnaires, the potential points of trouble in the schedules, and how these might be avoided or dealt with. They were also instructed on delicate topics, such as sexual and domestic assault, and told under what conditions they should use the self-completion, indirect method of questioning to the best advantage. Because a number of the items on the schedules were open-ended, interviewers were instructed about how to probe, what kind of information to look for, how to record responses accurately, and how to be sensitive to the gender dynamics of the process. The potential for referral of respondents to support services was emphasized, and all fieldworkers were equipped with appropriate materials for distribution. Finally, so that any difficulties might be identified and corrected early, interviewers engaged in mock interviews under supervision. After the briefing sessions, only those considered to be appropriately equipped to conduct the research were hired.

Interviewers were also supervised in the field. For purposes of this discussion, the key aspect involved supervised interviews. All interviewers were instructed to carry out no less than two and no more than three interviews before contacting the field supervisor to arrange a supervised interview. In this way, interviewers would have the opportunity to become comfortable with the interview schedule; however, if they were engaging a style that was unsuitable, this could be identified and corrected before too many interviews had been completed. After the supervised interview, the interviewer was briefed by the field supervisor, during which the strengths of the interviewer's style were reinforced. Also, points on which the interviewer might improve were raised by the field supervisor, who provided further instruction. In this way, the research team had the opportunity to view the entire range of interviewing on the project and to develop a greater degree of interviewer uniformity. In addition, the field supervision staff made follow-up visits to about 16% of the respondents. This strategy not only allowed for a check on the interviewers, but it also provided the research team with the opportunity to debrief respondents in cases in which it was necessary.

Finally, all of the interviewers were assigned a unique code that would allow for statistical control at the data analysis stage of the research. This strategy was not a new idea; researchers often use the interviewer as a variable in the study to control for interviewer effects. However, the unique strategy for the ICS was to allocate interviewers into a set of experimental conditions so that we might identify the conditions most conducive to disclosure. These experimental conditions are described in the following section.

Four Experimental Conditions

Methodological innovation often comes from methodological experimentation. Although it may be true that few researchers have the luxury to simply proceed with experimental methodologies, the wise researcher should, when possible, incorporate a methodological experiment as a way of providing empirical answers to methodological questions. The purpose of the ICS was not to conduct a methodological experiment; however, because much of the contemporary methodology employed in research on violence against women was based on assumptions and because the target sample was large (some 2,000 cases), it became clear that it would be possible to incorporate a methodological experiment into the survey.

Two questions were explored by the experimental design: Which interviewers achieve the higher rate of disclosure—males or females? Which method of questioning—direct or indirect—produces the higher rate of disclosure? In this way, there are two variables (sex of interviewer; method of questioning) with two values each (male vs. female; direct vs. indirect, respectively) that, when combined, yield four experimental conditions. If the interviewers were to follow instructions, about 250 female respondents would fall into each of the four conditions (i.e., 2,000 respondents, half of which are female, divided equally into four experimental conditions). The four conditions are labeled as follows:

- Female interviewers with female respondents questioned directly
- Female interviewers with female respondents questioned indirectly
- Male interviewers with female respondents questioned directly
- Male interviewers with female respondents questioned indirectly

At the conclusion of the fieldwork, the data were partitioned into these four experimental categories and the proportion of the overall disclosures—for both wife assault and sexual assault—attributable to each condition was articulated and compared. Let us now look at the results from this experiment.

Findings From the Experiment

Disclosures for sexual assault have been grouped into the four experimental conditions in Table 12.1. From Table 12.1, two important findings can be observed. First, in this sample, more respondents disclosed incidents of sexual assault to male interviewers than to female interviewers. About two thirds of all the sexual assault disclosures were attributable to male interviewers, with the remainder attributable to female interviewers. Second, disclosure rates were higher in the direct condition (about two thirds of cases

TABLE 12.1 Rates of Disclosure for Sexual Assault in Four Experimental Conditions

Experimental Condition	*Percentage of Victims Disclosing*
Female/Female Direct	29.6
Female/Female Indirect	7.4
Male/Female Direct	37.1
Male/Female Indirect	25.9
	100.0

BASE: All female victims of sexual assault, unweighted data.
SOURCE: MacLean, 1989, p. 211.

TABLE 12.2 Rates of Disclosure for Domestic Assault in Four Experimental Conditions

Experimental Condition	*Percentage of Victims Disclosing*
Female/Female Direct	28.2
Female/Female Indirect	10.3
Male/Female Direct	41.0
Male/Female Indirect	20.5
	100.0

BASE: All female victims of domestic assault, unweighted data.
SOURCE: Islington Crime Survey data file, 1986.

disclosed) compared to those in the indirect condition (about one third of disclosures).

Patterns of disclosures of wife assault are similar to those found for sexual assault. Disclosures for wife assault have been grouped into the four experimental conditions in Table 12.2. From Table 12.2, two important findings can be observed. First, as in the case of sexual assault, more respondents disclosed incidents of wife assault to the male interviewers. About 60% of all the wife assault disclosures was attributable to male interviewers, with the remainder attributable to female interviewers. Again, disclosure rates were higher in the direct condition (about 70% of cases disclosed) compared to those in the indirect condition (about 30% disclosures).

What do these two types of findings tell us about the most appropriate methodology for research on male violence? Furthermore, what do these types of findings tell us more generally about "gender-sensitive" research?

Approaches to answering these questions are explored in our concluding discussion.

Conclusion

Although the Islington Crime Survey is survey research, it offered the research team an opportunity to conduct a mini-experiment that would explore controversial issues in the measurement of violence against women. Emphasizing the tentative nature of our conclusions, we offer two findings for exploration in future research.

The first conclusion concerns the benefits of direct versus indirect questioning about male violence against women. As we have seen, the necessity for large samples means that victimization surveys are costly endeavors. As a consequence, much effort has been expended to reduce the costs of fieldwork. In this regard, telephone surveys and self-completed questionnaires are promising approaches to data collection. Besides reducing the costs of travel, they represent labor-saving methods. Significantly, there are grounds to believe that they also encourage higher rates of disclosure. If this latter argument is correct, all of these factors render telephone interviews and self-completed questionnaires more desirable than face-to-face interviews. As seen in Table 12.1, however, about two thirds of the disclosures of woman abuse on the ICS came from direct rather than indirect questioning. Thus, despite theoretical grounds for predicting that indirect questioning—such as self-completed questionnaires—reduces the anxiety of disclosing a personally sensitive life event, our empirical evidence suggests that face-to-face interviews are more conducive to disclosure by victims of woman abuse.

The second issue explored through the Islington Crime Survey concerns the ideal sex of interviewers for research on violence against women. Given the gendered nature of the subject matter, feminists have pointed to the need for gender-sensitive methods of research. Although much debate surrounds exactly what "gender-sensitive" research entails, conventional wisdom has led many writers to believe that female interviewers would be the most appropriate choice for research on violence against women. This conventional wisdom is based on two claims implicit in (much) literature on feminist research. The first claim, found in the work of the "first" woman sociologist, Harriett Martineau, is that women are likely to be better researchers than men when it comes to qualitative research, such as personal interviews. Although most draw this claim from the fact that women are socialized to a greater extent than men to be "good listeners," to be supportive in conversational contexts, and to decode nonverbal communication, this fact is often translated into an apparently self-evident assumption that women will *necessarily* exhibit these qualities when conducting research on women. The second claim, related to but distinct from the first, is that interviewing is inherently a feminist—therefore gendered—research method. This claim is implicit in the early work of British sociologist Ann Oakley (1981). She found it impossible to maintain a detached but seemingly personal relationship with women as they shared their experiences of motherhood. The problem for Oakley was that women often "asked questions back," primarily because, unlike her, they defined data collection in terms of friendship rather than research. In the final analysis, Oakley decided that interviewing women is a contradiction in terms because the traditional interview is a masculine paradigm. In its place, she suggested that interviewing should be a strategy for documenting women's own accounts of their lives. In effect, she regarded "sociological research as an essential way of giving the subjective situation of women greater visibility not only in sociology, but, more importantly, in society" (p. 48).

Much of the early research on violence against women benefited from the feminist promotion of qualitative research as a way for women to "tell their own stories" of abuse. For example, the works of Pizzey (1974), MacLeod (1980), and many others are filled with quotes and stories from women about their experiences of abuse. These stories identify the nature of the problem of woman abuse, including unsupportive and judgmental responses by "helping" agencies such as the criminal justice system, social services, and the general public. However, like much of the gender research during the 1970s and into the 1980s, most of this early work was exploratory in nature; although it was useful in advancing our understanding of the *nature* of woman abuse, it failed to provide the type of information necessary to develop effective strategies of intervention. Although the former requires a study of social processes through which male domination is maintained in small-group settings, the latter requires documentation of patterns across populations. For this reason, feminist approaches to violence against women currently embrace both qualitative and quantitative approaches. Few feminists continue to maintain that a single feminist methodology is either possible or desirable (Currie, 1988).

Feminists have made significant innovations in developing survey research technology that is sensitive to the gendered nature of research on violence against women. For the most part, these innovations attempt to address the complaint that survey research is problematic because it employs distanced measures that "objectify" victims and ignore the subjective elements of woman abuse (Kelly & Radford, 1987). One response by researchers has been to define violence and abuse in ways that include psychological and spiritual dimensions (MacLeod & DeKeseredy, 1996). Another has been to critically reconsider the conditions in which women are asked to disclose violence. Along these lines, the commonsense assumption has prevailed that women are more comfortable disclosing male violence to other women. However appealing, as shown by findings from the ICS, this assumption oversimplifies the nature of gender dynamics in everyday interactions, including those of the interview setting.

When we look at the findings from the ICS, it is apparent that the argument in favor of women-only interview teams conflates sex and gender. This strategy tends to valorize notions about gender characterized in the work of some radical feminists. In contrast to portrayals of women as empathetic listeners who are attuned to the needs of others, these writers portray men as inherently aggressive, controlling, and unable to empathize with the suffering of others. One logical conclusion of this position—one we do not support—is that only women can "do feminism." Furthermore, this position implies that gender dynamics occur between gender groups, not within gender groups (in this case, women). Suggested by Table 12.2, we need to reconsider how gender actually operates in the context of disclosing violence against women. We have noted earlier that patriarchal ideologies about male violence place the blame for woman abuse on women, and there is no reason to believe that many abused women will not subscribe to this view. For example, in a campus survey of violence against women, Currie (1995) was surprised to find that a significant proportion of undergraduate women held women responsible for rape through the ways they dressed or acted. Following from this, it is possible that an abused woman may relive feelings about her abuse that include anger, depression, and guilt, and may experience the interview as testifying to her failure as a "good woman." As shelter workers predicted and our data suggest, if abused women have internalized patriarchal ideologies that blame women, they may be reluctant to disclose to other women that they have failed in one of the most important missions in a woman's life: to "catch a good man." Regardless of how "sisterly" a feminist researcher may feel toward other women, there is no guarantee that respondents perceive other women as necessarily supportive.

In the final analysis, further research is required to better understand how gender operates in the research setting. Here we do not advance the position that male interviewers will necessarily elicit higher rates of disclosure on woman abuse, even though our data make it tempting to do so. Rather, we suggest that because gendered modes of interacting are learned behaviors, well-trained interviewers—male and female—can acquire a manner of interacting that is both gender-sensitive and characteristic of good interviewing practice.

In the ICS, training of fieldworkers was given precedence over simply selecting female interviewers with the expectation that women would "naturally" do better research. Training included gender-sensitization and education about male violence against women. This training probably accounts for more of the observed differences in disclosure than do sex-related factors. However, this is not to suggest that we can eliminate gender in the interview setting by producing a team of nongendered, androgynous interviewers. Rather, by recognizing the gendered nature of the interview as a social encounter, we can better prepare our interviewers to elicit disclosure of violence against women. In this way, estimates of the patterns of woman abuse will be more accurate than those produced by approaches that are not gender-sensitive.

In closing, sociologists are a long way from being able to stipulate exactly what constitutes "gender-sensitive" research. We offer three points for consideration. First, gender-sensitive research is aware of the effect of the social investigation of human relations. As a result, it actively attempts to ensure that the needs of respondents will be met in the research setting. Second, the sex of the researcher *does* make a difference when, as sociologists and as human beings, we enter the research setting. However, as argued here, the effect of gender is another matter. We suggest that although respondents may indeed react to the fact of whether a fieldworker is male or female, the interviewer does not necessarily follow a gender script. Third, because this latter point makes the picture more and not less complex, gender-sensitive research strives to identify how social attitudes about or by women and men enter into the research setting. As we have attempted to show here, their effects may not follow "commonsense" assumptions or wishful thinking on the part of researchers.

CHAPTER

13

Studying Violence Against Women of Color

Problems Faced by a White Woman

KIMBERLY A. HUISMAN

White middle-class women have been criticized by some for generalizing their own experiences to all women while excluding the experiences of women of color (hooks, 1984; Lorde, 1984; Mohanty, 1991). In recent years, however, many white feminists have been very careful not to speak of "women's experience" in a monolithic way and have begun to acknowledge that "women come only in different classes, races and cultures: there is no 'woman' and no 'woman's experience' " (Harding, 1987, p. 7). A debate remains, however, over whether white women should engage in cross-race research. Can a white female researcher studying the experiences of women of color enlarge our knowledge and understanding of the social world? Can white women understand the experiences of groups that have been deemed (by whites) as outsiders? Do white women have the right to peer into the lives of women of color? In this chapter, I will argue that cross-race research can be epistemologically beneficial if the researcher addresses particular methodological issues. Drawing from my own qualitative research, which focused on the specific needs of battered Asian women from various ethnic groups, I will discuss the challenges I faced and the methods and strategies I found most helpful throughout my research. Before turning to my own experiences, I will briefly discuss the debate in the literature over the legitimacy of cross-race research.

Debate Over the Legitimacy of Cross-Race Research

There is a long history of exclusion and marginalization of people of color in the United States. People of color are very familiar with being ignored or being reduced to a stereotype or a footnote in American discourse. One does not have to go very far to find examples of this; reading through a traditional high school history book illustrates this point well. What is important to note is that the perpetrators of this exclusionism have usually been white. Historically, white scholars have done more damage than good; people of color have been treated as objects rather than as subjects of historical experiences (Asante, 1993). No wonder there is considerable doubt over whether white scholars can produce knowledge about people of color. Patricia Hill Collins (1990) argues that,

> Because elite white men and their representatives control structures of knowledge validation, white male interests pervade the thematic content of traditional scholarship. As a result, Black women's experiences with work, family, motherhood, political activism, and sexual politics have been routinely distorted in or excluded from traditional academic discourse. (p. 201)

In social science literature, arguments about the legitimacy of cross-race research lie on a continuum. At one extreme on this continuum is the argument that race makes no difference when engaging in social research because we live in a "colorblind" society. Frankenberg (1993) refers to this as "color and power evasiveness." Those who argue that race is not of central importance "reduce race to a mere manifestation of other supposedly more fundamental social and political relationships such as ethnicity or class" (Omi & Winant, 1994, p. 2). Such theorists would argue that anyone can engage in cross-race research because race is not an important social category. Proponents of this perspective may be either entrenched in positivism, thus succumbing to the fallacy that there exists objective truth, or oblivious to the central role played by race and racial privilege in the United States. As Peggy McIntosh (1988) argues, those who have privilege have a tendency not to recognize their dominant position in society. Furthermore, many who are cognizant of the privilege afforded by race, class, or gender may feel a sense of entitlement about their privilege and employ white rationalizations of privilege (Feagin & Vera, 1995). Clearly, this approach to race ignores systems of power and denies the historical legacy of racism and discrimination in the United States.

Theorists at the other extreme of the continuum claim that race is the primary analytical category and therefore takes precedence over other social categories, such as class and gender. Such theorists argue that white women have no right studying women of color. For example, one theorist argues,

> Academic work is conducted within a social context in which racism means that black people are socially devalued and white people are socially valued. Most researchers are white, and as a result are likely not to share the same perspectives as black people. Research therefore must be suspect when conducted within the value systems of a racist society. This means that when comparisons are made between groups of black people and groups of white people research continues to construct white people as the norm and black people as abnormal by comparison. (Phoenix, 1987, p. 51)

In a similar vein, early standpoint theorists, who were greatly influenced by Marxist positivism, argued that minority groups possessed a clearer vision of the social world because of their oppressed position in society (Collins, 1990). In other words, groups that were pushed to the bottom of the social hierarchy possessed a clearer vision of oppression than groups that were more privileged. Advocates of this position were in search of "Truth" and failed to acknowledge that there are multiple perspectives and no absolute truth.

Somewhere in the middle of these two extremes lies an argument that views race, class, and gender as interlocking systems of oppression (Anderson, 1993; Collins, 1990; Glenn, 1986). Most proponents of this position agree that doing research outside of your race, class, or gender can be valuable as long as researchers are careful not to place their own experiences at the center and view the experiences of their research subjects as peripheral. Advocates of this position also acknowledge that all of these categories of oppression are equally important components that constitute the complex web of hierarchical societal arrangements. Their level of importance varies by context; in one context, race may be of primary importance, whereas in another, class or gender may take precedence. Although this paradigm is a strand of standpoint theory, which acknowledges that members of subordinated groups have unique viewpoints based on their own experiences, it does not regard these viewpoints as "absolute truth." Patricia Hill Collins (1990) argues that,

> Despite African-American women's potential power to reveal new insights about the matrix of domination, a Black women's standpoint is only one angle of vision. Thus Black feminist thought represents a partial perspective. The overarching matrix of domination houses multiple groups, each with varying experiences with penalty and privilege that produce corresponding partial perspectives, situated knowledges, and, for clearly identifiable subordinate groups, subjugated knowledges. No group has a clear angle of vision. (p. 234)

Although it is important to recognize that it may be more difficult to engage in cross-race research than same-race research, I believe that many of the problems encountered are not insurmountable. I agree with Margaret Anderson (1993), who acknowledges that "minority scholars are less likely to experience distrust, hostility, and exclusion within minority communities" that ultimately may affect their research findings (p. 41). However, I also agree with the claim that it is possible for white scholars to obtain epistemologically valuable information about race, particularly "when studying situations which are not directly concerned with theories of race, but in which race plays a part" (Edwards, 1990, p. 48). My research on wife battering is an example of this. I argue that women who are battered by their male partners and who view themselves as victims or survivors of battering are likely to experience a common resistance to male violence and domination that often takes precedence over issues concerning race. Although race played an important part in my research, I found that it was possible to overcome some divisions of race when studying violence against women. Because violence against women transcends all boundaries, including race, ethnicity, class, age, sexual orientation, and religion, there is some common ground on which one can stand when doing research in this area. However, as Reissman (1987) found in her research, gender congruency is not always enough to create shared understandings between the researcher and the subjects of research. Before addressing this important point, I will briefly discuss my own research, which I will continue to refer to throughout the chapter.

Brief Review of My Research

I became interested in wife battering during my first year of graduate school at a university located in a city on the East Coast. I was initially inspired to study violence against women by a professor who had been working in this area for over a decade, and I decided to further my understanding of wife battering by volunteering at a local domestic violence shelter. To work as a volunteer at the East Coast shelter, I had to complete a 40-hour training program. Toward the end of the training, my interest shifted from wife battering in general to wife battering in Asian communities. One of the guest speakers at the training session was a woman from Laos, who explained to us that the needs of battered Asian women are different from the needs of women from other racial and ethnic groups and that services for Asian women are practically nonexistent, particularly for Asian women who do not speak English. I was struck by the fact that, unlike most other racial and ethnic groups in the United States, Asians have no common language or culture. Despite the fact that they are all lumped together by mainstream society, each Asian ethnic group has its own unique language, culture, and history. By the time I left that training session, my head was spinning with ideas and questions, and it was then that I decided to do research in this area. Specifically, my research focused on identifying the specific needs of battered Asian women and delineating the various structural and cultural barriers that inhibit Asian women from securing help from mainstream social service providers.

In my research, I chose for several reasons to interview people who work with battered Asian women rather than interviewing the battered women themselves. First, the people I interviewed had extensive knowledge about and experience working with battered Asian women from various Asian ethnic groups and were able to elaborate on many of the issues in which I was interested. Second, because I was interested in the experiences of Asian women with deep historical roots in this country in addition to recently arrived immigrant and refugee women who did not speak English, I decided to interview bilingual service providers who had experience working with both populations. If I had decided to interview the women themselves, I would have been restricted to interviewing only English-speaking women. Third, because there is a stigma in many Asian groups about "airing your dirty laundry," it was questionable whether battered Asian women would be willing to discuss such a sensitive topic with me, a monolingual white woman.

To gain access to people who work with battered Asian women, I volunteered at domestic violence shelters that provided services for battered Asian women. I conducted my research in two stages. In the first stage, as mentioned previously, while residing on the East Coast, I volunteered at a battered women's shelter located in a city with a high Asian population. While later attending graduate school on the West Coast, I volunteered at a battered women's shelter that was established to meet the needs of Asian women. My decision to work in this setting was motivated by my desire to learn more about the communities, to increase my understanding of wife battering, to establish contacts, to gain trust, and ultimately to do my research.

Gaining initial access to the setting was not very difficult. Most shelters are underfunded, in need of extra help, and usually welcome volunteers. However, it didn't take long to realize that although I worked almost exclusively with other women in these settings, gender congruity, a mutual commitment to ending violence against women, and a feminist identity were not enough to form an immediate alliance with them. I met several challenges along the way, most of which centered around gaining trust. I will discuss these issues in the next section.[1]

Challenges of My Research

I was faced with many challenges in my research, but there were two that stand above the rest in terms of difficulty to overcome. In general, I was viewed as an outsider on two dimensions. First, I was the only white woman working at the shelter. Almost everyone I worked with at one time or another questioned my motivations for volunteering at the shelter. Although this was usually done in a very polite manner, I was acutely aware of their suspicions of me. I was met with questions such as, "Why are you interested in this topic?" and "Why are you doing this research?" Although at times I felt very isolated and insecure in this environment, overall, I remained hopeful that this obstacle could be overcome gradually.

Second, I was the only academic working in this environment. All of the women I worked with viewed themselves as activists and practitioners. Many of the women had earned their master's degrees in social work or family counseling and were much more concerned with activism and the practical, everyday experiences of women than in academic discourse. In fact, several of the women expressed very negative views of academia at one time or another. Generally, academics were considered to be "part of the problem, not part of the solution for battered women" (Hoff, 1988, p. 275). I found that this was exacerbated even further by my affiliation with a private university that has a reputation and legacy of being very conservative and elitist. In contrast, most of my coworkers had attended one of the state universities in the area, which were known for their more liberal and inclusive policies. Thus, there were not only racial differences but also perceived (not necessarily actual) class differences that expanded the chasm between us.

I feel that because of these two issues—my race and my affiliation with a private university—I was met with extreme caution and distance. I was acutely aware of this distance and, after careful thought, understood and accepted their skepticism. Initially, I was naive and saw myself as being aligned with them, and could not fully understand why they did not view me as being on their side. After all, we were all feminists working toward the same goal of ending violence against women.

Fortunately, over time I was able to overcome these two obstacles to a large extent, and this enabled me to establish relationships with my coworkers and proceed with my research. Overcoming these obstacles took time, commitment, and careful thought. I invested as much time and effort into volunteering at the shelter as possible, and I kept a journal of fieldnotes in which I explored the many obstacles and issues that were arising. These two approaches helped to facilitate my awareness and gain the trust of my coworkers. Thus, because of my awareness and understanding about how I was being perceived, I was able to respond in an advantageous way. I shared a similar experience to that of Lee Ann Hoff (1988):

> Overtly, my professional preparation was a clear liability in establishing trust and rapport; covertly, it was an asset in helping me understand the dynamic process and regulate my behavior accordingly. (p. 275)

To help alleviate the problems I faced, I took several steps, which I will discuss in the next section of the paper. I will address the different stages of my research and specifically discuss the methods and strategies I found helpful at each stage. Although I focus specifically on Asian women, to a large extent this discussion can be applied to studying wife battering among women of color in general and to a lesser extent, to studying groups with whom you do not share membership.

METHODS AND STRATEGIES EMPLOYED TO OVERCOME OBSTACLES

I employed various strategies to overcome the obstacles I faced throughout the research. I will address the strategies I found helpful at each stage of the research and conclude by delineating some of my findings. I believe that the strategies I used were paramount in allowing me to obtain rich, detailed information from the people I interviewed.

Stage I: Prior to Entry

There are two things that helped prepare me for my entry into this research setting: my feminist orientation and my training in qualitative methods. Without training in these two areas, I do not believe I would have gotten very far in this research. My research was guided by several goals of feminist scholarship throughout the entire process. Although there is no one feminist method, there are several features that are universal to feminist methodologies. First, there is the importance of doing research *for* women rather than just *about* women (Smith, 1974). I adhered to this principle throughout the entire research process, which included the final stage of writing my results. Because the primary goal of my research was to improve the lives of battered women, I felt it was exceedingly important to write in a way that was accessible to all women rather than writing solely for an academic audience. After I gained entry, it was very important for me to convey this goal to my coworkers because this very issue may lie at the heart of the rift between academics and practitioners. For researchers to "use" people for their own professional gain is not unheard of (Gorelick, 1991; Hoff, 1988).

A second important feminist principle that guided my research was viewing myself as being on the same plane as the people I interviewed (Billson,

1991; Harding, 1987; Stacey, 1988). Contrary to traditional positivist methodology, which views the researcher as the "knower" and the relationship between the researcher and the research subjects as hierarchical, feminist methodologies emphasize that

> the best feminist analysis . . . insists that the inquirer her/himself must be placed in the same critical plane as the overt subject matter, thereby recovering the entire research process for scrutiny in the results of the research. That is, the class, race, culture, and gender assumptions, beliefs, and behaviors of the researcher her/himself be placed within the frame of the picture that she/he attempts to paint. . . . Thus the researcher appears to us not as an invisible, anonymous voice of authority, but as a real, historical individual with concrete, specific desires and interests. (Harding, 1987, p. 9)

Another goal of feminist scholarship that guided my research was the importance of explicitly stating the values that guide research and of acknowledging that no researcher is ever "value-free" (Bograd, 1988; Yllö, 1988). I remained very cognizant of the importance of remaining self-reflexive and self-critical throughout the research process. Edwards (1990) points out that issues such as "class, race, sex, assumptions, and beliefs, should be explicated in terms of its [sic] effect upon the research and upon analysis" (pp. 479-480).

In addition to my feminist orientation, my training in qualitative methods was very helpful in preparing me for the research setting. While I was doing my research at the West Coast shelter, I was enrolled in an advanced qualitative methods course. In this course, I had the opportunity to discuss the problems I was confronting with my classmates, who provided me with invaluable feedback and advice. For example, I had the opportunity to have my fieldnotes and interview transcripts peer-reviewed, which proved to be very helpful. The course readings also shed light on some issues I would face in the research setting.

Stage II: Access and Initiation

As I mentioned earlier, gaining initial access was not that difficult. The problems I faced occurred after I entered the setting. However, several things facilitated my initiation into the environment. First, the 40-hour training that

I underwent at the West Coast shelter, which spanned a 4-week period, helped me immensely. During the training, I became acquainted with the shelter staff, my fellow volunteers, and many community activists who spoke at our training sessions. The training sessions enabled me to get acquainted with people who worked with battered Asian women in the community and who I hoped to interview at a later date. Also, I gained a lot of knowledge from this training. I learned about the nuances and complexities of Asian cultures and traditions. I learned that although women all over the world are subject to male dominance, patriarchy is a fluid concept that is conceptualized and manifested differently in various settings, and that meanings of patriarchy must be understood contextually (Hondagneu-Sotelo, 1992). As Michelle Bograd (1988) argues, "Wife abuse cannot be examined out of its particular sociohistorical context, which shapes its dynamics, its social acceptance, and its meaning" (p. 15). Working in a shelter for battered Asian women heightened my awareness about the sociohistorical context in which battering takes place. Thus, by immersing myself in the shelter environment and in the literature, I increased my cultural sensitivity and was better able to establish relationships and rapport with my coworkers and the women I interviewed. Furthermore, the knowledge I gained working in this environment enabled me to construct a semi-structured interview that covered issues I would not have been aware of if I had, instead, gone directly into doing interviews. In addition, my affiliation with the shelter helped me find people to participate in my study and provided me with more credibility than I would have otherwise had.

Stage III: Gaining Trust

Gaining the trust of my coworkers and the women I wanted to interview was difficult and took a long time. However, there are several strategies that I found very helpful in gaining their trust and acceptance. First, I found that flexibility was very important. I did not enter the setting with a rigid agenda about what I wanted. Rather, I entered the setting with an open mind and was more concerned about what I could give to the shelter than what I could get. This helped facilitate my adaptation and acceptance into the environment. I found that it is important to be open to unanticipated events that may force one to alter one's research to some degree or to reassess one's views and preconceived notions. This issue is also grounded in the feminist approach of viewing myself as the student rather than the expert.

A related issue I found helpful in gaining the trust and acceptance of my coworkers was patience. I took the time to get acquainted with the environment and my coworkers before pursuing my research goals. I did not want to come across as pushy or as having an agenda. I did not begin interviewing people until after I had been volunteering at the shelter for 3 months. By the time I was ready to interview people, I was well-acquainted with the protocol and norms of the shelter. I was able to go about scheduling interviews in a nonobtrusive way.

I was also very careful to show respect and consideration for the people I worked with. I tried very hard not to offend anyone or overstep my bounds. I made a great effort to show up to work on time, I welcomed any opportunity to attend social functions and seminars, I willingly agreed to work extra hours when necessary, and I assisted with several projects.[2] I viewed this as a form of negotiation. I felt better giving my time when I was needed, and this helped assuage some of the discomfort I felt about my underlying research agenda. The reciprocity that developed enabled me to view our relationships as symbiotic rather than one-way; my coworkers were benefiting from the volunteer time I put in at the shelter, and I was benefiting from their cooperation and participation in my research.

Stage IV: Interviewing

By the time I was ready to start interviewing, I had already been working at the shelter for 3 months, was familiar with how things were run, and had established relationships with several of my coworkers. One of the women who ran the shelter and was well-known and involved in the Asian communities turned out to be a key informant for my research. Although she would not agree to an interview, stating that I already knew what she thought, she provided me with a list of names to contact, told me I could use her name, and provided me with reading material she thought I might find helpful.

My relationship with this woman is a good example of what I went through to gain people's trust. When I began working at the shelter, she seemed very suspicious of my interest in this issue. On several occasions she asked why I was interested in wife battering in Asian families, how I became interested, and what my goals were in doing this research. At times these interactions became very uncomfortable because I felt as if I were being put to a test: She would quiz me about my knowledge of wife battering and my knowledge about Asian ethnic groups and cultures. However, over time, the tension between us subsided, and she took me under her wing and went out of her way to help me. I am very indebted to her for her help and support. My affiliation with the shelter and with this woman proved to be critical in recruiting participants for my study. This affiliation gave me a foot in the door and improved my credibility.

I believe that the steps I took in conducting this research were crucial. I don't believe I would have been able to develop the trust and rapport I achieved without employing the strategies I have outlined in this chapter.

Most of the interviews went very well. The average interview lasted 70 minutes, during which the participants usually spoke at length. On several occasions, when I first requested to schedule an interview, the women did not seem very interested and only reluctantly agreed to participate. In these cases, the interview often got off to a slow start, but in most instances the interviews ended up going very well and flowed more like a conversation than a question-and-answer session. Although the majority of my interviews went very well, there were a few that did not go well at all. For example, one interview with a woman whose trust I never gained was very uncomfortable. Rapport was never developed, and the interview was very awkward. Her responses were very short and curt, and I felt as if I was wasting her time. Following are two excerpts that illustrate this well.

Q: What kind of services do you provide at your shelter?

A: They are very well stated in the materials.

Q: What are some of the constraints that inhibit Asian women from seeking help?

A: I think you know what those are.

Fortunately, this was the only interview in which I felt completely uncomfortable. Yet I believe that had I not taken the steps outlined in this chapter, this example might be a more representative one.

Several interviews went extremely well, despite the initial skepticism of the participant. For instance, when I first requested to interview one woman, a Japanese-Korean lawyer who represents battered Asian women, she informed me that she would participate but that she could give me only 30 minutes of her time. When I arrived at her office, she was very standoffish at first and proceeded to question me about my intentions. However, once the interview got underway and I had explained my intentions in doing this research, everything started to flow and the interview ended up lasting 90 minutes. After the interview, she offered to photocopy some material for me that she thought would be helpful to my research.

Another woman, a Japanese lawyer, also questioned my intentions at the beginning. However, she appeared to be pleased with my responses to her questions, and the interview proceeded very well. In fact, throughout the interview she voluntarily provided me with the names of people she thought I should contact and interview, and at the end of the interview, she thanked me for taking on this study. Similarly, a Korean woman, who worked as a victims' advocate, expressed appreciation for my interest in this study:

> I think it's great that you're doing this. I think there needs to be something, some more work done in the Asian culture on the issues of domestic violence, and I give you a lot of credit for going into a community that's probably not very accepting of you because you're not one of us, so to speak, but hang in there doing this because it's so important.

Findings of My Research

Based on interviews with 18 Asian community activists and service providers, I found that battered Asian women, particularly recently arrived monolingual immigrant and refugee women, have distinct needs that differ from women of other racial and ethnic groups. In addition, there are numerous structural and cultural constraints that inhibit battered Asian women from securing help from mainstream social service providers.

The distinct needs of battered Asian women include the need for unbiased interpreters; community-based methods of outreach; and culturally hospitable shelters in which Asian food is provided, the staff is educated about Asian cultures, and culturally sensitive advocacy is available.

Cultural and structural constraints faced by Asian women include language, traditional cultural beliefs that are often grounded in patriarchal ideologies, immigration laws, extended family systems, lack of awareness about women's legal rights, stereotypes depicting Asians as the "model minority," racism in the United States and within some social service organizations, and the failure of the mainstream battered women's movement to fully incorporate the specific needs of battered Asian women into their policies and procedures.[3]

Conclusion

I used several strategies and methods to conduct this research. These included immersing myself in the environment in which I wanted to do my research; using feminist values and principles in my research; cultivating and maintaining relationships; and being flexible, patient, and respectful. These strategies facilitated my research to a considerable degree and illustrate that it is possible to engage in cross-race research.

Although my experiences also indicate that it may be more time-consuming and difficult to study groups that you are not a member of, I believe that to increase global awareness and overcome barriers of understanding, it is imperative for researchers to engage in cross-cultural and cross-race research. Through challenging restrictive, positivist methodological approaches, incorporating self-reflexivity into the research process, and acknowledging the existence of white privilege, more inclusive methodological frameworks can be developed. Although there are pros and cons to studying groups that you are not a member of, it is important that researchers and practitioners remain open to this type of research and realize that to raise global awareness we must learn to step outside of the concentric circles in which we live.

Notes

1. When discussing the obstacles I faced, I will be referring to my experiences at the West Coast shelter because I have been volunteering there for a longer period of time and because this shelter is run exclusively for Asian women, whereas the shelter on the East Coast provides services for women from various racial and ethnic groups.
2. This strategy proved to be very beneficial. As time went on, I was asked to assist with several projects, attend social functions, and was even asked to work as a shelter assistant, which required taking on a lot of responsibility.
3. For a detailed discussion of the findings of this research, see Huisman (1996).

References

Abbey, A., Ross, L. T., & McDuffie, D. (1995). Alcohol's role in sexual assault. In R. R. Watson (Ed.), *Drug and alcohol abuse reviews, Vol. 5: Addictive behaviors in women.* Totawa, NJ: Humana.

Abbey, A., Ross, L. T., McDuffie, D., & McAuslan, P. (1996). Alcohol and dating risk factors for sexual assault among college women. *Psychology of Women Quarterly, 20,* 147-169.

Adler, P. A., & Adler, P. (1987). *Membership roles in field research.* Newbury Park, CA: Sage.

Adler, P. A., & Adler, P. (1993). Ethical issues in self-censorship: Ethnographic research on sensitive topics. In C. M. Renzetti & R. M. Lee (Eds.), *Researching sensitive topics* (pp. 249-266). Newbury Park, CA: Sage.

Agar, M. H. (1977). Ethnography in the streets and in the joint: A comparison. In R. S. Weppner (Ed.), *Street ethnography: Selected studies of crime and drug use in natural settings* (pp. 143-156). Beverly Hills, CA: Sage.

Ageton, S. S. (1983). *Sexual assault among adolescents.* Lexington, MA: D. C. Heath.

American Psychiatric Association. (1987). *Diagnostic and statistical manual of mental disorders* (3rd ed. revised). Washington, DC: Author.

Amir, M. (1971). *Patterns in forcible rape.* Chicago: University of Chicago Press.

Anderson, M. L. (1993). Studying across difference: Race, class, and gender in qualitative research. In J. H. Stanfield II & R. M. Dennis (Eds.), *Race and ethnicity in research methods* (pp. 39-52). Newbury Park, CA: Sage.

Appelbaum, M. I., & McCall, R. B. (1983). Design and analysis in developmental psychology. In W. Kessen (Ed.), *Handbook of child psychology, vol. 1. History, theory & methods* (pp. 413-476). New York: John Wiley.

Arias, I., & Beach, S. R. H. (1987). Validity of self-reports of marital violence. *Journal of Family Violence, 2,* 139-149.

Asante, M. K. (1993). *Malcolm X as cultural hero & other Afrocentric essays.* Trenton, NJ: Africa World Press.

Ashmore, R. D., & DelBoca, F. K. (1987). *The development and validation of a structured inventory to assess the multiple components of gender-related verbal attitudes.* Paper presented at the Nags Head Interdisciplinary Conference on Sex and Gender, Nags Head, NC.

Babbie, E. (1995). *The practice of social research* 7th ed. Belmont, CA: Wadsworth.

Baer, J. S., Kivlahan, D. R., & Marlett, G. A. (1995). High risk drinking across the transition from high school to college alcoholism. *Clinical and Experimental Research, 19,* 54-61.

Barnes, G. E., Greenwood, L., & Sommer, R. (1991). Courtship violence in a Canadian sample of male college students. *Family Relations, 40,* 37-44.

Barrett, M., & MacIntosh, M. (1982). *The anti-social family.* London: Verso.

Beattie, V. (1992). *Analysis of the results of a survey on sexual violence in the UK.* Cambridge, UK: Women's Forum.

Beauchesne, E. (1995, August 18). Canada best place to live—with a catch. *Ottawa Citizen,* pp. A1-A2.

Beck, A., Ward, C., Mendolsohn, M., Mock, J., & Erbaugh, J. (1961). An inventory for measuring depression. *Archives of General Psychiatry, 4,* 53-63.

Becker, J. V., Skinner, L. J., Abel, G. G., Axelrod, R., & Treacy, E. C. (1984). Depressive symptoms associated with sexual assault. *Journal of Sex and Marital Therapy, 10,* 185-192.

Bergen, R. K. (1993). Interviewing survivors of marital rape: Doing feminist research on sensitive topics. In C. M. Renzetti & R. M. Lee (Eds.), *Researching sensitive topics* (pp. 197-211). Newbury Park, CA: Sage.

Bernard, J. (1973). My four revolutions: An autobiographical history of the ASA. *American Journal of Sociology, 78,* 773-791.

Bernard, M. L., & Bernard, J. L. (1983). Violent intimacy: The family as a model for love relationships. *Family Relations, 32,* 283-286.

Billson, J. M. (1991). The progressive verification method: Toward a feminist methodology for studying women cross-culturally. *Women's Studies International Forum, 14*(3), 201-215.

Blum, H. P. (1982). Psychoanalytic reflections on "the beaten wife syndrome." In M. Kirkpatrick (Ed.), *Women's sexual experiences: Explorations of the dark continent* (pp. 263-267). New York: Plenum.

Boeringer, S. B., Shehan, C., & Akers, R. (1991). Social contexts and learning in sexual coercion and aggression: Assessing the continuation of fraternity membership. *Family Relations, 40,* 58-64.

Bograd, M. (1988). Feminist perspectives on wife abuse: An introduction. In K. Yllö & M. Bograd (Eds.), *Feminist perspectives on wife abuse* (pp. 11-26). Newbury Park, CA: Sage.

Bohmer, C., & Parrot, A. (1993). *Sexual assault on campus: The problem and the solution.* Toronto: Maxwell Macmillan.

Bownes, I. T., O'Gorman, E. C., & Sayers, A. (1991a). Assault characteristics and posttraumatic stress disorder in rape victims. *Acta Psychiatrica Scandinavia, 83,* 27-30.

Bownes, I. T., O'Gorman, E. C., & Sayers, A. (1991b). Psychiatric symptoms: Behavioral responses and post-traumatic stress disorder. *Issues in Criminological and Legal Psychology, 17,* 25-33.

Boyle, K., & Anglin, M. D. (1993). "To the curb": Sex bartering and drug use among homeless crack users in Los Angeles. In M. S. Ratner (Ed.), *Crack pipe as pimp: An ethnographic investigation of sex-for-crack exchanges* (pp. 159-186). New York: Lexington.

Brownmiller, S. (1975). *Against our will.* New York: Bantam.

Bryden, D. P., & Lengnick, S. (1996). *Rape in the criminal justice system.* Manuscript under review.

Bumgartner, M. A. (1993). The myth of discretion. In K. Hawkins (Ed.), *The uses of discretion* (pp. 129-162). Oxford: Clarendon.

Cancian, F. M. (1992). Feminist science: Methodologies that challenge inequality. *Gender & Society, 6,* 623-642.

Chambers, G., & Millar, A. (1984). *Investigating sexual assault.* Edinburgh: HMSO.

Chancer, L. S. (1987). The "before and after" of a group rape. *Gender & Society, 1*(3), 239-290.

Chancer, L. S. (1993, Winter). Prostitution, feminist theory, and ambivalence: Notes from the sociological underground. *Social Text, 37,* 143-171.

Channels, N. L. (1993). Anticipating media coverage: Methodological decisions in criminal justice research. In C. M. Renzetti & R. M. Lee (Eds.), *Researching sensitive topics* (pp. 267-280). Newbury Park, CA: Sage.

Chesney-Lind, M. (1995, March). Towards a feminist praxis. Paper presented at the annual meetings of the Academy of Criminal Justice Sciences, Boston.

Clark, L., & Lewis, D. (1977). *Rape: The price of coercive sexuality.* Toronto: The Women's Press.

Clear, T. R. (1994). *Harm in American penology: Offenders, victims, and their communities.* Albany: State University of New York Press.

Cohen, J. M. (1994). Public violence and public obligation: The fulcrum of reason. In M. A. Fineman & R. Mykituk (Eds.), *The public face of private violence* (pp. 349-381). London: Routledge.

Collins, P. H. (1990). *Black feminist thought: Knowledge, consciousness, and the politics of empowerment.* New York: Routledge, Chapman and Hall.

Cook, J., & Fonow, M. (1984). Knowledge and women's interests: Issues of epistemology and methodology in feminist sociological research. *Sociological Inquiry, 56,* 2-29.

Cooney, M. (1994). Evidence as partisanship. *Law & Society Review, 28,* 833-858.

Crenshaw, K. W. (1993). Beyond racism and misogyny: Black feminism and 2 Live Crew. In M. J. Matsuda, C. R. Lawrence III, R. Delgado, K. W. Crenshaw (Eds.), *Words that wound: Critical race theory, assaultive speech, and the first amendment* (pp. 111-132). Boulder, CO: Westview.

Crenshaw, K. W. (1994). Mapping the margins: Intersectionality, identity politics and violence against women of color. In M. A. Fineman and R. Mykituk (Eds.), *The public face of private violence* (pp. 93-118). London: Routledge.

Crime Victims Research and Treatment Center. (1992). *Rape in America: A report to the nation.* Arlington, VA: National Victim Center.

Currie, D. H. (1988). At the crossroads: Feminism or science? In D. H. Currie (Ed.), *From the margins to centre: Essays in women's studies research* (pp. 176-192). Saskatoon: Social Research Unit.

Currie, D. H. (1995). *Student safety at the University of British Columbia: Preliminary findings of a study of student safety.* Report submitted to the Provost. Vancouver: University of British Columbia.

Currie, D. H., & MacLean, B. D. (1992). Women, men, and police: Losing the fight against wife battery in Canada. In D. H. Currie & B. D. MacLean, (Eds.), *Rethinking the administration of justice* (pp. 251-275). Halifax: Fernwood.

Currie, D. H., & MacLean, B. D. (1993). Woman abuse in dating relationships: Rethinking women's safety on campus. *Journal of Human Justice, 4*(2), 1-24.

Curtis, L. A. (1976). Rape, race, and culture: Some speculations in search of a theory. In M. J. Walker & S. L. Brodsky (Eds.), *Sexual assault: The victim and the rapist* (pp. 117-134). Lexington, MA: Lexington.

Deitz, P. E. (1978). Social factors in rapist behavior. In R. Rada (Ed.), *Clinical aspects of the rapist* (pp. 59-115). New York: Grune & Stratton.

DeKeseredy, W. S. (1988). *Woman abuse in dating relationships: The role of male peer support.* Toronto: Canadian Scholars' Press.

DeKeseredy, W. S. (1990). Male peer support and woman abuse: The current state of knowledge. *Sociological Focus, 23*(2), 129-139.

DeKeseredy, W. S. (1995). Enhancing the quality of survey data on woman abuse: Examples from a national Canadian study. *Violence Against Women, 1,* 158-173.

DeKeseredy, W. S., & Kelly, K. (1993a). The incidence and prevalence of woman abuse in Canadian university and college dating relationships. *Canadian Journal of Sociology, 18,* 157-159.

DeKeseredy, W. S., & Kelly, K. (1993b). Woman abuse in university and college dating relationships: The contribution of the ideology of familial patriarchy. *Journal of Human Justice, 4,* 25-52.

DeKeseredy, W. S., & Kelly, K. (1995). Sexual abuse in Canadian university and college dating relationships: The contribution of male peer support. *Journal of Family Violence, 10,* 41-53.

DeKeseredy, W. S., Kelly, K., & Baklid, B. (1992). *The physical, sexual, and psychological abuse of women in dating relationships: Results from a pretest for a national study.* Paper presented at the annual meeting of the American Society of Criminology, New Orleans.

DeKeseredy, W. S., & Schwartz, M. D. (1993). Male peer support and women abuse: An expansion of DeKeseredy's model. *Sociological Spectrum, 13,* 393-413.

DeKeseredy, W. S., & Schwartz, M. D. (1994). Locating a history of some Canadian woman abuse in elementary and high school dating relationships. *Humanity & Society, 18,* 49-63.

Delacoste, F., & Alexander, P. (Eds.). (1988). *Sex work: Writings by women in the sex industry.* London: Virago.

Delgado, R., & Stefancic, J. (1995). Images of the outsider in American law and culture: Can free expression remedy systemic social ills? In R. Delgado (Ed.), *Critical race theory: The cutting edge* (pp. 217-227). Philadelphia, PA: Temple University Press.

Delgado, R., & Yun, D. (1995). Pressure valves and bloody chickens: An assessment of four paternalistic arguments for restricting hate speech regulation. In L. Lederer & R. Delgado (Eds.), *The price we pay: The case against racist speech, hate propaganda, and pornography* (pp. 290-300). New York: Hill and Wang.

Delmar, R. (1986). What is feminism? In J. Mitchell & A. Oakley (Eds.), *What is feminism? A reexamination* (pp. 8-33). New York: Pantheon.

Derogatis, L. R. (1977). *Manual for the SCL.* Baltimore: Johns Hopkins School of Medicine.

Diana, L. (1985). *The prostitute and her clients.* Springfield, IL: Charles C Thomas.

Dobash, R. E., & Dobash, R. (1979). *Violence against wives: A case against the patriarchy.* New York: Free Press.

Dunlap, E., Johnson, B., Sanibria, H., Holliday, E., Lipsey, V., Barnett, M., Hopkins, W., Sobel, I., Randolph, D., & Chin, K. (1990, Winter). Studying crack users and their criminal careers. *Contemporary Drug Problems,* 455-473.

Dutton, D. G., & Hemphill, K. J. (1992). Patterns of socially desirable responding among perpetrators and victims of wife assault. *Violence and Victims, 7,* 29-40.

Dye, E., & Roth, S. (1990). Psychotherapist's knowledge about and attitudes toward sexual assault victim clients. *Psychology of Women Quarterly, 14,* 191-212.

Easterday, L., Papademus, D., Schorr, L., & Valentine, C. (1977). The making of a female researcher. *Urban Life, 6,* 333-347.

Edwards, R. (1990). Connecting method with epistemology: A white woman interviewing black women. *Women's Studies International Forum, 13*(5), 477-490.

Ehrlich, H. J. (1990). *Campus ethnoviolence and policy options.* Baltimore, MD: National Institute Against Prejudice and Violence.

Ehrlich, H. J. (1992). *Campus ethnoviolence: A research review.* Baltimore, MD: National Institute Against Prejudice and Violence.

Eich, E. (1982). Theoretical issues in state dependent memory. In H. L. Roediger III & F. I. M. Craik (Eds.), *Varieties of memory and consciousness* (pp. 331-354). Hillsdale, NJ: Lawrence Erlbaum.

Elliot, S., Odynak, D., & Krahn, H. (1992). *A survey of unwanted sexual experiences among University of Alberta students.* Research report prepared for the Council on Student Life, University of Alberta. University of Alberta: Population Research Laboratory.

Elliott, D. S., & Ageton, S. S. (1980). Reconciling race and class differences in self-reported and official estimates of delinquency. *American Sociological Review, 45,* 95-110.

Ellis, C. (1991). Emotional sociology. *Studies in Symbolic Interaction, 12,* 123-145.

Ellis, D., & DeKeseredy, W. S. (1996). *The wrong stuff: An introduction to the sociological study of deviance* (2nd ed.). Toronto: Allyn & Bacon.

Ellis, E. M., Atkeson, B. M., & Calhoun, K. S. (1981). An assessment of long-term reaction to rape. *Journal of Abnormal Psychology, 90,* 263-266.

Estrich, S. (1987). *Real rape: How the legal system victimizes women who say no.* Cambridge, MA: Harvard University Press.

Faith, K., & Currie, D. H. (1993). *Seeking shelter: A state of battered women.* Vancouver: Collective Press.

Feagin, J. R., & Vera, H. (1995). *White racism.* New York: Routledge.

Federal Bureau of Investigation (FBI). (1994). *Crime in the United States, 1993.* Washington, DC: U.S. Department of Justice.

Fekete, J. (1994). *Moral panic: Biopolitics rising.* Montreal: Robert Davies.

Fenstermaker, S. (1989). Acquaintance rape on campus: Attribution of responsibility and crime. In M. Pirog-Good & J. Stets (Eds.), *Violence in dating: Emerging social issues* (pp. 257-271). New York: Praeger.

Fielding, N. G. (1993). Mediating the message: Affinity and hostility in research on sensitive topics. In C. M. Renzetti & R. M. Lee (Eds.), *Researching sensitive topics* (pp. 146-159). Newbury Park, CA: Sage.

Fine, M. (1993). The politics of research and activism: Violence against women. In P. B. Bart & E. G. Moran (Eds.), *Violence against women: The bloody footprints* (pp. 278-287). Newbury Park, CA: Sage.

Finkelhor, D. (1984). *Child sexual abuse: New theory and research.* New York: Free Press.

Finkelman, L. (1992). *Report of the survey of unwanted sexual experiences among students of U.N.B.-F. and S.T.U.* University of New Brunswick: Counselling Services.

Frank, E., Turner, S. M., & Stewart, B. (1980). Initial response to rape: The impact of factors within the rape situation. *Journal of Behavioral Assessment, 2,* 39-53.

Frankenberg, R. (1993). *White women, race matters: The social construction of whiteness.* Minneapolis: University of Minnesota Press.

Frazier, P. (1990). Victim attributions and post-rape trauma. *Journal of Personality and Social Psychology, 59,* 298-304.

Frazier, P. (1991). Self-blame as a mediator of post-rape depressive symptoms. *Journal of Social and Clinical Psychology, 10,* 47-57.

Frazier, P., & Haney, B. (1996). *Sexual assault cases in the legal system: Police, prosecutor, and victim perspectives. Law and Human Behavior, 20,* 607-628..

Frazier, P., & Schauben, L. (1994). Causal attributions and recovery from rape and other stressful life events. *Journal of Social and Clinical Psychology, 13,* 1-14.

Frohmann, L. (1991). Discrediting victims' allegations of sexual assault: Prosecutorial accounts of case rejections. *Social Problems, 38,* 213-226.

Frohmann, L. G. (1992). *Screening sexual assault cases: Prosecutorial decisions to file or reject rape complaints.* Doctoral dissertation, University of California, Los Angeles.

Fromuth, M. E., & Burkhart, B. (1996, March). *The sexual abuse of women and girls: Backlash against the truth.* Paper presented at symposium on violence against women, Southeastern Psychological Association, Norfolk, VA.

Galton, E. (1975-1976). Police processing of rape complaints: A case study. *American Journal of Criminal Law, 4,* 15-30.

Gavey, N. (1991). Sexual victimization prevalence among New Zealand university students. *Journal of Consulting and Clinical Psychology, 59,* 464-466.

Gidycz, C. A., & Koss, M. P. (1991). Predictors of long-term sexual assault trauma among a national sample of victimized college women. *Violence and Victims, 6,* 175-190.

Gidycz, C. A., Coble, C. N., Latham, L., & Layman, M. J. (1993). Sexual assault experience in adulthood and prior victimization experiences: A prospective analysis. *Psychology of Women Quarterly, 17,* 151-168.

Gidycz, C. A., Hanson, K., & Layman, M. J. (1995). A prospective analysis of relationships among sexual assault experiences. *Psychology of Women Quarterly, 19,* 5-19.

Gilbert, N. (1991). The phantom epidemic of sexual assault. *The Public Interest, 103,* 54-65.

Gilbert, N. (1992). Realities and mythologies of rape. *Society, 29,* 4-10.

Gilbert, N. (1993). Examining the facts: Advocacy research overstates the incidence of date rape and acquaintance rape. In D. R. Gelles & D. R. Loseke (Eds.), *Current controversies on family violence* (pp. 120-132). Newbury Park, CA: Sage.

Gilbert, N. (1994). Miscounting social ills. *Society, 31,* 18-26.

Girelli, S. A., Resick, P. A., Marhoefer-Dvorak, S., & Hutter, C. (1986). Subjective distress and violence during rape: Their effects on long-term fear. *Victims and Violence, 1,* 35-46.

Glassner, B., & Loughlin, J. (1987). *Drugs in adolescent worlds: Burnouts to straights.* New York: St. Martin's.

Glenn, E. N. (1986). *Issei, nisei, war bride: Three generations of Japanese American women in domestic service.* Philadelphia, PA: Temple University Press.

Godenzi, A. (1994). What's the big deal? We are men and they are women. In T. Newburn & E. A. Stanko (Eds.), *Just boys doing business* (pp. 135-152). London: Routledge.

Goffman, E. (1963). *Stigma.* Englewood Cliffs, NJ: Prentice Hall.

Goffman, E. (1989). On field work. (Transcribed and edited by L. H. Lofland). *Journal of Contemporary Ethnography, 18,* 123-132.

Gorelick, S. (1991). Contradictions of feminist methodology. *Gender & Society, 5*(4), 459-477.

Gouldner, A. (1970). *The coming crisis in western sociology.* New York: Basic Books.

Green, G., Barbour, R. S., Barnard, M., & Kitzinger, J. (1993). "Who wears the trousers?" Sexual harassment in research settings. *Women Studies International Forum, 16,* 627-637.

Greenwald, A. G. (1976). Within subjects designs: To use or not to use. *Psychological Bulletin, 83,* 314-320.

Grillo, T., & Wildman, S. M. (1995). Obscuring the importance of race: The implications of making comparisons between racism and sexism (or other -isms). In R. Delgado (Ed.), *Critical race theory: The cutting edge* (pp. 564-572). Philadelphia, PA: Temple University Press.

Gruber, J. E. (1989). How women handle sexual harassment: A literature review. *Sociology and Social Research, 74,* 3-9.

Gurney, J. N. (1985). Not one of the guys: The female researcher in a male-dominated setting. *Qualitative Sociology, 8,* 42-62.

Gutek, B. A., & Koss, M. P. (1993). Changed women and changed organizations: Consequences of and coping with sexual harassment. *Journal of Vocational Behavior, 42,* 28-48.

Guttman, S. (1991) "It sounds like I raped you!" How date-rape re-education fosters confusion, undermines personal responsibility, and trivializes sexual violence. In O. Pocs (Ed.), *Human sexuality* (pp. 217-221). Guilford, CT: Dushkin.

Hall, R. (1985). *Ask any woman: A London inquiry into rape and sexual assault.* London: Falling Wall.

Hanmer, J., & Saunders, S. (1984). *Well-founded fear: A community study of violence to women.* London: Hutchinson.

Hans, V. P., & Vidmar, N. (1986). *Judging the jury.* New York: Plenum.

Hardesty, M. J. (1986). Plans and mood: A study in therapeutic relationships. In C. J. Couch, S. Saxton, & M. A. Katovich (Eds.), *Studies in symbolic interaction, Supplement 2: The Iowa school (Part A)* (pp. 209-230). Greenwich, CT: JAI.

Harding, S. (Ed.). (1987). *Feminism and methodology.* Bloomington: Indiana University Press.

Harmon, P. A., & Check, J. V. P. (1989). *The role of pornography in woman abuse.* North York, Ontario: LaMarsh Research Programme on Violence and Conflict Resolution.

Hatty, S. (1989). Violence against prostitute women: Social and legal dilemmas. *Australian Journal of Social Issues, 24,* 235-248.

Heise, L. L., Pitanguy, J., & Germain, A. (1994). *Violence against women: The hidden health burden.* World Bank Discussion Paper No. 255. Washington, DC: The World Bank.

Herman, D. (1988). The rape culture. In J. W. Cochran, D. Langton, & C. Woodward (Eds.), *Changing our power* (pp. 260-273). Dubuque, IO: Kendall/Hunt.

Himelein, M. J. (1995). Risk factors for sexual victimization in dating: A longitudinal study of college women. *Psychology of Women Quarterly, 19,* 31-48.

Hippensteele, S. K. (1996). Advocacy and student victims of sexual harassment. In B. Sandler and R. Shoop (Eds.), *Sexual harassment on campus: A guide for administrators, faculty and students* (pp. 293-313). Boston: Allyn & Bacon.

Hippensteele, S. K., & Chesney-Lind, M. (1995). Race and sex discrimination in the academy. *Thought & Action: The NEA Higher Education Journal, 11*(2), 43-66.

Hippensteele, S. K., Chesney-Lind, M., & Veniegas, R. (1996). On the basis of . . .: The changing face of harassment and discrimination in the academy. *Women and Criminal Justice, 8*(1), 3-26.

Hochschild, A. R. (1979). Emotion work, feeling rules, and social structure. *American Journal of Sociology, 85,* 551-575.

Hochschild, A. R. (1983). *The managed heart.* Berkeley: University of California Press.

Hoff, L. A. (1988). Collaborative feminist research and the myth of objectivity. In K. Yllö & M. Bograd (Eds.), *Feminist perspectives on wife abuse* (pp. 269-281). Newbury Park, CA: Sage.

Hoff-Sommers, C. (1994). *Who stole feminism? How women have betrayed women.* New York: Simon & Schuster.

Holmstrom, L., & Burgess, A. W. (1978). *The victim of rape: Institutional reactions.* New York: Wiley.

Hondagneu-Sotelo, P. (1992). Overcoming patriarchal constraints: The reconstruction of gender relations among Mexican immigrant women and men. *Gender & Society, 6*(3), 393-415.

hooks, b. (1984). *Feminist theory: From margin to center.* Boston: South End Press.

Hough, M., & Mayhew, P. (1983). *The British crime survey.* London: HMSO.

Huesmann, L. R., & Eron, L. (1992). Childhood aggression and adult criminality. In J. McCord (Ed.), *Facts, frameworks, and forecasts: Advances in criminological theory, vol. 3* (pp. 137-156). New Brunswick, NJ: Transaction Books.

Huisman, K. (1996). Wife battering in Asian American communities: Identifying the service needs of an overlooked segment of the U.S. population. *Violence Against Women, 2*(3), 260-283.

James, J., Withers, J., Haft, M., Theiss, S., & Owen, M. (1977). *The politics of prostitution.* Social Research Associates.

Janoff-Bulman, R. (1979). Characterological versus behavioral self-blame: Inquiries into depression and rape. *Journal of Personality and Social Psychology, 37,* 1798-1809.

Jensen, R. (1995). Pornographic lives. *Violence Against Women, 1,* 32-54.

Johnson, C. B., Stockdale, M. S., & Saal, F. (1991). A persistence of men's misperceptions of friendly cues across a variety of interpersonal encounters. *Psychology of Women Quarterly, 15,* 463-475.

Johnson, J. M. (1983). Trust and personal involvements in fieldwork. In R. M. Emerson (Ed.), *Contemporary field research* (pp. 203-215). Prospect Heights, IL: Waveland.

Jones, T., MacLean, B. D., & Young, J. (1986). *The Islington Crime Survey: Crime, victimization and policing in inner-city London.* Aldershot: Gower.

Junger, M. (1987). Women's experiences of sexual harassment: Some implications for their fear of crime. *British Journal of Criminology, 27,* 358-383.

Junger, M. (1990). The measurement of sexual harassment: Comparison of the results of three different instruments. *International Review of Victimology, 1,* 231-239.

Kahn, A. S., Mathie, V. A., & Torgler, C. (1994). Rape scripts and rape acknowledgment. *Psychology of Women Quarterly, 18,* 53-66.

Kanin, E. J. (1985). Date rapists: Differential sexual socializations and relative deprivation. *Archives of Sexual Behavior, 14,* 219-231.

Kanin, E. J., & Parcell, S. R. (1977). Sexual aggression: A second look at the offended female. *Archives of Sexual Behavior, 6,* 67-76.

Katz, B. L. (1991). The psychological impact of stranger versus nonstranger rape on victims' recovery. In A. Parrot & L. Bechhofer (Eds.), *Acquaintance rape: The hidden crime* (pp. 251-269). New York: John Wiley.

Katz, B. L., & Burt, M. R. (1988). Self-blame in recovery from rape: Help or hindrance? In A. W. Burgess (Ed.), *Rape and sexual assault II* (pp. 151-168). New York: Garland.

Kelly, K. D., & DeKeseredy, W. S. (1994). Women's fear of crime and abuse in college and university dating relationships. *Violence and Victims, 9,* 17-30.

Kelly, L. (1988). *Surviving sexual violence.* Minneapolis: University of Minnesota Press.

Kelly, L., Burton, S., & Regan, L. (1994). Researching women's lives or studying women's oppression? Reflections on what constitutes feminist research. In M. Maynard & J. Purvis (Eds.), *Researching women's lives from a feminist perspective* (pp. 27-48). London: Taylor & Francis.

Kelly, L., & Radford, J. (1987). The problem of men: Feminist perspectives on sexual violence. In P. Scraton (Ed.), *Law, order, and the authoritarian state* (pp. 237-253). Milton Keynes: Open University Press.

Kennedy, L., & Dutton, D. G. (1989). The incidence of wife assault in Alberta. *Canadian Journal of Behavioural Science, 21,* 40-54.

Kikuchi, J. J. (1988, Fall). Rhode Island develops successful intervention program for adolescents. *NCASA News,* 26-27.

Kilpatrick, D. G., Saunders, B. E., Veronen, L. J., Best, C. L., & Von, J. M. (1987). Criminal victimization: Lifetime prevalence, reporting to police, and psychological impact. *Crime and Delinquency, 33,* 479-489.

Kleiber, N., & Light, L. (1978). *Caring for ourselves: An alternative structure for health care.* Vancouver: University of British Columbia School of Nursing.

Kleinman, S., & Copp, M. A. (1993). *Emotions and fieldwork.* Newbury Park, CA: Sage.

Koss, M. P. (1985). The hidden rape victim: Personality, attitudinal, and situational characteristics. *Psychology of Women Quarterly, 9,* 193-212.

Koss, M. P. (1988). Hidden rape: Sexual aggression and victimization in a national sample in higher education. In A. W. Burgess (Ed.), *Rape and sexual assault* (Vol. 2, pp. 3-25). New York: Garland.

Koss, M. P. (1992). The underdetection of rape: A critical assessment of incidence data. *Journal of Social Issues, 48,* 61-76.

Koss, M. P. (1993). Detecting the scope of rape: A review of prevalence research methods. *Journal of Interpersonal Violence, 8,* 198-222.

Koss, M. P., & Cleveland, H. H. (in press). Fraternities and athletics as predictors of date rape: Self-selection or different causal processes? *Violence Against Women.*

Koss, M. P., & Cook, S. L. (1993). Facing the facts: Date and acquaintance rape are significant problems for women. In R. J. Gelles & D. R. Loeske (Eds.), *Current controversies on family violence* (pp. 104-119). Newbury Park, CA: Sage.

Koss, M. P., & Dinero, T. E. (1988). Predictors of sexual aggression in a national sample of college men. In V. Quinsey & R. Prentky (Eds.), Human sexual aggression: Current perspectives. *Annals of the New York Academy of Sciences, 528,* 133-147.

Koss, M. P., & Dinero, T. E. (1989a). Discriminant analysis of risk factors for sexual victimization among a national sample of college women. *Journal of Consulting and Clinical Psychology, 57,* 242-250.

Koss, M. P., & Dinero, T. E. (1989b). Predictors of sexual aggression among a national sample of male college students. *Annals of New York Academy of Science, 528,* 133-147.

Koss, M. P., Dinero, T. E., Seibel, C. A., & Cox, S. L. (1988). Stranger and acquaintance rape: Are there differences in the victim's experiences. *Psychology of Women Quarterly, 12,* 1-24.

Koss, M. P., Figueredo, A. J., Bell, I., Tharan, M., & Tromp, S. (in press). Traumatic memory characteristics: A cross validated mediational model to response to rape among employed women. *Journal of Abnormal Psychology.*

Koss, M. P., & Gaines, J. A. (1993). The prediction of sexual aggression by alcohol use, athletic participation, and fraternity affiliation. *Journal of Interpersonal Violence, 8,* 94-108.

Koss, M. P., & Gidycz, C. A. (1985). Sexual Experiences Survey: Reliability and validity. *Journal of Consulting and Clinical Psychology, 50*(3), 455-457.

Koss, M. P., Gidycz, C. A., & Wisniewski, N. (1987). The scope of rape: Incidence and prevalence of sexual aggression and victimization in a national sample of higher education students. *Journal of Consulting and Clinical Psychology, 55,* 162-170.

Koss, M. P., Goodman, L. A., Browne, A., Fitzgerald, L. F., Keita, G. P., & Russo, N. F. (1994). *No safe haven: Male violence against women at home, at work, and in the community.* Washington, DC: American Psychological Association.

Koss, M. P., & Oros, C. J. (1982). Sexual Experiences Survey: A research instrument investigating sexual aggression and victimization. *Journal of Consulting and Clinical Psychology, 50,* 455-457.

Koss, M. P., Woodruff, W. J., & Koss, P. G. (1991). Relation of criminal victimization to health perceptions among women medical patients. *Journal of Consulting and Clinical Psychology, 58,* 147-152.

Kosson, D. S., Kelly, J. C., & White, J. W. (in press). Psychopathy-related traits predict self-reported sexual aggression among college men. *Journal of Interpersonal Violence.*

Kramer, T., & Green, B. (1991). Posttraumatic stress disorder as an early response to sexual assault. *Journal of Interpersonal Violence, 6,* 160-173.

Ladner, J. (1987). Introduction to *Tomorrow's tomorrow: The black woman.* In S. Harding (Ed.), *Feminism and methodology* (pp. 74-83). Bloomington: Indiana University Press.

Lather, P. (1991). *Getting smart.* New York: Routledge.

Layman, M., Gidycz, C., & Lynn, S. (1996). Unacknowledged versus acknowledged rape victims: Situational factors and posttraumatic stress. *Journal of Abnormal Psychology, 105,* 124-131.

Ledwitz-Rigby, F. (1993). An administrative approach to personal safety on campus: The role of a President's Advisory Committee on woman's safety on campus. *Journal of Human Justice, 4,* 85-94.

Lee, J. (1989). Our hearts are collectively breaking: Teaching survivors of violence. *Gender & Society, 3,* 541-549.

Leonard, K. E. (1993). Drinking patterns and intoxication in marital violence: Review, critique, and future directions for research. In *Alcohol and Interpersonal Violence. Research Monograph-24 NIH Publication No. 93-3496.* Rockville, MD: National Institute on Alcohol Abuse and Alcoholism, National Institutes of Health, U.S. Department of Health and Human Services.

Levan, A. (1996). Violence against women. In J. Brodie (Ed.), *Women and Canadian public policy* (pp. 319-354). Toronto: Harcourt Brace.

Lofland, J., & Lofland, L. H. (1984). *Analyzing social settings: A guide to qualitative observations and analysis.* Belmont, CA: Wadsworth.

Lorde, A. (1984). *Sister outsider.* Freedom, CA: The Crossing Press.

MacIvor, H. (1995, April). The biopolitical agenda. *The Literary Review of Canada,* pp. 20-21.

MacKinnon, C. A. (1993), Feminism, Marxism, method, and the state: Toward a feminist jurisprudence. In P. B. Bart & E. G. Moran (Eds.), *Violence against women: The bloody footprints* (pp. 201-227). Newbury Park, CA: Sage.

MacLean, B. D. (1989). *The Islington Crime Survey 1985: A cross-sectional study of crime and policing in the London borough of Islington.* Doctoral dissertation, University of London.

MacLeod, L. (1980). *Wife battering in Canada: The vicious circle.* Canadian Advisory Council on the Status of Women, Ottawa: Ministry of Supply and Services.

MacLeod, L., & DeKeseredy, W. S. (1996). *Woman abuse: A sociological story.* Unpublished manuscript.

Maguire, P. (1987). *Doing participatory research: A feminist approach.* Amherst, MA: Center for International Education, University of Massachusetts at Amherst.

Makepeace, J. (1981). Social factor and victim-offender differences in courtship violence. *Family Relations, 36,* 87-91.

Malamuth, N. M. (1986). Predictors of naturalistic sexual aggression. *Journal of Personality and Social Psychology, 50,* 953-962.

Malamuth, N. M. (1989). The attraction to sexual aggression scale: I. *Journal of Sex Research, 26,* 26-49.

Malamuth, N. M., & Brown, L. M. (1994). Sexually aggressive men's perceptions of women's communications: Testing three explanations. *Journal of Personality and Social Psychology, 67,* 669-712.

Malamuth, N. M., & Dean, K. E. (1991). Attraction to sexual aggression. In A. Parrot & L. Bechhofer (Eds.), *Acquaintance rape: The hidden crime* (pp. 229-248). New York: John Wiley.

Malamuth, N. M., Linz, D., Heavey, C. L., Barnes, G., & Acker, M. (1995). Using the confluence model of sexual aggression to predict men's conflict with women: A 10-year follow-up study. *Journal of Personality and Social Psychology, 2,* 353-369.

Malamuth, N. M., Sockloskie, R. J., Koss, M. P., & Tanaka, J. S. (1991). Characteristics of aggressors against women: Testing a model using a national sample of college students. *Journal of Consulting and Clinical Psychology, 59,* 670-681.

Mandoki, C. A., & Burkhart, B. R. (1989). Sexual victimization: A vicious cycle? *Victims and Violence, 4,* 179-190.

Martin, P. Y., & Hummer, R. A. (1989). Fraternities and rape on campus. *Gender & Society, 3,* 457-473.

Mattley, C. (1994). *(Dis)courtesy stigma: Fieldwork among phone fantasy workers.* Paper presented at the annual meeting of the American Society of Criminology Annual Meetings, Miami, FL.

Maynard, M. (1994). Methods, practice and epistemology: The debate about feminism and research. In M. Maynard & J. Purvis (Eds.), *Researching women's lives from a feminist perspective* (pp. 10-26). London: Taylor & Francis.

McCahill, T. W., Meyer, L. C., & Fischman, A. M. (1979). *The aftermath of rape.* Lexington, MA: D. C. Heath.

McCann, L., & Pearlman, L. (1990). *McPearl Belief Scale.* South Windsor, CT: Traumatic Stress Institute.

McIntosh, P. (1988). *White privilege and male privilege: A personal account of coming to see correspondences through work in women's studies.* Working Paper No. 189. Wellesley, MA: Center for Research on Women, Wellesley College.

McMillen, L. (1990). An anthropologist's disturbing picture of gang rape on campus. *The Chronicle of Higher Education, 43,* A3.

Mies, M. (1983). Towards a methodology of feminist research. In G. Bowles & R. Duelli-Klein (Eds.), *Theories of women's studies* (pp. 117-139). Boston: Routledge & Kegan Paul.

Miller, E. (1986). *Street woman.* Philadelphia, PA: Temple University Press.

Miller, J. (1991). Prostitution in contemporary American society. In E. Grauerholz & M. A. Koralewski (Eds.), *Sexual coercion: A sourcebook on its nature, causes and prevention* (pp. 45-57). Lexington, MA: Lexington.

Miller, J. (1993). "Your life is on the line every night you're on the streets": Victimization and resistance among street prostitutes. *Humanity & Society, 17,* 422-446.

Miller, J. (1995). Gender and power on the streets: Street prostitution in the era of crack cocaine. *Journal of Contemporary Ethnography, 23,* 427-452.

Miller, J., & Schwartz, M. D. (1995). Rape myths and violence against street prostitutes. *Deviant Behavior, 16,* 1-23.

Mills, C. S., & Granoff, B. J. (1992). Date and acquaintance rape among a sample of college students. *Social Work, 37,* 504-506.

Mohanty, C. T. (1991). Under western eyes: Feminist scholarship and colonial discourses. In C. T. Mohanty, A. Russo, & L. Torres (Eds.), *Third world women and the politics of feminism* (pp. 51-80). Bloomington: Indiana University Press.

Moran-Ellis, J. (1996). Close to home: The experience of researching child sexual abuse. In M. Hester, L. Kelly, & J. Radford (Eds.), *Women, violence and male power* (pp. 176-187). Buckingham: Open University Press.

Morokoff, P. J. (1983). Toward the elimination of rape: A conceptualization of sexual aggression against women. In A. P. Goldstein (Ed.), *Prevention and control of aggression* (pp. 101-144). New York: Pergamon.

Morris, A. (1987). *Women, crime, and criminal justice.* Oxford, UK: Basil Blackwell.

Muehlenhard, C. L., & Cook, S. W. (1988). Men's self-reports of unwanted sexual activity. *Journal of Sex Research, 24,* 58-72.

Muehlenhard, C. L., Friedman, D. E., & Thomas, C. M. (1985). Is date rape justifiable? The effects of dating activity, who initiated, who paid, and men's attitudes toward women. *Psychology of Women Quarterly, 9,* 297-310.

Muehlenhard, C. L., & Hollabough, L. C. (1988). Do women sometimes say no when they mean yes? Prevalence and correlates of women's token resistance to sex. *Journal of Personality and Social Psychology, 54,* 872-879.

Muehlenhard, C. L., & Linton, M. A. (1987). Date rape and sexual aggression in dating situations: Incidence and risk factors. *Journal of Counseling Psychology, 34,* 186-196.

Muehlenhard, C. L., Powch, I. G., Phelps, J. L., & Highby, L. M. (1992). Definitions of rape: Scientific and political implications. *Journal of Social Issues, 48,* 23-44.

Muehlenhard, C. L., & Rogers, C. S. (1993, August). *Narrative descriptions of "token resistance" to sex.* Presented at the annual meeting of the American Psychological Association, Toronto, Canada.

Muehlenhard, C. L., Sympson, S. C., Phelps, J. L., & Highby, B. J. (1994). Are rape statistics exaggerated? A response to criticism of contemporary rape research. *Journal of Sex Research, 31,* 143-153.

Murphy, J. E. (1984). *Date abuse and forced intercourse among college students.* Paper presented to the Midwestern Sociological Society, Chicago.

Myers, M. B., Templer, D. I., & Brown, R. (1984). Coping ability of women who become victims of rape. *Journal of Consulting and Clinical Psychology, 52,* 73-78.

Niles, P. L., & White, J. W. (1989). *Correlates of sexual aggression and their accessibility.* Paper presented at the Southeastern Psychological Association, Washington, DC.

Norris, J., Nurius, P. S., & Dimeff, L. A. (1996). Through her eyes: Factors affecting women's perceptions of resistance to acquaintance sexual aggression threat. *Psychology of Women Quarterly, 20,* 123-145.

Oakley, A. (1981). Interviewing women: A contradiction in terms. In H. Roberts (Ed.), *Doing feminist research* (pp. 30-61). London: Routledge & Kegan Paul.

Olweus, D. (1993). Victimization by peers: Antecedents and longterm outcomes. In K. H. Rubin & J. B. Asendorpf (Eds.), *Social withdrawal, inhibition, and shyness in childhood* (pp. 315-341). Hillsdale, NJ: Lawrence Erlbaum.

Omi, M., & Winant, H. (1994). *Racial formation in the United States: From the 1960's to the 1990's* (2nd ed.). New York: Routledge.

O'Sullivan, L. F. (1995, August). *Consenting to noncoercive sex in heterosexual dating.* Paper presented at the annual meeting of the American Psychological Association, Boston.

Paglia, C. (1993). *New essays: Vamps and tramps.* New York: Vintage.

Pateman, C. (1988). *The sexual contract.* Cambridge: Polity Press.

Phillips, S. P., & Schneider, M. S. (1993). Sexual harassment of female doctors by patients. *New England Journal of Medicine, 329,* 1936-1939.

Phoenix, A. (1987). Theories of gender and black families. In G. Weiner & M. Arnot (Eds.), *Gender under scrutiny: New inquiries in education* (pp. 50-61). London: Hutchinson Open University.

Pierson, R. R. (1991). Violence against women: Strategies for change. *Canadian Woman Studies, 11,* 10-12.

Pineau, L. (1989). Date rape: A feminist analysis. *Law and Psychology, 8,* 217-243.

Pitts, V. L., & Schwartz, M. S. (1993). Promoting self-blame in hidden rape cases. *Humanity & Society, 17,* 383-398.

Pizzey, E. (1974). *Scream quietly or the neighbours will hear.* New York: Penguin.

Plass, M., & Gessner, J. (1983). Violence in courtship relationships: A southern sample. *Free Inquiry in Creative Sociology, 11,* 148-202.

Podhoretz, N. (1991, October). Rape in feminist eyes. *Commentary,* 29-35.

Pollard, J. (1993). *Male-female dating relationships in Canadian universities and colleges: Sample design, arrangements for data collection and data reduction.* Toronto: Institute for Social Research.

Pollner, M., & Emerson, R. M. (1983). The dynamics of inclusion and distance in fieldwork relations. In R. M. Emerson (Ed.), *Contemporary field research* (pp. 235-252). Prospect Heights, IL: Waveland.

Prescod, M. (1990). Discussion presented at the National Women's Studies Association annual conference. Akron, OH.

Randall, M., & Haskell, L. (1995). Sexual violence in women's lives: Findings from the Women's Safety Project, a community-based survey. *Violence Against Women, 1,* 6-31.

Rapaport, K., & Burkhart, B. R. (1984). Personality and attitudinal characteristics of sexually coercive college males. *Journal of Abnormal Psychology, 93,* 216-221.

Reinharz, S. (1992). *Feminist methods in social research.* New York: Oxford University Press.

Renzetti, C. M. (1992). *Violent betrayal: Partner abuse in lesbian relationships.* Newbury Park, CA: Sage.

Renzetti, C. M. (1995). Studying partner abuse in lesbian relationships: A case for the feminist participatory research model. *Journal of Gay and Lesbian Social Services, 3,* 29-42.

Resick, P. (1993). The psychological impact of rape. *Journal of Interpersonal Violence, 8,* 223-255.

Rhode, D. L. (1989). *Justice and gender.* Cambridge, MA: Harvard University Press.

Riessman, C. K. (1987). When gender is not enough: Women interviewing women. *Gender & Society, 1*(2), 172-207.

Roberts, C. (1989). *Women and rape.* New York: New York University Press.

Roberts, J., & Mohr, R. (1994). *Confronting sexual assault.* Toronto: University of Toronto Press.

Roiphe, K. (1993). *The morning after: Sex, fear and feminism.* Boston: Little Brown.

Romero, M. (1988). Chicanas modernize domestic service. *Qualitative Sociology, 11*(4), 19-333.

Ronai, C. R. (1992). The reflexive self through narrative: A night in the life of an erotic dancer/researcher. In C. Ellis & M. G. Flaherty (Eds.), *Investigating subjectivity* (pp. 102-124). Newbury Park, CA: Sage.

Rose, S., & Frieze, I. H. (1989). Young singles scripts for a first date. *Gender & Society, 3,* 258-268.

Rozee, P. D. (1993). Forbidden or forgiven: Rape in cross-cultural perspective. *Psychology of Women Quarterly, 17,* 499-514.

Ruch, L. O., & Chandler, S. (1983). Sexual assault trauma during the acute phase: An exploratory model and multivariate analysis. *Journal of Health and Social Behavior, 24,* 174-185.

Ruch, L. O., Amedeo, S. R., Leon, J. J., & Gartrell, J. W. (1991). Repeated sexual victimization and trauma change during the acute phase of the sexual assault trauma syndrome. *Women and Health, 17,* 1-19.

Russell, D. E. H. (1982a). The prevalence and incidence of forcible rape and attempted rape of females. *Victimology: An International Journal, 17,* 81-93.

Russell, D. E. H. (1982b). *Rape in marriage.* New York: Macmillan.

Russell, D. E. H. (1984). *Sexual exploitation: Rape, child sexual abuse, and workplace harassment.* Beverly Hills, CA: Sage.

Russell, D. E. H. (1990). *Rape in marriage* (2nd ed.). Bloomington: Indiana University Press.

Saal, F. E., Johnson, C. B., & Weber, N. (1989). Friendly or sexy? It may depend on who you ask. *Psychology of Women Quarterly, 13,* 263-276.

Sacco, V. F., & Johnson, H. (1990). *Patterns of criminal victimization in Canada.* Ottawa: Statistics Canada.

Sales, E., Baum, M., & Shore, B. (1984). Victim readjustment following assault. *Journal of Social Issues, 40*(1), 117-136.

Samoluk, S. B., & Pretty, G. M. H. (1994). The impact of sexual harassment simulations on women's thoughts and feelings. *Sex Roles, 30,* 679-699.

Samson, H. H. III, & Grant, K. A. (1990). Some implications of animal alcohol self-administration studies for human alcohol problems. *Drug Alcohol Dependence, 25,* 141-144.

Sanday, P. R. (1990). *Fraternity gang rape.* New York: New York University Press.

Sanday, P. R. (1996). *A woman scorned: Acquaintance rape on trial.* New York: Doubleday.

Santiago, J. M., McCall-Perez, F., Gorcey, M., & Beigel, A. (1985). Long-term psychological effects of rape in 35 victims. *American Journal of Psychiatry, 142,* 1338-1340.

Scheppele, K. L., & Bart, P. B. (1983). Through women's eyes: Defining danger in the wake of sexual assault. *Journal of Social Issues, 39*(2), 63-81.

Schwartz, M. D., & DeKeseredy, W. S. (1994a). *Male peer support, pornography and the abuse of women in dating relationships.* Paper presented at the annual meeting of the American Society of Criminology, Miami, FL.

Schwartz, M. D., & DeKeseredy, W. S. (1994b, December). "People without data" attacking rape: The Gilbertization of Mary Koss. *Violence UpDate,* 5, 8, 11.

Seiber, J. (1993). The ethics and politics of sensitive research. In C. M. Renzetti & R. M. Lee (Eds.), *Researching sensitive topics* (pp. 14-26). Newbury Park, CA: Sage.

Selkin, J. (1978). Protecting personal space: Victim and resister reactions to assaultive rape. *Journal of Community Psychology, 78,* 263-268.

Sessar, K. (1990). The forgotten nonvictim. *International Review of Victimology, 1,* 113-132.

Shainess, N. (1979). Vulnerability to violence: Masochism as process. *American Journal of Psychotherapy, 33,* 174-189.

Shim, Y. (1992). *Sexual violence against women in Korea: A victimization survey of Seoul women.* Paper presented at the conference on International Perspectives: Crime, Justice and Public Order, St. Petersburg, Russia.

Shotland, R. L. (1992). A theory of the causes of courtship rape: Part 2. *Journal of Social Issues, 48,* 127-143.

Shotland, R. L., & Hunter, B. A. (1992, August). *Women's "token resistance" and compliant sexual behaviors are related to uncertain sexual intentions and rape.* Paper presented at the annual meeting of the American Psychological Association, Toronto, Canada.

Siegel, J. M., Golding, J. M., Stein, J. A., Burnam, M. A., & Sorenson, S. B. (1990). Reactions to sexual assault: A community study. *Journal of Interpersonal Violence, 5,* 229-246.

Silverman, R. A. (1992). Street crime. In V. F. Sacco (Ed.), *Deviance: Conformity and control in Canadian society* (pp. 236-277). Englewood Cliffs, NJ: Prentice Hall.

Smith, D. E. (1974). Women's perspective as a radical critique of sociology. *Sociological Inquiry, 44,* 7-13.

Smith, D. E. (1987). Women's perspective as a radical critique of sociology. In S. Harding (Ed.), *Feminism & methodology* (pp. 84-96). Bloomington: Indiana University Press.

Smith, M. D. (1987). The incidence and prevalence of woman abuse in Toronto. *Violence and Victims, 2,* 173-187.

Smith, M. D. (1988). Women's fear of violent crime: An exploratory test of a feminist hypothesis. *Journal of Family Violence, 3,* 29-38.

Smith, M. D. (1990). Patriarchal ideology and wife beating: A test of a feminist hypothesis. *Violence and Victims, 5,* 257-273.

Smith, M. D. (1994). Enhancing the quality of survey data on violence against women: A feminist approach. *Gender & Society, 18,* 109-127.

Solicitor General of Canada. (1985). *Canadian urban victimization survey: Female victims of crime.* Ottawa: Ministry of the Solicitor General.

Soothill, K., & Walby, S. (1991). *Sex crime in the news.* London: Routledge.

Sparks, R. (1982). *Research on victims of crime: Accomplishments, issues and new directions.* Rockville, MD: U.S. Department of Health and Social Services.

Spence, J. T., Helmreich, R. L., & Holahan, C. K. (1979). Negative and positive components of psychological masculinity and femininity and their relationship to self-reports of neurotic and acting out behaviors. *Journal of Personality and Social Psychology, 37,* 1673-1682.

Stacey, J. (1988). Can there be a feminist ethnography? *Women's Studies International Forum, 11*(1), 21-27.

Stanko, E. A. (1977). *These are the cases that try themselves.* Doctoral dissertation, City University of New York.

Stanko, E. A. (1981-1982). The impact of victim assessment on prosecutors' screening decisions: The case of the New York County District Attorney's office. *Law & Society Review, 16,* 225-240.

Stanko, E. A. (1982). Would you believe this woman? In N. Rafter & E. A. Stanko (Eds.), *Judge, lawyer, victim, thief: Women, gender roles and criminal justice* (pp. 63-82). Boston, MA: Northeastern University Press.

Stanko, E. A. (1985). *Intimate intrusions.* London: Routledge.

Stanko, E. A. (1990). *Everyday violence: How women and men experience sexual and physical danger.* London: Pandora.

Stanko, E. A. (1994). Challenging the problem of individual men's violence. In T. Newburn & E. A. Stanko (Eds.), *Just boys doing business* (pp. 32-45). London: Routledge.

Stanko, E. A. (1996). Reading danger: Sexual harassment, anticipation and self-protection. In M. Hester, L. Kelly, & J. Radford (Eds.), *Women, violence and male power* (pp. 50-62). Buckingham: Open University Press.

Steketee, G., & Austin, A. (1989). Rape victims and the justice system: Utilization and impact. *Social Service Review, 63,* 285-303.

Stockdale, M. S. (1993). The role of sexual misperceptions of women's friendliness in an emerging theory of sexual harassment. *Journal of Vocational Behavior, 42,* 84-101.

Straus, M. A. (1979). Measuring intrafamily conflict and violence: The Conflict Tactics (CT) scales. *Journal of Marriage and the Family, 41,* 75-88.

Straus, M. A., Gelles, R. J., & Steinmetz, S. K. (1981). *Behind closed doors: Violence in the American family.* New York: Anchor.

Strauss, A. L. (1987). *Qualitative analysis for social scientists.* Cambridge: Cambridge University Press.

Strickland, W. (1991, April). *Institutional emotion norms and role satisfaction: Examination of a career wife population.* Paper presented at the meeting of the North Central Sociological Association meetings, Dearborn, MI.

Struckman-Johnson, C. (1988). Forced sex on dates: It happens to men, too. *Journal of Sex Research, 24,* 234-240.

Tolich, M. (1993). Alienating and liberating emotions at work. *Journal of Contemporary Ethnography, 22*(3), 361-381.

Tromp, S., Koss, M. P., Figueredo, A. J., & Tharan, M. (1995). Are rape memories different? A comparison of rape, other unpleasant, and pleasant memories among employed women. *Journal of Traumatic Stress, 8,* 607-627.

Turk, C. L., & Muehlenhard, C. L. (1991, June). *Force versus consent in definitions of rape.* Paper presented at the meeting of the Society for the Scientific Study of Sex Midcontinent Region, Kansas City, MO.

U.S. Department of Justice, Federal Bureau of Investigation. (1994). *Uniform crime reports.* Washington, DC: U.S. Government Printing Office.

U.S. House of Representatives. (1977). *Suspension of the National Crime Survey.* Washington, DC: U.S. Government Printing Office.

Ullman, S., & Siegel, J. M. (1993). Victim-offender relationship and sexual assault. *Violence and Victims, 8,* 121-134.

United Nations. (1995). *Human development report 1995.* Toronto: Oxford University Press.

Veit, C. T., & Ware, J. E., Jr. (1983). The structure of psychological distress and well-being in general populations. *Journal of Consulting and Clinical Psychology, 51,* 730-742.

Waldner-Haugrud, L. K. (1995). Sexual coercion on data: It's not just rape. *Update on Law-Related Education, 19,* 661-676.

Waldner-Haugrud, L. K., & Magruder, B. (1995). Male and female sexual victimization in dating relationships: Gender differences in coercion techniques and outcomes. *Violence and Victims, 10,* 203-216.

Walker, L., & Browne, A. (1985). Gender and victimization by intimates. *Journal of Personality, 53,* 179-195.

Warren, C. A. B. (1988). *Gender issues in field research.* Newbury Park, CA: Sage.

Warren, C. A. B., & Rassmussen, P. K. (1977). Sex and gender in fieldwork research. *Urban Life, 6,* 359-369.

Warshaw, R. (1988). *I never called it rape.* New York: Harper & Row.

Weed, F. J. (1995). *Certainty of justice: Reform in the crime victim movement.* New York: Aldine de Gruyter.

Weis, K., & Borges, S. S. (1973). Victimology and rape: The case of the legitimate victim. *Issues in Criminology, 8,* 71-115.

Weniger, R. H. (1978). Factors affecting the prosecution of rape: A case study of Travis County, Texas. *Virginia Law Review, 64,* 357.

White, J. W., & Bondurant, B. (1996). Gendered violence in intimate relationships. In J. T. Wood (Ed.), *Gendered relationships.* Mountain View, CA: Mayfield.

White, J. W., Donat, P. L. N., & Humphrey, J. H. (1996). Rape in our culture: A closer examination of the attitudes underlying sexual assault among acquaintances. *Journal of Psychology and Human Sexuality, 8,* 27-48.

White, J. W., & Farmer, R. F. (1992). Research methods: How they shape our view of sexual violence. *Journal of Social Issues, 48,* 45-60.

White, J. W., & Humphrey, J. A. (1991). Young people's attitudes toward rape. In A. Parrot & L. Bechhofer (Eds.), *Acquaintance rape: The hidden crime* (pp. 197-210). New York: John Wiley.

White, J. W., & Humphrey, J. A. (1994). Woman's aggression in heterosexual conflicts. *Aggressive Behavior, 20,* 195-202.

White, J. W., Humphrey, J. A., & Farmer, R. (1989). *Behavioral correlates of self-reported sexual coercion.* Washington, DC: Southeastern Psychology Association.

White, J. W., & Koss, M. P. (1991). Courtship violence: Incidence in a national sample of higher education students. *Violence and Victims, 6,* 247-256.

Wieder, G. B. (1985). Coping ability of rape victims: Comments on Myers, Templer, and Brown. *Journal of Consulting and Clinical Psychology, 53,* 429-430.

Williams, K. M. (1978). *The role of the victim in the prosecution of violent crime.* Washington, DC: Institute of Law and Social Research.

Williams, L. S. (1984). The classic rape: When do victims report? *Social Problems, 31*(4), 457-467.

Wolf, N. (1993). *Fire with fire.* London: Chatto & Windus.

Yllö, K. (1988). Political and methodological debates in wife abuse research. In K. Yllö & M. Bograd (Eds.), *Feminist perspectives on wife abuse* (pp. 28-50). Newbury Park, CA: Sage.

Index

About the Authors

HOBART H. CLEVELAND was formerly a practicing attorney and is currently a doctoral student in Family Studies at the University of Arizona. His primary scholarly interest is male sexual aggression, including its causes, prevention, and treatment.

DAWN H. CURRIE is Associate Professor of Sociology and Chair of Women's Studies at the University of British Columbia, where she teaches both feminist sociology and women's studies. Her areas of research and publication include feminist research, social justice, and feminist cultural studies. She is currently completing a book-length manuscript on fashion magazines and their adolescent readers. This interest in women's fashion is being extended through fieldwork in Sri Lanka on garment workers. She completed her PhD in Sociology at the London School of Economics in 1988.

WALTER S. DEKESEREDY is Professor of Sociology at Carleton University in Ottawa. He has published dozens of journal articles and book chapters on woman abuse and left realism. He is the author of *Woman Abuse in Dating Relationships: The Role of Male Peer Support*; with Ronald Hinch, coauthor of *Woman Abuse: Sociological Perspectives*; with Desmond Ellis, coauthor of the second edition of *The Wrong Stuff: An Introduction to the Sociological Study of Deviance*; with Martin Schwartz, coauthor of *Contemporary Crimi-*

nology and *Sexual Assault on the College Campus: The Role of Male Peer Support* (forthcoming); and with Linda MacLeod, coauthor of *Woman Abuse: A Sociological Story* (forthcoming). In 1995, he received the Critical Criminologist of the Year Award from the American Society of Criminology's Division on Critical Criminology. In 1993, he received Carleton University's Research Achievement Award. Currently, he is coeditor of *Critical Criminology: An International Journal* and serves on the editorial board of *Women & Criminal Justice.*

PATRICIA A. FRAZIER is Associate Professor in the Counseling and Social Psychology Programs in the Department of Psychology at the University of Minnesota. She received a PhD in Counseling Psychology and Social Psychology from the University of Minnesota in 1988. Her research interests include sexual assault, sexual harassment, coping with stressful life events, and the interface between psychology and law.

SUSAN K. HIPPENSTEELE is a research psychologist and the victim's advocate for students, faculty, and staff at the University of Hawaii at Manoa. Active in antidiscrimination research and policy development as a graduate student, she was hired as the first victims' advocate for this 20,000-student campus shortly after earning her PhD in Psychology in 1991. Her current research examines student and faculty experiences with campus ethnoviolence, emphasizing the relationships among victims' experiences with racism, sexism, and homophobia in multiple minority settings. She also works as a consultant to plaintiff attorneys and to universities and colleges developing victim advocacy and support programs on campus.

JENNIFER K. HUFF is a graduate of both the sociology masters program and the Honors Tutorial College undergraduate program at Ohio University. Currently, she is acquiring additional perspective and expanding her knowledge of social services through her work for a state agency that helps consumers with disabilities obtain employment.

KIMBERLY A. HUISMAN is working on her PhD at the University of Southern California. Her research interests include violence against women, gender, race, and ethnicity.

JOHN A. HUMPHREY is Professor of Sociology at the University of North Carolina at Greensboro. His research has focused on interpersonal violence, including criminal homicide and suicide, alcohol and other drug abuse, and sexual aggression. He has been coprincipal investigator with Jacquelyn W. White of a longitudinal study of the risk of sexual and physical assault among undergraduates.

MARY P. KOSS is Professor of Family and Community Medicine, Psychiatry, and Psychology in the Arizona Prevention Center at the University of Arizona (Tucson). She is the cochair of the American Psychological Association Task Force on Male Violence Against Women, which published *No Safe Haven: Violence Against Women at Home, at Work, and in the Community,* winner of the 1994 Washington EdPress award for outstanding book on a social concern. She is coauthor, with Mary Harvey, of *The Rape Victim: Clinical and Community Interventions,* and her national study on college students' experiences with sexual aggression is the subject of Robin Warshaw's *I Never Called It Rape.* She is associate editor of *Violence and Victims* and consulting editor to many more journals, including, among others, *Journal of Clinical and Consulting Psychology, Gender and Health, Journal of Interpersonal Violence, Violence Against Women,* and *Criminal Behavior and Law.*

BRIAN D. MacLEAN currently teaches criminology at the Richmond campus of Kwantlen University College. He completed his PhD in Sociology at the London School of Economics and Political Science, where he was a Commonwealth Scholar. He has authored, coauthored, or edited 12 books and over 35 articles in books and scholarly journals on the subject of crime and society. He is the founding editor or coeditor of three journals and has published over 40 editions of various academic periodicals. In 1992, with Dragan Milovanovic, he was awarded the Distinguished Achievement Award from a division of the American Society of Criminology.

CHRISTINE MATTLEY teaches sociology at Ohio University. She received her PhD from Washington State University in 1984 and has published on the self and self-concept in such journals as *Symbolic Interaction* and *Journal of Family Violence.* Her current research focuses on emotion, emotion-work and the self, and the emotion-work of sex workers.

JODY MILLER is Assistant Professor of Criminology and Criminal Justice at the University of Missouri at St. Louis. Her research interests are gender, adolescence, and delinquency. She is currently involved in a study of female gang involvement in "new" gang cities. She has numerous publications, including "Gender and Power on the Streets: Street Prostitution in an Era of Crack Cocaine" in the *Journal of Contemporary Ethnography.*

VICTORIA L. PITTS is completing her PhD in sociology at Brandeis University. She has published in *Justice Quarterly, Humanity & Society,* and *Race, Class and Gender in Criminology: The Intersections.* She has taught for Bradford College.

CLAIRE M. RENZETTI is Professor and Chair of Sociology at St. Joseph's University, Philadelphia. She is editor of *Violence Against Women: An International, Interdisciplinary Journal* (Sage) and of the book series, *Gendered Justice: Women, Crime and Law.* With Jeffrey Edleson, she coedits the Sage *Violence Against Women Book Series.* She has published eight books and numerous book chapters and journal articles. Her current research interest is women's use of violence.

MARTIN D. SCHWARTZ is Professor of Sociology at Ohio University. He has written more than 60 articles, chapters, edited books, and books on a variety of topics in such journals as *Criminology, Deviant Behavior, Justice Quarterly,* and *Women and Politics.* He has been teaching women's studies courses on violence against women since the late 1970s. A former president of the Association for Humanist Sociology, he is the winner of a lifetime achievement award from the Division on Critical Criminology of the American Society of Criminology and has never been convicted of a major felony. He is the coauthor of *Contemporary Criminology, Sexual Assault on the College Campus: The Role of Male Peer Support,* and *Corrections: An Issues Approach,* now in its 4th edition, and the coeditor of *Race, Class and Gender in Criminology: The Intersections.* He serves as deputy editor of *Justice Quarterly* and on the editorial boards of a number of publications, including *Violence Against Women; Race, Class & Gender;* and *Teaching Sociology.*

LISA M. SEALES is a doctoral student in the Counseling Psychology Program at the University of Minnesota—Twin Cities. Her research interests lie in the areas of interpersonal relationships, gender stereotyping, and family systems.

ELIZABETH A. STANKO, Reader in Criminology, worked for 13 years teaching sociology and women's studies at Clark University, Worcester, Massachusetts, moving to London in 1990 to take her position at Brunel University's Law Department. She is the author of *Everyday Violence* (1990) and *Intimate Intrusions* (1985) and an editor of texts on gender and crime (most recently, *Just Boys Doing Business: Men, Masculinities and Crime* with Tim Newburn, 1994). She has published widely on issues of prosecutorial discretion, violence, violence against women, and crime prevention. She is currently writing *The Good, the Bad and the Vulnerable,* a critique of victimization, to be published by Sage in 1997.

JACQUELYN W. WHITE is Professor of Psychology at the University of North Carolina at Greensboro. Her research focuses on interpersonal violence, specifically violence against women in intimate relationships. She has been coprincipal investigator with John A. Humphrey on a longitudinal study of sexual and physical assault among undergraduates.